PRAISE
RULE

"*Rule 62* is a serious dose of Gen-X wisdom for a world bereft of common sense. Optionality and hard work, shades of gray and rigid self-discipline, focus and flexibility, pragmatism and expectations—Jared's penchant for juxtapositions in manageable chunks will jar, entertain, and move you to healthy introspection."

—ED MARSH
Founder, veteran, independent director

"Not your typical self-help fluff—this one's got bite, humor, and a whole lot of truth."

—JENNIE READS

"I consider meditation to mean focusing one's thoughts to better understand a matter. *Rule 62: Meditations on Success and Spirituality* embodies this concept across a serious-lighthearted spectrum. Looking for a book that inspires, provokes thought, disagrees with you, and can make you laugh—often in short order? You have one right here."

—DAN ALLEN
Retired accountant and transactional attorney

"As a longtime reader of Dillian's financial newsletter, I've always come for the market insights and stayed for the comedic philosophy and life advice. If you're here for the latter, *Rule 62* offers 79 essays packed with hilarious, no-nonsense counsel on living a meaningful life. Dillian's wisdom shines through in a style that's closer to stand-up comedy than Immanuel Kant. Pick it up today, and as he suggests: Don't take yourself too seriously."

—CHRISTIAN HOFFMANN
Head of fixed income, Thornburg Investments

"I've been reading Jared's daily investing newsletter for over ten years now. *Rule 62* is a collection of his most insightful and meaningful pieces, the ones I would typically forward to friends and family."

—JOHN BELLIS
Head trader at J. Goldman & Co. LP

"This highly entertaining read is a series of non-stop reality checks that make

you think deeply about your own beliefs and the beliefs of others. It truly helps you understand why others do what they do and what you should be doing to be a better version of yourself. Highly recommended!"
—MICHAEL VASKO
Vice president of sales, MotoSleep

"Dillian writes about heaven and hell, sin and selfishness. He writes about blow and vomit, death, South Carolina, and Paris Hilton's prowess as a DJ. Some people would run the other way. I encourage you to lean in."
—JAMES BLANDFORD
Senior producer, The Great Courses

"Jared's writing style is like no other, from the time I read his first book I was hooked. I was telling a friend about *Rule 62*, and described the essays as a series of meditations. I like to read one at a time and ponder them because I can fit them easily into a busy schedule."
—LIZ DEFOREST
Private investor

"Of all the investment newsletter writers I've subscribed to over the past 15 years, Jared Dillian is the only one I still read religiously every week. And speaking of religion, in *Rule 62* he has now injected spirituality into his technical analysis to good effect. His take on things is mercurial—like the god Mercury who was, in fact, the god of financial gain, eloquence and communication. Perfect! You should read this book not in one sitting, but more like reading one chapter a day as a daily meditation."
—DEAC MANROSS
Apple Computer (retired)

"Ever wish you had that wise older brother whom you could lean on for key advice in life, especially during challenging times? Someone who can guide, enlighten, and even illuminate your own journey, simply by sharing his own experiences and anecdotes? Jared Dillian may not literally be that family member, but *Rule 62: Meditations on Success and Spirituality* is certainly a formidable distillation. Delve in, learn plenty and enjoy the ride, as this military veteran, former Lehman Brothers trader, newsletter writer and the author of six acclaimed books imparts his wisdom in this poignant and memorable collection of essays."
—SHANE STEIN
Film producer, record producer, author and composer

"A genuinely enjoyable and engaging read! It draws you in with sharp wit, delivers

unexpected laughs, and unsettles with truths you'd rather not confront—all while keeping you thoroughly entertained."
—LAURENCE BLACK
Founder, The Index Standard

"Jared's lucid story telling coupled with his unique understanding of the human condition and ability to see around life's corners, provides his readers with depth and actionable insights that improve personal, professional, and spiritual outcomes. This collection of essays is like your favorite bag of potato chips—absolutely impossible to put down until you have consumed them all!"
—MICHAEL DOUGLIS
Global account manager

"Most people will not publicly discuss their regrets, mistakes, body image or ruminations on mortality. Jared lays it all out there in plain view. Revealed herein is the wisdom gleaned from a decades-long climb over the mountain of mental illness and addiction. Maybe you're stuck, and you want to get unstuck. Maybe you want to be friends with God and your boss. Maybe you just want to make more money and be happy. This book will help you achieve all of the above. This is the book you write in your 50s to your 20-year-old self. Or just gift *Rule 62* to your 20-year-old nephew—hopefully he'll read it before he's 40. In your hands is an instruction manual for a happy, useful life."
—MICHAEL KAWOCHKA
Associate broker, Daniel Gale Sotheby's International Realty

"*Rule 62* is a latter-day Book of Proverbs. It's 79 essays full of insight, wit, LOL vulgarity, and wisdom. It's not a book to be devoured—rather sampled, considered, and revisited. Whether it's about tipping, the nature of evil, cats, or death, the lessons are timeless."
—TAI WONG
Host and market commentator, Global Money Talk

"Jared Dillian was born in the 20th century and will die in the 21st and that's about as much as you can pin him down. *Rule 62* is impossible to genre-lize—kind of memoir, kind of self-help, kind of Americana reportage, kind of human nature excavation. And full of brutal, uncomfortable honesty that brings light to dark places. Some of *Rule 62* made me cry, a whole lot of it made me laugh, some of it horrified me, pretty much all of it made me consider some particular thing in a different way. You'll want to read it fast—try and read it slow."
—LAURA MUNDOW
Chief Marketing Officer

First published in 2025.

Paperback ISBN: 979-8-9909447-2-5
eBook ISBN: 979-8-9909447-3-2

Copyright © 2025 Jared Dillian

The moral right of the author has been asserted.

All rights reserved; no part of this publication may be reproduced, stored in a retrieval system, or transmitted in any form or by any means, electronic, mechanical, photocopying, recording, or otherwise without the prior written permission of the Author. This book may not be lent, resold, hired out or otherwise disposed of by way of trade in any form of binding or cover other than that in which it is published without the prior written consent of the Author.

While every effort has been made to ensure that information in this book is accurate, no liability can be accepted by the Author for any loss incurred in any way whatsoever by any person relying on the information contained herein.

No responsibility for loss occasioned to any person or corporate body acting or refraining to act as a result of reading material in this book can be accepted by the Author.

The scanning, uploading, and distributing of this book via any means without permission of the Author is illegal and punishable by law. No part of this work may be used or reproduced in any manner whatsoever to train or inform artificial intelligence or to teach any computerized system in any way.

Book design by Christopher Parker

JAREDDILLIAN.COM

RULE 62

MEDITATIONS ON
SUCCESS AND
SPIRITUALITY

Jared
Dillian

AVAILABLE BY
THE SAME AUTHOR

NON-FICTION

No Worries:
How To Live a Stress-free Financial Life

Those Bastards:
69 Essays on Life, Creativity, and Meaning

Street Freak:
Money and Madness at Lehman Brothers

FICTION

Night Moves:
And Other Stories

All the Evil of This World:
A Novel

CONTENTS

Foreword by Matt Zeigler — ix

Say Yes to Things — 1
Love — 5
Powerlessness — 9
My Ego is Not my Amigo — 14
Leaves in a Swimming Pool — 18
How to Handle Failure — 23
Give the Gift of Time — 28
Do Hard Things — 32
Having a Healthy Relationship With Money — 36
American Ninja Warrior — 41
Integrity — 45
Don't Chop Down the Tree — 49
Punctuality — 53
People Don't Change — 57
Rule 62 — 61
I Am Generation X — 66
A Students Work for C Students — 70
Legacy — 74
Sinners and Saints — 78
Winning — 82

The Best Days are Ahead	87
Restraint	91
Time Management	95
Perseverance	100
Tipping	105
Regrets	109
Happiness	113
The Purpose of the Body	117
Sleep is my Superpower	121
The Goodness of People	126
The Hustlers	130
The Creators	135
Procrastination	140
Tardive Dyskinesia	144
ASMR and Cringe Memories	148
Intelligence	153
Pessimism	157
Harder Than it Looks	161
Greatness	165
You Only Die Once	169
Every Sinner Has a Future	173
The Road to Hell	177
Loneliness	182
The Nature of Evil	186
Be Conscientious	191
What is Your Contribution?	195
Gratitude	199
The Thrill Seekers	203
Finish What You Start	207
Critical or Commercial Success	212
Compliments	216
Letter to My 22-Year-Old Self	221
Trauma	227

CONTENTS

Depression	231
The Futility of Planning	236
Class	241
The 80% Solution	246
Obsessive-Compulsive	250
Why Some People Get Rich and Others Don't	254
Spirituality	259
Never Enough	264
Creativity is Work	268
Living in the Present	272
Risk	276
The 60/30/10 Asshole Rule	281
Joy	285
Contempt Prior to Investigation	290
Moments That Change Your Life	295
I'm Offended	299
Mental Obsessions and Letting Go	303
A Full Life	308
Acceptance	313
Forward Motion	317
Power	321
I Love Pain	325
Fear	330
Resentment	334
Signs	339
Happiness is a Choice	344
Acknowledgments	349

FOREWORD
BY MATT ZEIGLER

THE FIRST TIME you read Jared Dillian, I'm pretty sure you're supposed to laugh at least once at the word "dirtnap," note two or three things you think sound smart, and then go back to a sentence that you read four or five minutes ago and say out loud, "Who does this schmuck think he is?"

Not long after I got my copy of *Night Moves* in the mail (Jared's 2024 short story collection), I was reading it on the couch, next to my wife who was deeply focused on a book of her own. "Okay, what is it?" she asks, because I'm doing what I always do, vibrating while I'm supposed to be sitting still and reading like a normal human, crinkling pages and making noises while underlining and earmarking stuff. "This guy," I tell her, "*this* guy. I mean, I read this sentence and then I'll flip to this other one, because—the sheer range! He goes from Buk-level poetic to puke-level dude-stuff, and he somehow owns and captures it all so perfectly. He's nuts."

After I showed her the two bits, she tells me, "I see what you mean," and then, "You know I'm trying to come up with dinner here?" She had been reading a cookbook until I interrupted her. "Seriously," she continues, "why'd you have to show me that second bit?" She wasn't wrong. Why did I have to show her that? And, to be fair, this was probably her first or third direct exposure to Jared's writing, at least with his name attached to it. "Who does that schmuck think he is?" she says. "Exactly. I don't know either," I respond.

In my case—and maybe in yours—by the 50th time you've read Jared (either because you signed up for one of his mailing lists or people keep forwarding you his stuff, usually at odd hours of the night), you come to peace with the fact that the same soul-bottoming-out questions are triggered inside of you every time. That's who this schmuck apparently thinks he is. The guy who makes you wonder, "Am I like *that*?" Or reflect, "Oh, I know somebody *just like that*." And say, "Uh-oh, I've been there, but *do I have to remember what 'there' is like right now?*"

This whole extracurricular existential crisis continues until, at some point, you click reply to one of his newsletters, trade some messages, record a podcast together, and somehow end up with a blank open Word document and the hazy memory of agreeing to write a foreword.

So. Where to start? How about "Who does this schmuck think he is?" Good idea. Let's unpack that. This is a foreword, after all. If we're here, we might as well do it right.

The most common non-complimentary message I receive after someone notices me publicly interacting with Jared goes something like, "A lot of people seem to like that guy, and I don't get it. Maybe I'm dumb or insensitive or something, but either way, I trust your judgement. What are you seeing that I'm not?"

My answer always starts, "Do you know what the word *sonder* means?" Nobody ever does. So I get to tell them—modestly, because both my mom and my dad's mom before her were English teachers, and I don't word-shame—"*Sonder* is the feeling you get when you realize everybody else's life is as complicated, as rich in detail, and as emotionally all over the place as yours is."

I tell them, "Whatever made you ask me this question, I need you to make a bet, in your heart, that you don't know something about Jared, but you're curious enough to find out—and doing so is worth it. The only thing I know for sure about him is that whenever I talk to him, he seems to think he's simple and straightforward, but when I read him, I always feel like something important and complex and meaningful is being revealed, and I'm hungry in the most magical way to learn more. That's *sonder*-ness. It's special, probably a little insane, but it's exactly what I respect most about his work."

I don't know if my sonder explanations have earned Jared any readers, but I do know he writes with truth, rhythm, and mystery, so that if the curiosity bug embedded in his work bites you, you're going to keep coming back. Even when it's weird (and it gets weird). Even when it punches you in the gut (*oh yeah*, that too). Even when you're swinging wildly back and forth between wanting to give the guy a hug because he's curled up in the fetal position on the floor of a psychiatric ward, to wanting to punch him in the face because "Why'd the husband in that short story have to die in a tragic accident right after the fight with his wife?"

"*Why?*" and "*What?*" That's the sound of sonder. That's the sound of writing that's forcing you to feel something, even if you don't have the words for what it's making you feel. I can't tell you if it makes the writing good. I can't tell you if it makes the writing good for *you*. I can only point out, whatever reaction you have to Jared's writing in the pages ahead, his gift is that he is going to trigger you to respond, and he is far less concerned with where that trigger leads you, and much more focused on writing to make sure that both you and he know you are very much alive and going through this together.

That's who I think this schmuck thinks he is. Now let's talk about this book. I need you to know what you're about to get yourself into.

Rule 62 is a reference to an Alcoholics Anonymous in-joke, which means it's as much a reference to drinking yourself stupid as it is to loving yourself as a sober person. It's actually a reflection on the whole self-affirmed, 100% authentic, alcoholic redemption arc—where we accept how all the nasty bits are essential, even if they're horribly embarrassing, because they're a part of baring our souls honestly and something about that is beautiful. Buk and puke, remember? Don't forget it. The AA Rule 62 reads, "Don't take yourself too damn seriously." Jared, by choosing this title, as best as I can tell, is urging us all to be somewhere between serious enough and not too serious, as we stumble away from this book to ask ourselves, "What happened?"

There's his essay "Love," where he admits to thinking his wife is not only the most beautiful woman in the world, but that he's somehow managed to never have told her that. If you're paying attention, you'll see how he does his thing. He makes moments zoom in and out around you, where you can hear the anxious metronome in his head click-click-clacking away with stuff like:

> "My wife probably inherited her grandparents' longevity. There is a very good chance that she'll live to 100 or more. I, on the other hand, have a history of heart disease and cancer in my family. The men in my family rarely make it into their 60s. I might have ten years left, for all I know."

Where does that leave you? More important, where does that *lead* you? Yes, I texted my wife after I typed this quote, and it's all good. I also showed her the line, "The best husband in the world might be five-eleven and you would never know," and reminded her that she knows, because, well, I'll show you my driver's license if you can't figure it out. Time isn't linear, even if the stories are with Jared. Where he leaves you and leads you on the not-so-random walks is everything.

Take the comments about his dad from another story:

> "I treasure my childhood—I treasure the freedoms that I had. But I long for something resembling a normal relationship with my parents. My father was something of an amateur stock trader—when I told him that I got a job at Lehman Brothers, I begged him to come to New York and see the trading floor. He would

have loved it. He never came. When my first book was released, he sent me a one-sentence email. Nothing about the second or third books. When I texted him that I published my first column at Bloomberg, he sent me a picture of a lizard. I haven't spoken to him in years. What I would give to be a Millennial, and for my life to be complete."

Do you have whiplash from what he's doing yet? When he's talking about his life, he takes you from the present, to the distant future beyond his lifetime, then to the end of his life, then back in time to whenever the men in his family signed off. This temporal sonder, this invitation into the out-of-order experience of another person's life, is what makes his writing stick to your ribs long after you've finished reading. It's not booze, it's not a drunken stumble that never quite nourishes you. This is chicken soup, with some hints of crushed red pepper you didn't expect—and, after the shock, you realize you liked it.

He lives Rule 62. He follows it through each one of these essays. And he attacks all manners and moments of life with a sober thoughtfulness and honesty. I attempted to honor it in this foreword, and I really hope you don't put this book down until you hit the end (I didn't). And, when you get to the end—indeed, even the end of a single essay—just see what you felt. Ponder whatever experiences are getting caught in your throat or that need to be wiped off your shoes. This is what great art is supposed to do—it's supposed to create a moment, to spawn and spur some sonder, when another person's life feels as real and complicated as your own.

Go make something out of that. If it's not obvious, I don't know who this schmuck thinks he is. I don't really care, either. I just want more art in the world that does what his art does for me.

One last personal request before you start. When you finish this and you inevitably decide to write your own thoughts down, be sure to ask Jared to write your book's foreword. I'll be busy experiencing the sonder of my own life, just as you'll be experiencing his. But honestly, my real request is, don't stop reflecting, just like Jared won't stop writing. No matter what either of you think. No matter who that schmuck thinks he is, or thinks you are, or who you think you are—don't take it too damn seriously.

MATT ZEIGLER
March 2025

SAY YES TO THINGS

In the summer of 1993, during the interregnum between my official Coast Guard Academy duties and my sophomore year, I took a short trip to visit with my half-brother in Georgia. His mother had rented a condo at Lake Lanier. I had no experience with the place; I would learn later that it was something of a redneck vacation spot. There was a water-slide park, among other things. We spent a few days jackassing around in the summer sun.

One night, we went to the movies to see *The Firm*, the legal thriller starring Tom Cruise and Wilford Diabeetus Brimley. It was a low theater, wider than it was long, with an enormous screen, and if you remember what going to the movies was like back then: a lot of people went to the movies. The theater was packed, with not a single empty seat. We got there a bit on the late side, so ended up about six rows from the front. I went in first, my brother followed me, and I sat down to the left of a mixed-race girl about my age. She smiled.

I sat and looked straight ahead. Out of the corner of my right eye, I spied on her. She was with her boyfriend—or her brother—I could not tell which. She had long curly hair in ringlets held back in a ponytail, and glasses. She seemed happy, the type of happiness that is only attainable by being 18 years old, with a maximum of possibility and a minimum of responsibility. She was well cared for, well parented, that much I could tell. She smelled of water lilies.

The movie begins. About 15 minutes in, I attempt to place my right arm on the armrest, bumping into hers. She did not yield; our arms stayed there, touching. I looked over at her and smiled, and she smiled back, shrugging. Something funny happened in the movie; we looked at each other and smiled again. I could feel every micrometer of her arm touching mine. Her hand was just out of reach. Over the next 30 minutes, I moved my hand slowly, imperceptibly, until it was within range of hers. Unexpectedly, she grasped it, and I felt the electricity coursing through us. We held hands for the rest of the movie. I looked at her again—still smiling, but mostly I was looking at the boyfriend. He was completely disengaged, staring at the screen or possibly asleep.

When the lights came on, I was presented with a dilemma. *Do I ask for her number or not? What about the boyfriend?* I wasn't much in the mood to get my ass kicked in a movie theater. But the boyfriend was the least of my concerns. I played the tape forward. I get her number, and go back to Connecticut. We write each other letters. I talk to her on the payphone outside the company dayroom. I save all my money to buy a plane ticket to see her. There was the possibility of explosive sex, but relative to the amount of effort I would have to expend to have it, it seemed too hard. I didn't know anything about her. Maybe her family was ultra-religious. Maybe being a dental hygienist was the best she could do. Maybe a lot of things. She stood there, looking at me expectantly, wishing, hoping that I would ask for her number, with the boyfriend trailing behind, and I could only manage a grim smirk as I fled the theater behind my brother.

Easily one of my biggest pet peeves is when someone says they have no regrets. Really? Every course of action in your dumb life has been the correct one? You've never had a lapse in judgment? I have lots of regrets. I regret not asking for that girl's number. I do. Not because things would have turned out better—they undeniably would have turned out worse. But these days, I try to say yes to things. When given a choice between taking an opportunity and not taking an opportunity, I always choose the former. Because, as the great Joaquín Andújar once said, *you never know*. Introduce a little chaos into your life and see what happens. It's like a binomial tree. You could go this way, or that, and then this way, or that. The only thing we know for sure about your current path is that it's boring.

I don't regret doing things; I regret not doing things. I regretted not getting an MFA and pursuing a career in writing. I regretted that for two-and-a-half decades. Ultimately, my Coast Guard career didn't work out, but I don't regret giving it a try. I would have regretted not trying it. Lehman came to an ignominious end, but I don't regret that either. I regret saying no to things. I passed on going to my youngest brother-in-law's graduation, because I was "too busy" at work. It was important to him, too. If you want me to go to a graduation, wedding, bar mitzvah, dance recital, or baseball game, I will be there—because today I say yes to things. Note: weddings are optional, funerals are mandatory.

The world opens up with possibilities when you say yes to things. It puts you in a position where you can help people. It is a cure for isolation. You learn things and have new experiences. This is a typical example: Someone invites you to do X. You say, I don't really do X. X is not my kind of thing. *Come on, let's go do X.* No, I'm not going to do X, I'm going to stay home and watch TV. But if you said yes to X, I can almost guarantee that you would enjoy it more than you thought you would. For a lot of people, X might be opera or ballet. For me, X is fishing. There is a get-together of finance people in the woods of Maine that I have avoided for years because I don't like fishing. Fishing isn't my thing.

The only exceptions to the rule of saying yes to things are when someone asks you if you want to do drugs or something illegal. While that may indeed expand your horizons, the potential consequences are usually not worth it.

The point here is to be constantly exposed to new things, new people, new places, and new ideas. When I went back to grad school, I knew for sure that I would be exposed to new people and new ideas. I had to be open to receiving them. Calling someone closed-minded is an insult, but the truth is that just about all of us are closed-minded in some way. *Soccer is boring. Art museums are dumb. Your family sucks. No, no, no* we say, over and over again, closing ourselves off to life. The people who really close themselves off to life are the people who go to the same bar after work every day and get loaded with the same drunks talking the same shit all the time. I had a dear friend from the Academy who never posted on Facebook, but every day he would "check in" to the local bar. His world was pretty small.

I will give you an example of a time I said yes to something: A high school friend gave me the opportunity to go watch professional wrestling with him at the Hammerstein Ballroom in New York City. My first instinct was to say, no, I'm not coming, I'm going to stay home and watch TV. Wrestling is fake and dumb. But I went, and it was one of the most fantastic nights I have ever had in my life. My guess is that you have never been to a professional wrestling match. You should really go. It's an experience. And you'll have a much greater respect for the wrestlers once you do. The highlight was when the referee went to kick one of the wrestlers and his shoe flew off, hit the balcony, and landed squarely in my friend's lap.

As for the girl. For sure, social anxiety was part of it. I have never been particularly outgoing. But I felt like I was going to make my life unnecessarily complicated. Only an insane person says no to pretty girls who hold the hands of complete strangers in movie theaters. Only a complete dildo doesn't get the number. Oh well—things worked out for the best.

But they don't always.

LOVE

I DON'T KNOW A thing about love. Traders typically don't. Trading is transactional—I will do something nice for you, if you do something nice for me. There is no unconditional love in trading. Business relationships continue until they end, when they no longer make economic sense. This is the world that I lived in for a long time. Your worth was measured in terms of what you could do for me.

Unconditional love goes something like this: *I will love you no matter what. There is nothing that you could do that is so awful that would make me stop loving you.* Or, *I will love you until you learn to love yourself.* The people in finance that I know don't usually learn about unconditional love until they have children. Then they post a lot of photos of them on social media.

Many people learn about unconditional love from their pets. But it is easy to love pets unconditionally, because they can never betray you. Cats and dogs will never let you down. They won't cheat on you, they won't lie to you, they won't fail to live up to your expectations. Children can grow up to be stinkers and hate you in adulthood. Pets never will. As such, a relationship with a cat or a dog is very simple and pure—

and this is why the death of a pet is frequently more traumatic than the death of a person. Relationships with people are complicated.

I do know that love is an action, not a feeling. People get cause and effect reversed—they think that they feel love, which compels them to perform esteemable acts towards another person. It is the other way around. You perform esteemable acts towards another person, and then you feel love. I took an oath when I got married that I would love my partner in sickness and in health, until death do us part. If you're not shitting your pants when you get married, I don't know what to say to you. At our wedding, I was doing okay until the organist played the first chord, at which point I almost fainted. In the last 25 years of our marriage, there has been a lot of sickness. There have been good times, and profoundly bad times. If we had tapped out during the bad times, we wouldn't have experienced the love that we have today.

On the mantle among the family photos is a picture of my wife's grandparents. Her grandfather is still alive, at age 100. Her grandmother passed away a few years ago, at age 93. They were married for about 70 years. They are the only photos on our mantle aside from us and the cats. I suspect my wife put them there out of admiration—not just for their longevity, but the depth and strength of their relationship. Over the course of 70 years, there would have been a lot of ups and downs, and probably many points along the way when one or both of them could have pulled the ripcord. I doubt they ever gave it a moment's thought.

A relationship evolves over time. First, you are lovers. Then, flesh being what it is, that goes away, and you are friends. Over time, the relationship deepens, and then you become soulmates. I have been with my wife for longer than I was raised by my parents. A friend of mine got married about ten years ago, and he said that on his honeymoon, he and his bride sort of ran out of things to say. That's not a good sign. They're still married, and doing better than I expected, which is terrific. I can tell you that, after 25 years of marriage, we have never run out of things to say, though we have told the same stories over and over again. My wife tells the same stories all the time, and I just let her. Now, we are getting old and the memory is going and we *really* tell the same stories over and over again. I like them better each time I hear them.

My wife probably inherited her grandparents' longevity. There is a very good chance that she'll live to 100 or more. I, on the other hand, have a history of heart disease and cancer in my family. The men in my family rarely make it into their 60s. I might have ten years left, for all I know. I like to joke with my wife that she'll be married to me for 40 years, and then she'll be married to some other dude for 40 years. And he'll probably be a complete tool. But that's okay—I wouldn't want my wife to become old and eccentric, rattling around in a big house with a bunch of cats, wearing dark sweaters. I wouldn't want it for myself. Personally, I'm not very good at being alone. My wife went on a project for a summer back in 2013, and I lost the TV remote on the second day, and then didn't watch TV again for the next six weeks. I'd be the first to test the thesis that one can survive on Chipotle alone. But most of all, I would miss her exceptionally dry sense of humor and her snarky comments on everything that passes by. At this point, we are each one half of a whole.

And I know that our relationship will grow deeper as we get older. We don't have children (as a matter of choice)—we just have each other. Our parents will grow old and pass away, and then it will be just us with the cats, and we'll lose the cats eventually, too. It will just be us. The stable, sane centrist and the crazy, volatile risk-taker. As we've gotten older, we're doing that thing where we're starting to look alike. We're even starting to dress alike. We disagree on politics, a little; we each have one or two pet issues that we're inflexible on. We each have our own roles in the relationship—I'm the dreamer, the big idea guy, and she executes on the details. We're building a house together. We heard from everyone that couples get divorced over building a house. We haven't had one argument yet, though the financial risk stresses me out sometimes. In short, we're a team, and a pretty good one at that.

I have achieved a lot in my life: degrees, books, professional success, money, and music. But if you want to know what I'd like to be remembered for, it's that I was a loving husband to my wife for many years. Every once in a while, you see successful people who've been married a bunch of times—I had this guy who was married four times say to me that he kept picking the bad women. I was like, dude, you are the one common denominator in all of these marriages. Maybe it's not them—maybe it's you? I occasionally run across these people with multiple kids from multiple marriages and messy divorces and their personal life is in an absolute shambles, and I don't really care how much money they have—I wouldn't trade places with them, ever. I wouldn't trade places with Elon Musk. I said that on Twitter one time, and I got shithoused in the replies. *You wouldn't trade places with Elon Musk? The richest man in the world?* No, I would not, because he has never experienced the love that comes with being in a loving relationship that spans decades. In my opinion, I am far richer. And if someday I ever get divorced, it will have been my greatest failure.

We don't maintain photo albums. We tried for a few years in the beginning, then got too busy. I figure Facebook has all the important photos. But I don't need them. I remember all the important moments—and the unimportant ones, too. Every minute, every second of a 25-year marriage (plus an eight-year courtship) condensed into a feeling—the feeling I hope I will have on my deathbed, as I pass peacefully into the next life while holding hands with my lifelong companion and best friend.

That's really all that matters, isn't it?

POWERLESSNESS

I DON'T KNOW IF you've ever had this experience, but let's say you text or call someone and they don't text or call you back. You immediately think that they hate you. Now, there are a million reasons why someone might not return a text or call. Maybe they missed it. Maybe they are busy. Maybe they didn't think that a response was expected. But you stew on it. You obsess over it for days and weeks, preoccupied with the idea that someone out there, somewhere, doesn't like you. It's the last thing you think about before you fall asleep, and the first thing you think about when you wake up. You try to will that person to call you with the power of your mind, through some kind of force you send through the atmosphere.

News flash: you are not in charge of what other people think of you.

You're not! When someone told me this, back in 2006, that I am not in charge of what other people think of me, it was like I had been struck by lightning. *I am not in charge of what other people think of me?* I thought I was. I thought a lot of things back then. I thought I could make the stock market do what I wanted it to do. I really did. I thought I could will the stock market higher or lower. I thought I had control over it. I thought I had control over a lot of things.

I didn't, and we don't, and there is a word for this: powerlessness.

If you really think about it, we are not in control of much of anything. As I drive to work in the morning, I am not in control of traffic. I could be sitting there in my car like a chump, and there is not much I can do about it. I am also not in control of whether or not I get rear-ended. Some drunk could be looking at Instagram models on his phone while he's driving, and it is going to ruin my day. I am not in control of whether people unsubscribe to my newsletter. I am not really in control of my investment performance. I think I am, but I am not. I am not in control of politics. I am not in charge of who becomes president. I am not in control of my taxes; that gets decided for me. I am not in control of the economy. I am not in control of interest rates. I am not in control of whether I get fired from one of my writing gigs. I am not in control of whether people dance to my music. I am not in control of the health of my cats. They will eventually get sick and die, and there is not much I can do about it. I am not in control of whether my new house gets built on time. I am not in control of how much it is going to cost. I am not in control of my own health. I am not in control of my wife's health, or that of any of my family members.

As it turns out, I am in control of very little. Now, you may look at this list, and think you have control over some of these things. Like your investment performance. Do you, really? Of course not. Some of the smartest people in the world get clobbered in the markets every year. Other people get lucky over and over again. It is mostly random. And this is where people get into trouble, because they think that investment performance is a function of work and effort. You can work 22 hours a day, and it makes no difference. You can work two hours a day, and it makes no difference. Change my mind.

I am not in control of people and things. I am only in control of how I respond to people and things. I am in control of my attitude. I am in control of my feelings. That is the essence of being human: we can choose our response to things. Many years ago, I was listening to a public speaker tell the story about the death of his wife—two teenagers dropped a cinder block off an overpass and it landed on her windshield, instantly killing her. They never found the kids. I suppose he could have loaded his shotgun and gone out in search of the perpetrators. That is not the response he chose. He handled it with grace, even forgiving the killers for their actions. It was one of the most powerful messages I have ever heard.

Keep in mind that I don't believe in determinism of any kind. I never believed any of that Martin Armstrong bullshit. And I don't believe any of the Fourth Turning bullshit, either, though I do like reading about generational studies. I don't believe that tragedies are "God's will." But since we're on the subject, I do believe that God won't give us anything that we can't handle—no matter how horrible the circumstances. And when I am faced with a serious challenge, I often think to myself, "What am I supposed to learn from this?" There is a lesson in everything. I am also not a believer in the idea that everything happens for a reason, but I do believe that life's obstacles are opportunities to respond to adverse circumstances with poise.

Someday, something awful, something entirely out of my control, is going to happen to me. It is a statistical certainty. How I respond to it will be up to me.

We are all going to die, one day. How will you choose to respond to the news that you are in checkmate, that you have a limited amount of time left on planet Earth? Will you handle it gracefully, fearlessly, or will you panic and drag everyone down with you? How will you handle the death of a parent, or child? That's not to say that you shouldn't mourn in these situations—there is a time and a place for mourning. And there is a time and a place for asking for help. But your burden shouldn't become someone else's. And it's funny, because some of our favorite stories as a society are those of people responding with grace and fortitude in times of extreme hardship. Like Viktor Frankl, and John McCain. We read these stories over and over again, and pass the book recommendations around on Twitter. *Dignity* is a very underused word these days.

One great litmus test of spiritual fitness is how you respond when you are in a car accident. Do you fly out of the vehicle, flapping your arms like a signalman, screaming obscenities at the other driver? Or do you calmly approach the other vehicle and ask the driver if he or she is okay—even if the accident was their fault? How you respond in these situations says a lot about you. Accidents suck bad enough as it is. It is a massive inconvenience, because now you have to deal with insurance and police and getting your car fixed, and nobody has time for that, and you don't need to exacerbate the situation by acting like an asshole. I sideswiped a guy on Highway 17 Bypass in Myrtle Beach in 2021, the first collision with another vehicle that I had ever caused, and when we pulled over, he held up his hands in the *what the fuck?* gesture, and I just shrugged and said, "I'm sorry," and then he was totally cool. Nobody's hurt. It's a hassle, but it's not the end of the world. I don't remember his name, and I will never see him again, but I will never forget the decency he showed me that day.

Another test of spiritual fitness is when you are fired from your job. When you've been fired, you're typically thinking about yourself, but I encourage you to think about the feelings of the poor person who had to deliver the news. Firing people isn't easy for anyone involved, and the last thing you need to do is to scream and yell and make a hard situation even more difficult. The best thing to do in these situations is to be classy: thank them for all the opportunities and wish them the best in the future. And guess what: if you exit gracefully, you will leave on good terms and with good feelings, and you never know, you might be needed at some point in the future. People lose sight of this in the moment. Remember, you can choose your response to things. Another recommendation: pause before you speak or act.

Now, the thing about powerlessness is that there is a certain class of people—politicians, CEOs, financiers, people in positions of authority—that really believe that they can direct the activities of everyone that works for them. Guess what: things would work just fine if they weren't there. They would work just fine if *you* weren't there. And that's the spiritually beautiful aspect of libertarianism: spontaneous order and the unplanned. When you examine Communism, really what it is, is a spiritual sickness, the idea that one person can control the activities of an entire population and its economy, and can optimally direct the actions of millions of people. And with loss of control comes fear, and with fear comes violence. The Western world, with its capitalism and liberal democracies, is spiritually enlightened, though we seem to be regressing on that front.

With powerlessness comes courage. To be in possession of the idea that nothing is within your control, but whatever happens, everything will be okay—that is the only real power. It always is okay, in the end.

MY EGO IS NOT MY AMIGO

I FIRST HEARD THAT saying, *my ego is not my amigo*, about five years ago, and thought it was pretty cool. Then I heard it a bunch more times and it sort of lost its coolness. Now, everyone is saying it. But it makes for a good title.

I will speak as an investment professional for a moment—life gets a lot simpler when you figure out that pretty much everyone in the markets is motivated by ego. They're not actually trying to make money. They're trying to look good. They want to be liked. They crave affection and admiration. This describes about 95% of people in finance. They would rather lose money privately than be wrong publicly.

There are deep psychological reasons for this. Notice that this phenomenon is even more pronounced among Generation X. Our Boomer/Silent Generation parents didn't pay any attention to us when we were kids. They didn't go to our Little League games, they didn't go to our graduations, and in some cases, actively shit on us or campaigned against us. They seemed indifferent to the possibility that we could be greased by a cement truck when out riding our bikes without helmets.

Boy, what parenting. Of course, the pendulum has swung completely back the other direction, and the Xers are compounding the errors of the Boomers by raising Zoomers that have pretty high opinions of themselves.

I see this on Twitter every day. *Look at me. Praise me. Tell me how awesome I am.* I'm not saying I don't do it, because I absolutely do. But I'm conscious of it, and I try to keep a lid on it. Your ego is not your amigo, especially in the world of finance.

But finance is depraved. I came of age reading a lot of Ayn Rand, who said that your ego was a good thing. Reasonable people can disagree on this. You don't want to think you're a piece of shit, but if you are going around thinking you're God's gift to _____, you're going to make a nuisance of yourself. Really, the solution here is to be right-sized. Your opinion of yourself should be correct. Your insides should match your outsides.

Not long ago, my therapist told me that I was full of myself, which sounds confrontational, but in that context it really wasn't. I do have a pretty high opinion of my writing ability. I do have a pretty high opinion of my DJing. When it comes to investing, I am pretty humble—there are a lot brighter financial minds than me out there. I am good at what I do, and I stay out of trouble, which is enough. But it made me wonder—is there some aspect of my personality that leads people to believe, like my therapist, that I have a big ego? Is this holding me back in life?

There is that old saying about the guy who was born on third base and thinks he hit a triple. That certainly doesn't describe me. I was born in the on-deck circle, and I am a self-made man. I think you will see that is one thing that self-made men have in common—they have a pretty high opinion of their abilities. Because they did it themselves, with no help. If I ever become super-famous, maybe someday people will travel to look at my childhood home. They will see that it is… small. I grew up with my divorced mother and my grandmother, who passed away when I was 14. We were not buying ribeye steak, let's put it that way. A social scientist would have looked at me, at age seven, and declared my case hopeless. And here I am. So yes, I have a pretty high opinion of myself, not least from having dealt with some serious health issues along the way.

One thing I always try to be is teachable. I don't have all the answers, and I am constantly seeking to improve. For the five-and-a-half years that I wrote for Bloomberg Opinion, I was constantly trying to improve as a columnist. I'm writing short stories, and it's very clear that I don't know what the hell I'm doing. Even in my financial newsletter, which I have been doing for 15 years, I am continually trying to get better. You have to be open to feedback. Sometimes feedback is painful, but if you're hearing the same thing from a number of different people, chances are, they are on to something. The day I stop being teachable is the day that my career comes to an end.

I talked about being right-sized, and how your insides should match your outsides. I strive to have my image of myself match up with other people's image of me. And my image of myself varies from day to day. Some days I think I'm a hero, other days I think I'm a piece of crap, which is often a function of being bipolar. Neither are true. Really, I'm just a bozo—like everyone else—trying to figure it out as I go along.

One thing finance people like to do (especially on Twitter) is cultivate an air of invincibility—draw attention to the calls that go right, and ignore the ones that don't. Three of the most powerful words in the English language are *I was wrong*. If more people said those three words, the world would be a better place.

The worst thing that can happen to you is that you become wildly successful. I look at athletes, movie stars, successful people in finance or tech, and they're superstars, legitimate superstars—they have legions of adoring fans who are constantly telling them how great they are. It is very difficult to stay grounded under such circumstances. I've had a middling amount of success—I've made some money, but nothing I've ever done has really gone hockey-stick—and it goes to your head. And a large ego can justify not-so-nice treatment of other people. Years ago, I was watching something on TV where Sylvester

Stallone's house help basically had to treat him like a god. If he entered the room, they had to bow their heads, avoid eye contact, and shuffle backwards out of the room. You may think to yourself that there is no way you would act like that if you had that kind of fame. I beg to differ. It can happen to all of us.

I have had a tiny amount of fame. I will be walking down the street somewhere, and someone will say, *hey, you're Jared Dillian!* And then they will want to take a selfie. I don't want to leave you with the impression that this happens all the time, but I will say that it has happened 30–40 times over the years. It happened when I was on vacation in Greece. It happened, of all places, in Carmel, Indiana. It's happened on planes and subways. I've had random people fist-bump me walking down the sidewalk in New York. I won't say that it's fun. It's very, very weird. It's a good opportunity to stay right-sized, is what it is. And it makes me wonder what life would be like for truly famous people, movie stars and such. You could never leave the house. It would be hell. The interesting thing is that finance is the one profession where you can have the money without the fame—and then people want the fame, too! It isn't enough to be stupidly rich. Everyone has to love you.

You can't not have an ego, or else you will be a doormat. If you didn't have an ego, you wouldn't dare to take risks, because you would think that you were incompetent to execute on them. But there is a pretty good chance that you are not as smart, likable, or as important as you think you are. I know that is certainly the case with me.

LEAVES IN A SWIMMING POOL

A MAN STANDS AT the edge of his swimming pool, holding a leaf skimmer. The pool was installed in 2006 when a great, expansive second floor was added to the house, increasing its value significantly. But time and the elements have taken their toll on the pool deck—the stone is marred with dirt and grime, and the outdoor furniture is faded.

The man swings the leaf skimmer back and forth in the pool, trying to scoop up every last leaf, deposited there from the oak that hangs over the north end of the pool, mocking him. If it weren't an oak, he would have had that tree removed long ago. "Damn all these leaves in this damn swimming pool," he says, cursing his misfortune, thinking about all the bullshit he has to deal with on a daily basis.

At this point his wife approaches from behind and says, "Darling… you have a swimming pool."

I looked it up. Eight percent of houses in the U.S. have a swimming pool, and that includes the cheap, lowbrow, above-ground types. You have a swimming pool, you are already in the top 8%. What in the actual fuck do you have to complain about? If you are in the top 8% of households in the U.S., that probably means that you are in the top 0.3% of households in the world. And you're complaining about leaves in a swimming pool. Earth to asshole: *You have a swimming pool.*

We have it so good. We have such an unbelievably high standard of living, with every technological convenience at our disposal. We have dishwashers and washing machines, and we even have these little robots that you talk to and they turn on the music. And some giant faceless corporation spent $25 billion on that gadget, losing boatloads of money on it in the hopes that you would buy their stuff. Life is awesome. Life is amazingly awesome. And this country is so rich that people in the bottom half, or even the bottom quarter, have it pretty good. There is literally nothing to complain about.

Years ago, I used to run around with a—for lack of a better word—poorer crowd of people in Myrtle Beach. What I found by hanging out with them was that I had the most extravagant luxury problems in the world. One time I was with these people, and everyone was talking about their problems, stuff like, *I can't pay my rent*, or, *I might go back to jail*, and I was like, "Ugh! My literary agent isn't returning my emails!" And people looked at me like I was nuts. There is a saying: *If you're with a group of people and you all put your problems in the middle of the room in a big pile, chances are you would want your problems back.* This is a pretty strong argument for not complaining about shit.

My brother and I are like Felix and Oscar. We have a lot of things in common, especially the scatological humor and dick jokes, but in some ways we are diametrically opposed. My brother doesn't complain about stuff—even when things are really going pear-shaped, he is always looking on the bright side and trying to spin it into a positive. This used to piss me off. And now I get it—your thoughts become your words, and your words become your actions, and if you are really a negative person, complaining about things all the time, you are going to manifest negativity in your life. If you wish for bad things to happen, bad things will happen. I have seen people do it over and over again.

To wit: I am writing this poolside at the Condado Vanderbilt in Puerto Rico. I am on a lounge chair overlooking the damn ocean. We were assigned to Room 262. We looked out the window—we were right over the hot tub, and unfortunately, the hot tub is open until midnight. There is noise. I'm not super-sensitive to noise, but my wife is. We discussed changing rooms. We talked to our travel agent, and we learned that the hotel tried to do right by us and upgrade us to a huge suite—it just happened to be in a bad location. The last thing I want to do is put this on my travel agent who works very hard to make sure his clients are happy. It's all good. Think of what a high-maintenance prick I would be if I threw a temper tantrum and demanded a room on a higher floor. Think of the optics of this for a second: rich guy is annoyed by voices coming from the hot tub outside his giant luxury suite. Life is pretty good—it doesn't have to be perfect.

My least favorite place in the world, hands down, is the Hamptons. I went once, years ago, and I will never go back (unless I have a DJ gig). And the reason I hate the Hamptons is because it is full of super-rich jackasses who think everything has to be perfect. I went to a fish shop at one point, this little place in East Hampton that sells fresh fish. I was waiting to pick up an order. A pencil-necked old guy was unhappy about the extra 30 seconds it was taking to be served, so he went behind the counter, *into the freezer*, and started yelling at the poor Mexican guy who worked there. I've seen people in the Hamptons get into fuck-you screaming matches over a parking space. It's nuts. This magical place, where everything is absolutely perfect, and people find reasons to be unhappy. In fact, they are unhappy pretty much all the time.

I've seen the same phenomenon in Los Angeles as well. As you know, the weather in Los Angeles is perfect, every day. There are inconveniences, like the traffic, but Californians have worked hard on making California perfect, and it is pretty great. I was in a café on the ground floor of an office building (this was back in 2007 or so), and this gorgeous, impeccably dressed young woman was at the cash register, getting her lunch, and she says to the cashier, "Were you giving me attitude?" And then they got into a screaming match on a perfect day where everyone was wearing perfect clothes and smelled great and everyone had a phone number in their bank account. I was like, you people are nuts.

I think if you grow up with not a lot, you tend to have a different perspective on this. Let's put it this way: I wasn't going to luxury hotels overlooking the ocean when I was a kid. Last week, I was at the construction site of my new 10,000-square-foot home, and I tripped over a piece of rebar. Punched a hole in my new $700 black suede boots. An old friend of mine says you're allowed to be upset about something for 24 hours. I was upset for about 20 minutes. Am I really going to be the guy that complains about ruining a pair of boots on the construction site of his multimillion-dollar home? I chunked them in the trash and ordered new ones, without giving it another thought.

I have another longtime friend who is unfailingly positive. He's the guy who gave me DJ lessons back in 2008. Sometime around 2013, we were taking some classes at Dubspot on 14th Street in New York. Dubspot was a great electronic music/DJ school that went tits up in 2016. I was taking an Ableton class with a bunch of 13-year-old dubstep producers. Anyway, my friend and I leave Dubspot and take a cab back to his apartment. Back in his apartment, about 15 minutes later, he says, "Shit! I left my laptop at Dubspot." At this point I'm freaking out—*dude, dude,* and he looks at me and says, very calmly, "I think it's going to be okay." I'm going nuts in the cab all the way there and his heart rate hasn't gone up a beat. We get to Dubspot, he goes inside, and the laptop is right in class where he left it. Nothing to worry about. He says that a lot: *I think it's going to be okay.* And the magic of that statement is it always is okay, and even if it's not, it's still okay. *Bridge of Spies*, starring Tom Hanks, was a decent movie, but the best part about it was the Communist spy. He'd be about to be sentenced to death for espionage, or swapped to the Russians who would torture and kill him. Tom Hanks would ask him, "Aren't you worried?" And he'd turn around and say, deadpan, "Would it help?"

I think this to myself when I'm on a plane and the wi-fi isn't working. Talk about first-world problems. A real problem is if one of my cats dies. And if that doesn't make any sense to you, change "cats" to "kids" and you will get the picture. Everything else is gravy. Go ahead. Say all the mean things you want to me on Twitter. At least I have Twitter.

HOW TO HANDLE FAILURE

WRITING ABOUT FAILURE is easy, because it comes naturally to me. I have failed at nearly every single thing that I have done:

- First of all, I was physically abused as a child.
- I was raised by a single mother in not-quite poverty.
- I was bullied occasionally.
- I was held back a year in Little League.
- I got poor grades in middle school.
- I got poor grades in high school.
- I didn't make the varsity baseball team.
- I got spit out the bottom of the tennis team.
- I almost got in serious trouble one time.
- I got poor grades in college in spite of having the third-highest SAT scores in my class.
- I almost got kicked out of college, which would have effectively ended my career in the Coast Guard.
- An injury ended my wrestling career.

- I was denied a command endorsement.
- I never made senior vice president at Lehman Brothers.
- I was paid half as much as my peers.
- Ultimately, I failed at Wall Street.
- I spent three weeks in a psychiatric ward.
- I have battled a variety of addictions.
- I have the slowest-growing newsletter in the history of newsletters.
- My first book was a failure.
- My second book was a failure.
- My radio show was an expensive failure.
- My essays are a failure.
- Almost none of the mountains of content I have created over the years has ever gone viral.
- My music career is a struggle, to say the least.

There have been some successes along the way. But I have failed far more than I have succeeded.

I have about 1,000 words to go. Now, I could write something treacly and embarrassing about grit and resilience, which is a fashionable thing to write about these days. There are millions of essays like that out there. They could be written by ChatGPT.

I want to tell you that failure is really, really hard.

One of my toughest failures was my first book, *Street Freak*. I had such high hopes for that book. I mean, how could a book about Lehman Brothers, released only three years after the financial crisis, on the same day that Occupy Wall Street started, underperform? I am not much for airing dirty laundry in print, but let's just say that the book ended up with the wrong publisher and the wrong people and everything that could go wrong, went wrong. And it was heartbreaking. I was bitter about that for years. The book was remaindered, you know. I'd tell you the sales figures, but they're pathetically low. When I tell people those sales figures privately, they're shocked.

And the reason they're shocked is because that book has become part of the Wall Street lexicon, held in the same regard as *Liar's Poker* and the other great Wall Street memoirs. Think of it this way: there are only a few hundred business books published by the Big Five publishers every year, mostly by people who are already famous in one way or another, and *Street Freak* was one of them. And it had a huge impact on people. I've had so many people reach out to me to share their struggles with mental health.

So it really is a matter of framing. All the failures I listed earlier could also be viewed as successes. If I had gotten the command endorsement my first tour in the Coast Guard, I'd likely still be in the Coast Guard. Or not—if I had gone through those same mental health struggles while in the military, I would have received a lower standard of care. And I would have lost my security clearance, and bounced out of the service in ignominy. So things worked out for the best. And if I had made SVP at Lehman Brothers, I'd likely still be on Wall Street, too—and freaking miserable, and a nervous wreck. So things worked out for the best.

When I reflect on my life, every hardship I've gone through, every failure I've experienced, has been for a reason. It wasn't suffering for suffering's sake. There was something I had to learn from each of those experiences. So you fail, and you learn, and you get smarter, and you fail at different things, and you learn, and you get smarter still. But you never quit. There is a time to quit, eventually, but if you quit before it's time to quit, it's undignified. And if you give up, and never try anything again, you are a loser. And I don't use that word lightly.

Writing is a particular source of suffering. Sometimes when I think about my middling writing success, I think about my favorite writer of all time: Barry Hannah, the greatest writer who ever lived, who never sold more than 7,000 copies of any of his books. And yet, many of the world's great writers consider Barry Hannah to be their favorite writer. At the time of writing, my Substack has 5,426 subscribers. It gets a huge amount of engagement—read rates in the high 60%s, dozens upon dozens of likes, but it doesn't grow. And somewhere out there, some 25-year-old nincompoop has clickbaited and growth-hacked his way to 50,000 subscribers. So I keep doing what I am doing, and plow forward with the idea that if you just keep putting in the time and writing something approximating literature, then good things will happen.

In 2016, leading up to the release of my novel *All the Evil of This World*, I got 100 galleys printed and sent them out to luminaries in print, TV, and Twitter. I might as well have been told to go fuck myself. Nobody helped. At one point, I sent a Twitter direct message to an editor at *Fortune*, angling for a review, but I accidentally referred to him as an editor at *Forbes* in the DM. He took a screenshot and tweeted it, ridiculing me. My heart was pounding. My ears were hot. This book was shaping up to be another failure, and this asshole was mocking me. I was sitting in my office, and I remember talking to myself—I never talk to myself. I said, *Get back on the horse, and set about sending out more cold DMs and emails*. None of it hit. The book generated a huge amount of controversy, resulted in scores of negative reviews on Amazon, and never sold more than 3,000 copies.

Framing: I consider it my greatest achievement, and I'm not kidding.

Nothing I have done has ever gone parabolic, and I have done a lot of things. At the time of writing, I have a third book coming out, and a fourth. I have high hopes for the fourth. But who knows—maybe it will be yet another failure. People close to me know that I am always working on a bunch of projects simultaneously in the hopes that something will take off. Nothing ever does. But I keep trying. I never give up. And there has been a great deal of suffering along the way.

The corollary to all of this is that suffering is how we grow. Look at any successful person, and they have scars. There is an old saying: *After 20 years, he was an overnight success*. Whenever we see a successful person, we don't see the years, even decades of work that goes into it. And as for the 25-year-old nincompoops, that success is transitory. They have never experienced love. They have never experienced pain. And the first time life throws them a curveball, they'll shrivel up and blow away. Successful people give off the impression that life is easy. But nothing could be further from the truth. They are sitting on top of a big pile of failures.

Life hands you a bag of shit sometimes. Bad things do happen randomly, though not very often. It's about how you clean up the mess. For as many professional failures as I've had, my life has been relatively free of tragedy. No car accidents, no cancer, no unexpected deaths of family members. I've been lucky, and some people have real problems. It really is all about your attitude. And remember, if you're going through hell, keep going.

GIVE THE GIFT OF TIME

I KNOW PEOPLE HAVE feelings about this, but I never give money to panhandlers. Never have. There are the usual concerns about how they're probably just going to score drugs with the money, but that's not really why. We all have a desire to help people. But a dollar doesn't really do anything. What is needed is to take that person to rehab, get them an apartment, get them cleaned up, get them a haircut, get them new clothes, and spend six months coaching them and following them around to make sure they get a job and become a productive member of society. But nobody has the time for that shit. So they give them a dollar, not because it really accomplishes anything, but because it eases their conscience. It's not really about the homeless person, it's about you. We give that dollar with the idea that a dollar might momentarily ease this person's suffering, and that is something, but maybe it does and maybe it doesn't. Maybe it just goes to drugs. The point is, it's not really helping.

Help is for the people who want it, not for the people who need it.

What is really needed is to donate time, rather than money. But that's true of a lot of things, right? A common phenomenon among rich people is they start writing checks to a lot of different charitable organizations. Sometimes this is done with the best of intentions. Sometimes this is done with the intent to get their name on the donor wall. And rich people tend to have lots of money, but not a lot of time. For sure, the money helps. But if rich people were generous with their time, rather than their money, it would be more meaningful.

It applies to me as well. I have donated to a local animal shelter. Years ago, someone suggested that I put on some old jeans and a T-shirt and go down there and scoop litter boxes. Truthfully, I would make the time to do that—working with your hands gets you out of your head—but animal shelters can be very sad places. I don't think I could handle it. So I write checks, and leave the really hard problems to someone else. That seems to be my role here. But I'm doing what all the other rich people do—donating money, not time.

Nobody has time. People just want to throw money at a problem and hope it goes away. San Francisco has been doing this with its homeless population for decades, with little to show for it. They spend billions upon billions of dollars, and they have hundreds of mental health professionals and social workers working on this, and it seems to have the opposite effect of what is intended. Help is for people who want it, not for people who need it.

But when I say "nobody has time," I'm not just talking about philanthropy, I'm talking about our dealings with family and friends. The most precious gift we could give someone is our time. Say you have a cousin who is struggling financially. You could throw money at the problem, and give him five thousand bucks, which would assuage your conscience, but my guess is it probably wouldn't help. You would be throwing good money after bad. Or you could give him the gift of time, buy a plane ticket, fly out to East Frogkick, sit down at the kitchen table, go through all his income and expenses and credit card statements, make a budget, and teach him a little discipline.

It could be done—few financial problems are intractable. And sometimes you offer to help and the help is refused. But nobody wants to jump on a plane and fly out to East Frogkick. Who has time for that? You have a job and a spouse and a house and some kids and some pets and church and karate or whatever else you do with your spare time, and maybe if you ignore this problem with your broke cousin long enough, it will go away. That's the way most people behave. *I'm just going to pretend this isn't happening and maybe it goes away.*

Time is more valuable than money. Jeff Bezos donated $10 billion to fight climate change, hoping that people would think he was a little less of an asshole. Ten billion dollars. It had no effect on public opinion whatsoever. They were still putting guillotines outside his house. Now, let's say that Jeff Bezos goes around meeting kids who are terminally ill with cancer in the hospital. How do you think people react to that? Sure, there will always be left-wing dicks who doubt his intentions, but my guess is that most people would view that pretty favorably. The difference: he is giving time rather than money.

Jeff Bezos's time is super important. He is being pulled in a bunch of different directions. My time is also important. Even at my level, I am being pulled in a bunch of different directions. But there are a handful of people—20, maybe—who, if they were struggling, I would be on a plane to East Frogkick to be with in a second. Or, at a minimum, I would pick up the phone. They say you really find out who your friends are in times of trouble. The people who will give you the gift of time.

As I've mentioned, I spent three weeks in a psychiatric ward in 2006. Do you want to know what I remember about that experience? I remember the people who visited me. In fact, I remember everyone who helped me during that period of my life. Keep in mind that a lot of progress has been made in educating people about mental illness since then. In 2006, there was still a strong stigma. Trust me, I know exactly who visited me back then, 17 years later. I'm not friends with all of them—people go in different directions. But I will never forget that they gave me the gift of time when I was at the most vulnerable point in my life.

You can tell a lot about someone by how they spend their time. Some people spend a lot of time with their kids—that's their priority, and that's fine. I spend a lot of time working (and with my cats). Some people spend a lot of time playing video games, and that says something too. If you really want to figure out why one or more aspects of your life isn't working, make a time chart. For a week, write down what you are doing for every 15-minute increment of the day. What you will probably see is that there is a lot of time that is not well spent. You will probably see that you spend an inordinate amount of time on leisure activities, like games, sports, TV, or social media. You will also see that you do not spend as much time working as you thought. You will also see that you are really not quite as busy as you thought. There is probably someone out there who needs your help, who is explicitly asking for your help, and you say that you do not have enough time. That's bullshit. We all have time. I swear to God, you have time. You don't even have to get on a plane to East Frogkick. All it takes is a phone call.

I am where I am today because of a handful of people who gave me the gift of time when I needed it the most. When you throw money at a problem, it is so… antiseptic. You lose the personal connection between the donor and the recipient, especially when the money passes through a third party, which is the reason why all social welfare programs eventually fail. And if they succeed in the meantime, it is because of the efforts of caregivers and social workers who actually give a shit. Very few problems have been solved by throwing money at them. Nearly all problems have been solved by one person spending time with another.

This isn't to say that you should never give money. Money has its place. But giving money is easy. You can always make more money. You can't make more time.

DO HARD THINGS

Back when I was writing for Bloomberg Opinion, the one piece I wrote that went insanely viral was the one where I took a giant dump on the CFA program. That kept me busy for a couple of months. I've never gotten so much hate mail in my entire life, and some of it was personal. I should have expected it. People worked hard to accomplish a goal, and I told them that it was a huge waste of time. Nobody likes to hear that.

I am a big proponent of doing hard things. Even the CFA, but we'll return to that in a second. I am even a proponent of doing hard things for the sake of doing hard things, because it raises your self-esteem. You set a goal, you work really hard to achieve it, overcoming a bunch of obstacles in the process, and at the end of it, you look back and say, *I did that*. You do this once, and you do this twice, and you do this dozens and hundreds of times over the course of your life, and that is a life well lived.

It doesn't have to be a professional achievement. Playing the guitar is hard. If you spend a few thousand hours learning it, and you get passably good at it, that is an achievement. Going back to school is hard. You're an adult, you're established in your career, and you find yourself doing homework and sitting in class with a bunch of 24-year-olds, and you jump through a bunch of hoops, and at the end of it, you get a diploma. That is an achievement. Even doing a giant fucking jigsaw puzzle is an achievement. That is probably the best example of doing something hard for its own sake—you get absolutely nothing out of it but the feeling of accomplishing something difficult.

A funny thing about being a newsletter writer and media personality for a bunch of years is that it gives you some pretty interesting insights into human nature. I find myself constantly at odds with people who have never done hard things. The people who have done hard things—run a hedge fund, for example—generally don't criticize, because they know how hard it is to create something. No, I have run-ins with the types of people who, when faced with a choice between something hard and something easy, took the easy path every time. When you've never accomplished anything, when you don't have that lived experience, when you don't know what it's like to build something, it's easy to be critical. The old saying is: *Those who criticize the most, contribute the least*. It is absolutely true.

I have done many hard things in my life. One that I don't talk about all that often was trying out for the wrestling team my senior year in high school. Yes, I waited until my senior year of high school to join the wrestling team. And it wasn't just any wrestling team—my school had won the state championships six years in a row. It was a juggernaut wrestling team. I was pretty much a fatso at that point in my life, and I was trying to get in shape because I would be going to the Coast Guard Academy the following year. The tryouts lasted a week. A hundred kids would try out, and the workouts were so hard that typically there would only be 20-30 left at the end of the week. Incredibly, I made the team. I finished with a 4-4 JV record that year, which certainly wasn't going to get my name on a plaque somewhere, but I did it. The tryouts were hard, but the practices were even harder. Running up and down stairs for hours, puking, it was nuts. And after I accomplished that, the Coast

Guard Academy was easy in comparison. Looking back, the four months that I did wresting in high school probably had a bigger positive impact on my life than anything I have ever done. And it was so improbable—fat Mr. Magoo tries out for one of the strongest wrestling teams in the country, and makes it. I ended up dropping 27 pounds, by the way.

And then I went to the Coast Guard Academy. Why do this to yourself? I didn't even like the water! I did it because it was hard. Bill Clinton spoke at my graduation. After we threw our caps in the air, we tumbled into a giant scrum on the field, and I found myself face to face with my freshman roommate, who was from West Virginia. We started doing this happy-happy dance on the field, embracing each other. I remember the look on his face. *We did it.* Four years of bullshit, of isolation, of mental torture, and we made it. I thought at the time that it was the hardest thing I would ever do, but it wasn't—not by a long shot.

Sometimes doing the hard thing leads to more money. This is often the case—but not always. Sometimes people do hard things for not a lot of money. Sometimes people do hard things for the one-in-a-million shot of making a lot of money—and they fail. And that is okay, too. There is a DJ/producer who calls himself Marsh—real name Tom Marshall. The guy looks like Waldo, with his horizontal-striped shirts and round glasses. He's got an incredible sound, a melodic mix of deep and progressive, and he is the king of the Anjunadeep label. He tours a lot. If I were to guess, he is probably making a few hundred thousand dollars a year, which is decent, but there are certainly ways to make a lot more money with a lot less work. But he's the best at what he does, he's famous (in certain circles), and he's doing what he loves. I've seen him play live before—he sure does look like he's having fun. It doesn't look like a job.

Sports are hard. I have said that I think marathons are dumb. This is true—but not the first one. You run a marathon, and then you get to say that you ran a marathon for the rest of your life. People do this, and then they put the oval 26.2 sticker on the back of their car, because they are really proud of it. I get it. You did a hard thing, and you're proud of it. I played racquetball in Myrtle Beach from 2010-2020. I used to hit the piss out of the ball. I ended up placing third in the top division of the city-wide tournament, right before the start of the pandemic. I was pretty proud of that, but at that point I had reached the limits of my abilities. People get good at tennis, they get good at golf, they get good at jiu-jitsu, and they are proud of it. Terrific. It's a lot of work, and remember: nobody has to do this stuff. Likewise, chess is hard. I have a lot of respect for people who are good at chess, because boy do I suck at chess. Poker is freaking impossible. I had some early success with poker and thought that I might take it more seriously, but it turned out to be a lot harder than I thought.

And sometimes things turn out to be too hard. You do the mental mathematics and you say, *well, I am going to put 10,000 hours into this, and this is what I am going to get in return,* and you decide that it isn't worth it. And you might find something enjoyable if you do it avocationally, but if you spent 10,000 hours on it, it wouldn't be enjoyable. And that's okay, too. I have done my 10,000 hours on music, and I can tell you that it is a grind sometimes, and while performing is fun, the gigs can be busts too. There are times when I feel like giving it up, because the work/reward ratio is so low. But it's good for the soul.

I have my objections to the CFA. First of all, I don't like credentialism, and second of all, there is no discernible benefit to getting a CFA. It doesn't really help you get a job, and it doesn't really help you get paid more. But if I had to write that op-ed all over again, I would say that the CFA is hard, and that hard things are worth doing, and you will feel a big sense of accomplishment when you're done. I would just rather spend my time doing other things, and that's a matter of personal preference. But it got people thinking about their motivations for doing the CFA, which is a good thing.

If you find your life unfulfilling, there is a 99% chance it's because you're not doing hard things. I don't care if you're making quilts. Do something hard, and try to be the best at it.

HAVING A HEALTHY RELATIONSHIP WITH MONEY

There are two types of people in this world: Cheap Fucks (CFs)—people who spend a little—and High Rollers—people who spend a lot. That shouldn't surprise anyone—we all know examples of each. What is surprising is that there are so few people in the middle. And the people in the middle, the tiny minority of them, are the only ones with a healthy relationship with money.

I have stories. Boy, do I have stories of mind-bogglingly stupid financial behavior out of CFs and High Rollers. Unfortunately, the people involved all read my stuff so I will not be able to share them here. Maybe over drinks sometime. Let me just say that your relationship with money is important, because it affects all your other relationships. If you cheap out on college for your kids, everyone is going to end up in therapy. If you blow cash on six-figure cars when you make five figures, everyone is going to end up in therapy.

I came from a CF family, at least on my mother's side. There were extenuating circumstances: we lived in Connecticut, the biggest cheap fuck state in the entire country. Connecticut is filled with women in their late 50s with bowl cuts and L.L. Bean sweaters and turtlenecks calculating out 15% tips to the penny with the tip calculator cards they keep in their purse. Connecticut is the land of separate checks, Venmo-ing for gas, and paying for things with coins. You may have heard the term *Nutmegger*, a slightly derogatory term for a CF Connecticutian. I grew up this way. I got a passbook savings account at the age of eight, and started depositing my allowance in there. The only money I didn't save were the quarters I plunked into the *Xevious* machine at the arcade. I graduated high school in 1992 with $2,000, which was compounding at eight percent. My friends blew their cash on stupid shit, and I laughed at them. This was my life.

You might say that I had an unhealthy relationship with money. You know how you know when you have an unhealthy relationship with money? When someone borrows ten bucks off you and it causes you stress. When you give precisely zero to charity. When you get Starbucks gift cards as Christmas gifts. When paying for something, even something as simple as parking, causes you pain. You are not in control of your money—your money is in control of you. It is your master.

I'll go further and say that you know you have an unhealthy relationship with money when you are living below your means. When you have a seven-figure bank account, and you're living in a 1200-square foot house and driving a Saturn of early 2000s vintage. When you shop for clothes at Target—or even Walmart. When you can afford the JW Marriott but you stay in a goddamn Super 8. When you are causing yourself discomfort in order to save money when there is really no reason to be saving money—that is how you know that you have an unhealthy relationship with money.

The converse is also true, naturally. The High Rollers are the people who live above their means. The fancy cars, the fancy houses, the fancy vacations. The person who spends too much is a terrible cliché, because these are the people that personal finance guru Dave Ramsey shits on all the time. Yes, people spend too much money. But people also spend too *little* money. I bet if some social scientist ran a poll somewhere, what he or she would find is that the latter far outnumber the former. Ramsey, the dick that he is, isn't the only one. We've farmed literally thousands of personal finance experts in this country, and they all say the same thing: *Make your coffee at home. Consume less.* By the way, the amateur personal finance expert is a thing, with the FIRE movement and Van Life. I like my personal finance like I like my porn: done by professionals.

There is a pervasive belief that consumption is bad. This belief exists on both ends of the political spectrum. The left wants you to consume less because consumption is bad for the environment. The right wants you to consume less because luxury is considered a sin. The solution is in the middle: to consume the right amount relative to your income, and to live at your means. Not above your means, not below your means, but *at* your means. If you make seven figures, you should not be buying used middlebrow cars. I am morally opposed to this. Cars are the ultimate personal finance litmus test, because they're terrible investments, what with the depreciation and maintenance, and people view them as status symbols. I will also tell you that an $80,000 car is twice as nice as a $40,000 car, which is twice as nice as a $20,000 car. It is more pleasurable to own and to drive. So if you have the money, you should buy a nice car. Stop being a cherry.

There is another pervasive belief that people are not saving money unless they're denying themselves small luxuries. People will be thirsty instead of spending a dollar on an Arizona iced tea at the gas station. The discomfort that they experience by being thirsty reinforces their belief that they are virtuous by forgoing consumption. I know, because I used to do this. Now, if I am hungry, I buy food. If I am thirsty, I buy something to drink. If I am sleepy, I get a hotel room. That is literally what the fucking money is for.

Yes, there are people who have problems with spending and going into debt. They are the object of ridicule of thousands of personal finance experts. In my experience, they are not too common. If you really want to know the state of personal finance in this country, talk to a waiter or waitress, and ask about all the horrible tips they get, like when a family with three kids sits down in a place like Olive Garden, and the kids smash food into the table and leave snot and barf everywhere, and the parents leave a $4 tip. Or when 12 women go out to a sushi lunch, and get 12 separate checks, and then spend the next 15 minutes arguing about who got what roll. These people are far more common than the couple that gets a $65 dinner, slaps down a hundo, and gets in their car and leaves. We did this to ourselves—we created a nation of cheap bastards.

So the goal here is to have a healthy relationship with money. You don't want the porridge to be too hot or too cold, but just right. How do you know when you have a healthy relationship with money? When you no longer stress about money. People who spend too much experience stress—they're always worried about how to make the next credit card payment. People who spend too little experience stress—they're agonizing over every penny. The goal is not only to experience zero stress about money, but to not even think about it at all. I have an assignment for you: try to go a week without even thinking about money. I bet you can't do it. It's a lot harder than you think. Everywhere we go we are bombarded by financial decisions. *Shit, the price of gas is high these days. Shit, Chipotle is $20 nowadays. Shit, my HOA dues went up this month.* Do any of these things cause you stress? If so, that provides an insight into your psychology.

Unfortunately, because my livelihood is tied to the financial markets, I have to think about money all the time. And sometimes I make a bad trade, and I have my ass in a sling. If I could make the same amount of money by just writing books and essays and short stories, trust me, I would. That is my curse—I think about money all the time. I even dream about it. But it's inescapable if you live in a capitalist country. You are at the mercy of wages, and you are at the mercy of prices. I'd still rather have that than the alternative. And maybe one day I will get to the point where I can just write short stories and make a living, though I probably won't live that long.

Like I said in the beginning, your relationship with money affects all your other relationships. People don't remember what you said, they remember how you made them feel. Also, separate checks are for candy-asses. I pay, then you pay. We take turns.

AMERICAN NINJA WARRIOR

There are a lot of Navy SEAL books out there. People like to take life advice from Navy SEALs, I guess. Especially on Wall Street. Finance folks hold the military in high regard, especially the special forces people. If you were to identify the core competency of a Navy SEAL, it is that he can withstand a superhuman amount of physical pain—and keep pressing forward.

I have known a handful of SEALs in my lifetime. In 2017, I think, I was at the Navy base on Coronado Island and met several of them. One of them was running an Ironman a week for an entire year. The guy was nothing special—six feet tall, maybe 185 pounds, but he probably could have killed me with his bare hands. That's nice, I guess, but I'm not sure why we're taking life advice from these people. And here's the reason: just because you are physically disciplined, does not mean you are mentally or emotionally disciplined. And mental and emotional discipline is what it takes to succeed in life—not how fast you can run an Ironman.

I know what you're thinking—don't you have to be mentally

disciplined to be physically disciplined? Like, if you're running a marathon (which I have) and you hit the wall (which I have), don't you have to be mentally tough to keep running and finish the race, instead of quitting? Well, yes—but that is a specific kind of mental toughness. Having what it takes to dig deep and finish a race is, yes, mental toughness. But that variety of mental toughness doesn't translate into other kinds of mental toughness. I have seen actual former special forces people crumble under the pressure of a trading floor, or shrivel up and die after people say mean things to them online. Just because you can run a sub-three marathon does not mean that you are going to succeed elsewhere in life. I'd repeat that sentence, but you can just go back and read it again.

And yet for years, I saw the bulge-bracket banks wave in dozens and hundreds of military people (myself included) because they conflated being tough with being smart, or conflated being tough with having an ability to manage risk. More often than not, you had a trading floor full of money-losing tough guys. This is a generalization, and there are exceptions. I can tell you that in my personal experience at Lehman Brothers, there were far more military folks that failed than succeeded. But it never changed the mythology around tough guys, and it never changed the recruiting practices. At least by now I think the Navy SEAL books are played out.

You want to see mental toughness, go find someone who is struggling with some hard-core mental illness (severe anxiety, severe depression, bipolar disorder, BPD, or schizophrenia, for starters) who suits up and shows up and does their best day in and day out. If you've ever been in the throes of it, you know. Of course, this is not to be confused with the person with mild unipolar depression who is feeling a little blue and spends two weeks on the couch watching the soaps. That's not to belittle that person's experiences, which are absolutely real and debilitating, but the person with severe mental illness who can dig deep and keep going in spite of that crippling psychic pain is a hero in my book. That is some Navy SEAL shit, right there. I'm not afraid of bombs and bullets—I'm really not. I'm afraid of the inside of my own head.

But we tend to celebrate physical achievements over mental achievements, don't we? I was scrolling through Facebook earlier today and I saw that a local friend of mine posted that he had just run his second half marathon. Not too fast, but he finished it. Bring on the likes and comments. I know this guy, and I know his personal struggles, and I can tell you on the list of his personal accomplishments, running a half marathon is far, far down the list. He's fought some demons bigger than you or I could ever imagine, and won. But the half marathon goes on Facebook. I have a few bodybuilder friends on Facebook, too. Lots of work, lots of discipline (especially around diet—yeesh), but that don't impress me much. Physical fitness is a funny thing—we look at someone who is fit and we make assumptions about what kind of character they have—that discipline must translate into something else, we think. Oftentimes, it doesn't. Lots of times, these people will have 580 credit scores or failed marriages or lives in personal turmoil. Conversely, we look at someone who is a fat fuck and we make assumptions about what kind of character they have. You can't judge a book by its cover.

So what is toughness? I would say that toughness is persevering in the face of some pretty great obstacles. Navy SEALs get all the credit because those obstacles are visible. *Let's carry logs around and simulate drowning and sleep for two hours over the course of a week.* And no, I'm not saying I can do that, because I can't. But Navy SEALs couldn't do what I do. And they couldn't do what you do, either.

For the average person who is persevering in the face of some fairly large obstacles, those obstacles are invisible. I mentioned mental illness, but poverty is another. Whenever I hear some story about a guy who rides his bike 20 miles to get paid ten bucks an hour on a Labor Ready job, that is some perseverance right there. Raising children could be another, especially special needs children, though I have no personal experience with that. Working two jobs and going to school at the same time. The point is that toughness comes in all shapes and sizes, and

I don't particularly appreciate being lectured on toughness by some asshole who runs ultramarathons and then gets a book ghostwritten about it, or some admiral who thinks that making your bed every day is the key to success in life.

It's all a matter of priorities. Physical fitness just isn't that important to a lot of people. Maybe they have other shit to do. Maybe they're working 18-hour days. Maybe they have a family. I should add that the reason that Navy SEALs are in such good shape is because it is pretty much their job to be in shape. Even when I was in the Coast Guard, taking two hours at lunch to go to the gym was a perfectly accepted practice. I had vastly more respect for the guys and gals who got up at 3:30 a.m. to work out in the basement of their homes in New Jersey so they could be at their desk at 6 a.m. on Wall Street. I place a high value on sleep, so that is a choice I would never make. Dwayne Johnson spends a fair amount of time in the gym and eats 700 pounds of cod a year. He has a lot of money riding on it. It doesn't mean he should be president.

When I look around, I see a lot of tough people. I see a lot of people who are carrying burdens that none of us would be willing to carry. Those are the people who should be writing self-help books. I've said this before, but it applies here, too: if you're going through hell, keep going.

INTEGRITY

INTEGRITY MEANS A lot of things to a lot of people. I define it as: *doing what you say you are going to do.*

Small example. Someone invites you to a party. You RSVP that you are going. Three hours before the party, something comes up. It is now inconvenient to go to the party. Do you stay home and take care of the minor emergency, or do you press on and go to the party, because that is what you said you were going to do?

Big example. You get married. Hot stranger attempts to seduce you. You made a promise, right?

An example that many of us will be faced with in the private sector: You have an employee that is doing exceptionally well at his job. You promise to give him a huge raise or bonus at the end of the year. The end of the year comes around, and the company has done not so well and there is less money to go around. You can still give him a huge bonus, but it would be problematic, because there would be less money to go around to more politically important people. Do you keep your promise?

Let me tell you how I do things. From 2001-03, I lived in Hoboken, New Jersey, at which point I moved two towns up the road to West New York. But for a time, I was still getting my hair cut at a barber shop in Hoboken. One day I had a haircut appointment and goofed and got on the wrong bus to West New York instead of Hoboken. I got off at the first stop in Weehawken and sprinted two miles, in my suit, in the summer, so I wouldn't miss my appointment in Hoboken. I arrived completely disheveled, dripping with sweat. I told them what happened, and they were like, *dude, you could have just missed your appointment,* and I said, no way was I going to miss that appointment. I do what I say I am going to do.

I am in the business of not letting people down. I do manage to let people down from time to time, like if I have a Zoom call and I don't put it on my calendar and I space. That actually happens a lot. But I don't intentionally let people down. I'm disorganized, but I have integrity.

There are some people who you just cannot count on under any circumstances. They say one thing, and do another. My nephew has a friend he calls "Flakemaster 5000" because the guy just absolutely never shows up to anything. So what happens? Whenever he says he is going to a party or an event, everyone is like, *surrrrrre you are,* and nobody takes him seriously. He's the Flakemaster. Whereas if I tell you I am going to be somewhere at a certain time, I will be there—a half hour early. I can be counted upon. There is a professor friend of mine at Coastal Carolina University who I go out to lunch with from time to time. I flaked on him twice in a row, both times because I had my ass on fire at work and was so engrossed in writing that I completely missed the reminders on my phone. I felt pretty bad about that. Nowadays, when we go out to lunch, I set about a half-dozen reminders to spare myself any further embarrassment.

I mentioned marriage. Marriage is a funny one—you make this promise in your 20s that you're never going to scrog with another person in your life. It's a bit early to be making that promise, to say the least. And then there are opportunities. And you are tested. I can say that I am not great-looking and I look grumpy all the time and I don't really give off any vibes, so it is pretty rare that I am tested. And the older you get, the easier that promise is to keep. There is more money at stake, there are kids, there are houses, everything is so much more complex, and you're going to trade all this money and experience all this pain for just five seconds of bliss. Infidelity looks like a pretty bad deal, the older you get. And then you find yourself with a secret life, buying extra phones and telling lies and making excuses and it is all impossible to keep track of after a while. Just a bunch of chaos. I prefer to keep my life simple.

And then there are things like dentist appointments. If you don't show up to a dentist appointment, you are an asshole. You are literally stealing money from the dentist. The dude has to run a business. What's wild is when people who actually run businesses do this to dentists. The funny thing about all of this is that appointment-based businesses (dentists, doctors, hairstylists) now use technology to remind the shit out of you so you don't forget. My hairstylist uses something called Vagaro to manage appointments, and I'm getting text messages three days out, then two days, then the day before. I suppose this cuts down on the Flakemasters, but it kind of clogs up my phone. I don't generally miss haircut appointments—after three weeks, I'm getting pretty shaggy and it starts to bug me. But the doctor's appointments every six months are a bit tougher. I put those in my phone and set it to remind me two weeks ahead of time, and by that point, circumstances may have changed. Then I call the doctor's office and reschedule the appointment. We used to do all this on paper.

In the Big 5 personality test, one of the attributes is conscientiousness. Conscientiousness, for the purposes of the test, is the tendency to be responsible, organized, hard-working, goal-directed, and to adhere to norms and rules. That's not quite integrity—there's nothing in there about keeping promises—but it's close. I score about in the middle in terms of conscientiousness—I have the best of intentions, but I am not very organized. I will say that I am very good with deadlines, because I deal with them all the time. But if I give you my word that I am going to do something, I will do it. And if I ever tell you "I swear on my cat's life…" you know that is as good as gold. I recall the scene in *Jerry Maguire* where the father of the college football player shakes hands with Tom Cruise and says that his word is "strong as oak" and then proceeds to throw him under the bus. I suspect that a lot of people behave this way when there is money involved. I mean, that pretty much describes all of Wall Street. Call me old-fashioned, but I am one of those people who believes that verbal commitments are binding, just like signed contracts. It's probably because I used to transact hundreds of millions of live deltas that way. As a trader, if your word wasn't your bond, you would have a very short career.

Most people, when thinking of the word integrity, believe it only applies to the big stuff: marriages and such. But it applies to the little stuff, too. Some people compartmentalize and keep big promises but let the little ones go. And some people are conscientious and keep the little promises but then screw up the big ones. Integrity is about keeping your word in all situations—big and small. In *Ocean's Eleven*, when Matt Damon and Brad Pitt are observing Terry Benedict, Matt Damon says, "That guy is a machine." Benedict, played by Andy Garcia, is a man of integrity, which is another way of saying that he does what he says he is going to do. And there is a saying that I came up with, years ago:

> *There is no commodity in this world so rare as the man who does what he says he is going to do.*

I used to work with a guy years ago who would miss deadlines and fuck things up all the time. His boss would come over to him, and ask him where the deliverable was, and he'd start flapping his arms around and say "O.B.E." O.B.E. stood for Overcome By Events. But that's the key—if you're a person of integrity, then you will never be overcome by events. You're in the no-matter-what club. You will get it done, no matter what. You will be there.

DON'T CHOP DOWN THE TREE

I'VE WRITTEN FIVE short stories in the last six months. Some of them are better than others. One of them is excellent. One of them got published. I can tell you that the last six months have been some of the happiest of my life, writing these dang short stories. It is because I am using imagination, which I don't get to use very often in my day job.

About my day job. My day job is writing about finance. I do it very well—I might be the best at it, or nearly so. But after 18 years of doing it, it is getting a little tedious. That isn't a statement about writing or finance or writing about finance; if you do anything for 18 years you will start to get sick of it. Problem is, I make a lot of money doing it, so it is hard to stop. But if you asked me what I really wanted to spend the rest of my life doing, it would be writing fiction.

I recently had a discussion with my literary agent about this. I told him that my goal is for my fifth book to be a short story collection. I added that I didn't want to self-publish it. He told me how hard it was, and having read some of my fiction, sort of implied that it's not good enough—at least, not yet. He said that even the indie presses that might pay you a $2,000 advance are flooded with submissions, and that it's a one-in-a-thousand shot. Well, you have to climb the mountain, and this is the hard thing, so naturally I want to do the hard thing. The easy thing would be to publish another finance book, which I could write in the time it takes for me to take a long piss, and sell a buttload of copies.

Part of this is ego. I don't want to be known as a financial writer; I want to be known as a writer. Period. And I am pretty versatile, and I can do a lot of different things, so I should be able to do it. But really I should stick with what I am good at, and just write financial stuff. I could be the best at it, and it wouldn't take anywhere near as much effort.

You see this all the time in the corporate world—a company goes public that is good at doing a specific thing, and it does this thing for 10–20 years, and then they get bored and they open up a new business line, and it ends up being a distraction, and it ends up bringing the whole thing down. Goldman Sachs wanted to get into consumer finance and found out that it was a lot harder than it looked. Twitter wants to become a bank. That would be a mistake. Even the banks are not so good at being banks. Banking is a hard business, and it is probably better left to the bankers. Hotel companies are really good at running hotels. Credit card companies are really good at issuing credit cards. A credit card company should probably not build a hotel, and vice versa. You're getting into things you know nothing about, and you're going to be way out of your depth, like Goldman was with Marcus. Being smarter doesn't count for anything. There's a lot of institutional knowledge that gets passed down over generations. If you're wondering why monopolies or oligopolies exist, this is why. People have been wondering for years when some wiseass is going to come along and disrupt Bloomberg, which is badly in need of disruption. It is very, very hard. And the chat feature basically made Bloomberg invincible.

That's not to say that you should never try to change careers. It's just going to be hard. And it is a lot easier for you to change careers than it is for Twitter to become a bank. Individuals are more adaptable than organizations. People reinvent themselves all the time. But it is rare. When was the last time you heard of a professional athlete who went on to have a successful career in something that had nothing to do with sports? Broadcasting doesn't count. I guess Steve Young became a successful attorney. Any others? Not many. You're really good at throwing the ball, but after a while, age and gravity take over, and you stop throwing the ball at age 40, and the problem is you have half your life ahead of you and you have no freaking clue what to do. Bernie Williams plays the guitar, but not well enough to be as successful playing the guitar as he was playing centerfield. You get the idea.

In MBA-speak this would be known as a *core competency*. You get really good at doing a thing, you should probably keep doing that thing and exploit it for all the money and success that you can. Instead of screwing around with short stories, I should probably be spending that time trying to grow my business. I don't spend a great deal of time thinking about it. Chances are, life will make that decision for me. Maybe I'll get so rich writing about finance that it will afford me the time to spend on other projects that get my creative juices flowing. Or maybe not.

This is kind of the purpose of a hobby, or avocation. You do this thing which makes you money and pays the rent and puts food on the table, except that's not the thing that makes you happy, the thing that makes you happy is some other thing that you could never in a million years be financially successful at, so your life is a struggle to find balance between spending time on the thing that makes you money and the thing that makes you happy. I think that is the right way to look at it. I bet you a million zillion dollars that David Solomon would rather be known as a DJ than the CEO of Goldman Sachs. I bet you. And everyone knows this. And the problem is that everyone knows this. Everyone knows that David Solomon would rather be a DJ and Goldman is his day job, so he is perhaps not as focused on being the CEO of Goldman Sachs, which gets people worried. I have a DJ hobby, too, but I get it. But I have long since resigned myself to the fact that in order for me to be more successful as a DJ, I would have to expend a huge amount of effort that I'm not really willing to expend. So I play my five gigs a year and that is it. Paris Hilton is a DJ, too, you know. I love Paris Hilton, but maybe that is a topic for another essay. She's legitimately good. Not really my style—she plays a lot of Bob Sinclar-style house music— but she's terrific. A lot of people think her success is due to her notoriety as a socialite. I assure you it is not.

So maybe the solution is to not chop down the tree that gives you all this delicious fruit. Keep doing the thing that you are good at, and in your spare time, you can do the thing that you are passionate about. Every once in a while, you find these people where their avocation is their vocation, the people who are passionate about their jobs as I am about my hobbies, and they eat, breathe and sleep finance, consulting, or whatever it is they do, and they become the best at it. There are a lot of people like that in finance. People who put in 20-hour days running hedge funds and such. Honestly, if I'm in a room with a bunch of Wall Street folks, and they start talking about finance, I get bored. I'd rather talk about literature or culture or music. I like what I do—if I hated it, I couldn't do it, but I don't eat, breathe, and sleep it. I've always told people that if I ever make a fuckton of money, I'm going to build a club in Myrtle Beach. I will do that. I've been in a lot of really cool clubs in my lifetime, and I have ideas about what makes a good club. I'd love to see that become a reality.

The other thing is that if you have a hobby or passion project, if you start doing it full-time, there is a very good chance that you won't enjoy it as much. It turns into a job, and jobs suck. I assure you that if I were a professional DJ, playing 200 gigs a year, flying all over the place, dealing with scurrilous nightlife people, that too would get old. If I had to write short stories like it was my job, it would probably get old. Or maybe not. But I can tell you that I am more energized to do these things when I have a limited amount of time to do them. You can't spend 20 hours a day on music. You just can't.

Take note of the first rule of wind walking—don't let go of something until you've got hold of something else. You take a decade or two to build up this skill, and it's worth a lot of money, and you don't want to just walk away from it. Of course, I did that once in my life—and I've never been happier.

PUNCTUALITY

My mother is the most punctual person I know.

A few years ago, we had a Halloween party at our house. The party started at 8 p.m. My mom showed up at 6:30 p.m. This was unwelcome, because we still had a bunch of things to do to get ready for the party, and my mom wanted to gab and hang out. She left at 8:15, just as people were starting to arrive. She had put on a costume and everything.

Back in the mid-2000s, my mom took me to my first NASCAR race up in New Hampshire. We stayed at a hotel in Manchester. She informed me in no uncertain terms that we would arrive at the track at 7 a.m., so we could get the best parking. It was about a 45-minute drive to the track, which meant we had to get up at 5 a.m. So we get up at zero dark hundred, drive to the track, park right next to the entrance, go inside, and... there was nobody there.

The race started at 4 p.m.

What ensued was five hours of crushing boredom. We were the only people in the stands until noon. This was before smartphones, and I hadn't brought a book, so there was really nothing to do, except for sit in the bleachers and sizzle like a burger for five hours. I have never been that bored in my entire life. At around noon, the vendors started opening up their trailers for business. I spent some time in the Skoal trailer, getting my picture taken with the Skoal girls. I checked out all the Big Johnson T-shirts. We still had four hours until the race started.

The race finally begins at 4 p.m. I don't know if you've ever been to a NASCAR race, but it's awesome. It's impossible to describe the feeling of being next to the track when cars are whizzing by at 180 miles per hour. It's a huge amount of fun. But after about 30 laps, my mom starts packing her shit. *Time to go,* she says—*we have to beat the traffic.* We waited nine hours to watch 15 minutes of a race. I managed to convince her to stay a little longer.

This is madness, of course. And look. I am all in favor of not being late to things. Being late is rude, which should be obvious. But being excessively early to things is a function of anxiety. It is said that Janet Yellen gets to the gate three hours before her flight. She would rather sit in the airport for three hours than deal with the uncertainty of a missed flight. This is not someone who is comfortable with risk, and neither is my mom. Interestingly, they are about the same age.

I think all of us acquire our code of conduct somewhere in life, maybe from your parents, maybe from church—for me, it was marching band. And in marching band, they told us that if you were early, you were on time, if you were on time, you were late, and if you were late, you were dead. I heard that again in the military. So I do not make a habit of being late for things. But there are some situations in which etiquette dictates that you want to be a little bit late for things. Like a party. Showing up on time for a party is très gauche—you want to give the hosts a little extra time to get things set up if they need to.

My current intern generally shows up to work about 1–5 minutes late. I have never said anything, on the principle that 1–5 minutes is small stuff, and the small stuff doesn't matter. Yet, if you are in an apprenticeship role of any kind, particularly in finance, you would prefer to get there 30 minutes early, before your boss, and be sitting there bright-eyed and bushy-tailed, ready to start the day. Let me clarify this by saying that

PUNCTUALITY

I am not a morning person. I get up at about 6:30 every day, and if I set my alarm for any earlier than that, I am plenty grumpy and end up hitting the snooze button a bunch of times. I just cannot haul my ass out of bed. When I was at Lehman, I had to be at my desk, open for business, at 7 a.m., which meant getting up at 5:30 at the latest. No fun. There were some guys who got to work at Lehman at 6 a.m., which meant that if they were getting a workout in before work, they were getting up at 3:30. Insanity. What the fuck are you going to do for three-and-a-half hours before the market opens? I always felt like this was some kind of dick-measuring contest to see who could get in the earliest. But that was Wall Street in the 2000s. People worked their asses off. I am nostalgic for those days, for sure.

Punctuality is a cultural thing, and being on time means different things in different parts of the country. In California, people are late. At Berkeley, everything starts ten minutes late: they call it Berkeley Time. If a class is listed for 10:10 a.m., it starts at 10:20. And if you throw a party, expect people to show up two to three hours after it starts. If you show up on time, you will be the only person there for two hours.

America is basically the only place in the world where things start on time and end on time, with the possible exceptions of the British, the Germans, the Swiss, and the Scandinavians. Lots of places in Southern Europe and Latin America expect meetings to start one hour late. Africa takes it to another level. Meetings start several hours late, and there are a lot of speeches and pomp and circumstance that need to happen before you get down to business. I took a class on this in business school, about doing business in different parts of the world, and dealing with all the cultural predilections. In Asia, if someone hands you a business card, you take it with both hands and stare at it for a moment. In the U.S., I am always a little put out when I hand a business card to someone and they jam it in their pocket without even looking at it.

I personally get to the airport about one hour and 45 minutes before the flight. It's the Myrtle Beach airport, and it's not too big, but you have to be careful because sometimes in the summer, the TSA line is out the door. Lots of times in New York, I will get to the airport three hours early, but that's because there is an Amex lounge there, and I can get some food and spread out and work with my headphones on. I generally don't mess around getting to the airport in NYC—you never know about the traffic. But I am not one of these people who rolls up to the airport half an hour before the flight. I will add that, in my lifetime, I have never missed a flight on account of being late. If I have down time, I just get the laptop out and work. It's really about stress minimization. I don't like the feeling of being late and wondering if I am going to make my flight. I don't like the stress. So I get there early, and my travel is completely stress-free. Also, at my age, I am not running through an airport. The last time I sprinted through an airport was about eight years ago, and I was actually in decent shape back then. Never again. I'll just miss the flight.

Think about the airline business, and how precarious it is, where food, bags, fuel, pilots, crew, and everything else has to be carefully choreographed to the minute, and there are a lot of ways that things can go wrong, and not many ways that things can go right. I was on a flight recently that was delayed because of a broken seat. And think about how upset people get when flights are even five minutes late. I like this culture of punctuality that we have here. I mean, the stock market opens on time. Can you imagine if people were loosey-goosey about the stock market and it just opened whenever people got around to it? Everything must work with precision. I visited Switzerland once. All my meetings were on time, which suited me just fine.

One last thing. If you are late for whatever reason, you must apologize. Even if it is a lame excuse. If you are late too many times with too many lame excuses, people will think you are a shithead. Don't be a shithead.

PEOPLE DON'T CHANGE

IF THERE IS a person in your life whose behavior bothers you—it's probably not going to get better.

People don't change. Someone who is an alcoholic will always be an alcoholic. Someone who is a thief will always be a thief. Someone who is a sex addict will always be a sex addict. Someone who is a gambler will always be a gambler. Someone who is an adulterer will always be an adulterer. Unwanted behavior keeps going, and going, and going.

How often have you seen this play out: Parents are dismayed to learn that their 15-year-old is smoking pot. They ignore it for a while, thinking it is harmless, but then it turns into Adderall, pills and cocaine. Soon the teenager has a full-blown drug problem, and he is flunking out of school. The parents ride to the rescue, going to the school to talk to his teachers to convince them not to fail him. The kid swears he will never do drugs again, but he is caught again within a few weeks. They take the kid to a therapist first, but 15-year-olds don't do so well in therapy, so that inevitably fails. They take the kid to outpatient drug treatment, to no avail. Finally, the kid goes to rehab for a month. Swears he will stay clean. Mom and dad think that things are finally back to normal. Caught with drugs again two weeks later. Thus continues a decade-long cycle of time in jails and institutions, with the parents bailing him out every step of the way. After years of this, the parents eventually tire of rescuing him all the time, and let him fail. The kid (now 25 years old) becomes homeless, where he is robbed, raped, and assaulted. Unspeakably awful things happen to him.

And then, magically, he gets sober. And it sticks.

People don't change… *until they do.*

And when they do, it is a miracle. But inevitably what has to happen is that person has to hit bottom, where things absolutely cannot get any worse. Bottoms vary. People with a high bottom get to keep their jobs and spouses. People with a low bottom have to lose everything before they learn.

It may seem as though I am focusing on addiction. I'm talking about all behavior that we find unpleasant. It could be chewing your fingernails. It could be obsessively washing your hands. It could be yelling at your kids. It could be watching porn. Behaviors have a tendency to continue until there is a significant emotional event. Until you lose, or are about to lose, someone or something you care about. Maybe you chew your fingernails, and you go on a date with someone you like a lot, and you catch them staring at your finger jank, and then they never talk to you again. You lost something. That is a significant emotional event. There is a saying: *I don't change when I see the light, I change when I feel the heat.*

Funny thing about our criminal justice system. Yes, you have criminals with long rap sheets who spend their entire lives rotating in and out of jail. But a lot of people, having once had contact with the legal system, are suddenly scared straight. One DUI and getting booked and photographed and fingerprinted is all it takes. They will never drink and drive again. They may never drink again. That was a bridge too far. So I've found that getting arrested is often the best thing for people. It is the significant emotional event that they needed to get clean. For others, jails and institutions have no effect. They're on an elevator going down, and they're going to get off in the basement. Which may mean death. I've known some people who were just never able to figure it out. They had no bottom. It got worse, and worse, and worse—and they ended up dying.

If you have a family member whose behavior bothers you, just know that it's not going to change, and not only is it not going to change, there is nothing that you can do to make it change. Not only that, anything you do to try and change this behavior will be completely counterproductive and actually make the situation worse. If you've heard the term codependence before, that's what I am talking about. When you bail someone out of jail, literally or figuratively, what you are doing is depriving them of their bottom. Because of your efforts, it will take longer for that person to hit bottom and figure it out. And this is a risk, because some people never figure it out, and they die. But if you continue to intervene, they will never get better—and neither will you. You have to let go.

Allowing someone to fail is not easy—especially when the consequences can be so great. But it is necessary. By the way, this concept is not just limited to family affairs—it's in business and economics, too. Companies that are failing will continue to fail. Turnarounds are rare. Everyone loves to bet on a turnaround. But the entire system is at risk if companies are not allowed to fail. No bailouts, right? That's as true for individuals as it is for corporations. If you bail out a spouse, child, or family member, you may be temporarily easing their pain, but you are creating the conditions for the behavior to continue far out into the future. People must be allowed to fail—otherwise, nobody learns.

We know why people get sick—we have no idea why they get better. There is no explanation for when someone suddenly figures it out and turns it all around. I can tell you what the precondition is: the person has to want to get better. Some people *want* to want to get better—no, you have to want to get better. Remember, sick people want to stay sick. It's easy. It's what they know. All the chaos, all the unmanageability, it becomes familiar after a while. As the loved one of a person suffering from addiction, you have to understand that there are significant psychological barriers to getting better. You hope that the person doesn't have to lose everything to get it, but oftentimes they do.

In the mid-2000s, I was suffering from pretty severe OCD, which mostly took the form of repeatedly locking my front door. It may sound benign, but it was actually crippling—45 minutes each morning of ritualized behavior, just trying to get out the door and go to work. It followed me to South Carolina, where I had to double check that I closed the garage door each morning. After a few weeks of driving back to the house multiple times to check the garage door, I knew I had hit bottom. I had to develop some pretty sophisticated psychological techniques to get past this fear of leaving the garage door open. I used to think about something else—like work—to distract my mind as I was driving away from the house. Twenty minutes later, I would remember the garage door, but by then I was almost at work and I was committed. I would get home in the evening to find the garage door closed, which reinforced my belief that everything was okay. In other words, it was a lot of work. And it still flares up from time to time. But I have developed tools to deal with it. That's not the only behavior I've had to change in my life, but it is the only one that I am willing to write about.

If there is some aspect of you that you don't like, something that you wish you could change, why don't you change it? Because it's hard. Because it's a lot of work, that's why. It's really, really hard. But you know what? You can ask for help. Change is difficult, almost impossible—but it can be done. So no, people generally don't change—but when they do, it is glorious.

RULE 62

ALWAYS REMEMBER RULE 62: *Don't take yourself so damn seriously.*
Many years ago, I was invited on a prominent financial podcast. You have probably heard of it. I was excited to go on—some of the guests were the biggest names in finance, and it was an honor to be asked. Unlike most podcasts I go on, I actually did a little preparation.

This was in the years before Zoom. Nowadays, when you do a podcast, you can typically see the person you're talking to, which helps. But we were just doing this over Skype. No big deal. So I go on the podcast, and there are some brief introductions, and the host starts going: *Mi mi mi mi mi mi! Harrrumph harrumph harrumph. Mi mi mi mi mi mi!* Clearing his throat like he is some kind of opera singer.

And then when he starts talking, he's talking in this overly exaggerated Howard Cosell/Ryan Seacrest voice, like he's the color commentator on a Knicks game or something like that. I was dying. I actually did terrible on the podcast, and I was never invited back, because it was all I could do to keep myself from cracking up about this ding-dong who took himself *so damn seriously*.

I'm guessing that most of the people who read this work in the financial industry in some capacity. Maybe they run billions of dollars at a hedge fund. Maybe they are a senior managing director at a bank. Maybe they have CFAs or any number of professional designations. Maybe they are even CEOs.

The one nice thing I will say about the financial industry is that the egos tend not to be too out of control—or maybe that is just a function of the people I hang out with. The thing about working in finance is that finance is a very humbling profession, and the market has a tendency to take you out and wax you like a surfboard when you start running around telling everyone how important you are. I will say, however, that there are some pretty big egos in the financial pundit business. I have spoken at a bunch of conferences, and these talking heads take themselves very seriously. They expect to be treated like stars, and I'm not kidding.

Of all the people in the world that I don't get along with, it's generally the people who take themselves super-seriously. I don't take myself seriously at all. I'm a ding-dong with a newsletter. Okay, I have some books, and okay, I was a columnist for a while, and I do some other things, but I am just another bozo on the bus. And eminently fallible. I am wrong often. Funny thing about the financial pundit business—people hate to be wrong, and they really hope you won't bring up their bad calls. They'll ignore it, and hope it goes away. That's a function of taking yourself too seriously.

But like I said, the egos are not so bad in finance, relatively speaking. They are bad elsewhere. They are especially bad in the public sector and academia. Professors get a lot of mileage out of being a professor. People frequently put *comma PhD* in their Twitter handle. I mean, they're completely entitled to do it, it's just interesting that they do it. I'm entitled to put *comma MFA* in my Twitter handle, and I'm not going to do it. The only place it really belongs is in official correspondence or your email signature. But the thing about having an advanced degree is that it leads the holder of the degree to think they're smarter than everyone else. I'm sure some PhDs will dispute that, but it is absolutely true. But just because you know elemental truths about history, anthropology, English, physics, or math, doesn't mean you know all truths. My experience has shown that people without advanced degrees tend to do a better job of predicting the future than people with advanced degrees. Having a PhD means you are an expert on some specific things, while someone with an MBA knows a little about a lot of things. Always trust the generalists to get it right.

Of course, this is an essay on humility. And I'm sure you've had this experience, where you're at the airline counter, trying to check in, and the airline employee is a complete mook, and it's taking forever, and it's getting screwed up, and you're tempted to say *don't you know who I am?* Oh boy. If you ever find yourself saying *don't you know who I am*, then you are taking yourself way too seriously. There is a very good chance that the airline employee doesn't know who you are, or care. And just because you are famous in finance circles, doesn't mean you are famous in all circles. Never, ever throw your weight around. I wonder if a guy like Morgan Stanley strategist Mike Wilson has difficulty getting restaurant reservations, and I wonder if he's ever been tempted to tell the maître d' who he is. I mean, in the financial world, he's a big deal. Everyone knows who he is. In the rest of the world, nobody cares. And even if you truly are a celebrity, like a real celebrity, never do this. Just sit with the hoi polloi. See the difference in public opinion on Keanu Reeves and James Corden. I sincerely hope I am never that famous, but if I am, I hope most of all that it never goes to my head.

When you take yourself too seriously, you have a deep-seated need to impress people. Quick story: I was in Miami recently, and I was sitting down to lunch with a bunch of New York people. Some of them I knew, some of them I didn't. I was sitting next to this guy I didn't know, who was involved in tech somehow and had made a bunch of money, and was pals with Richard Branson and spent a lot of time on Necker Island. I was sitting there quietly, as I usually am, and someone at the table mentioned that I had written some books, and the guy perks up and goes on Amazon and sees all my books, and says to me, "You're just the silent assassin over here!" I just shrugged. I don't feel a need to talk about myself and my accomplishments in social situations. I'm not a self-promoter. In fact, I am allergic to self-promotion. I believe in a philosophy of attraction, rather than promotion—keep putting out good work and you will attract the right people.

I am friendly with someone who was once a bat boy for the Yankees. He told me a lot about the players and their egos. All of this was told to me in confidence, and out of deference to him I'm not going to reveal any clubhouse secrets, but let me just say that it was very interesting to hear about who had big egos and who considered themselves to be humble servants. Because if you're a ballplayer, you're really nothing special. Aaron Judge is nothing special. He plays a game for a living, in his pajamas. You really have to think about what you're placed here on this earth for. This is what I believe I am placed here on this earth for: To ease people's burdens, if only for a few moments. To uplift and entertain and inform. Before leaving earth, I want to know that I left a positive impact, and that impact is measured in the number of people whose spirits I lifted. That's it. You can call it altruism if you want, but if I do this, I make more money.

I've sure you've had this experience where you're having a conversation with someone and you're talking about a third party, and the other person will say: *he's not a good person*. Whoa! Where does that come from! Really, it comes down to how you treat people. If you're the type of person to shit on the airline ticket agent, to shit on the Uber driver, to shit on the valet, to mistreat people who you believe are less than you, you are not a good person. I refer to this phenomenon as *sucking up and punching down*. Being nice to people who you think can help you, while crapping on everyone else. If you've ever read Dale Carnegie, you know this is not the way to do things. And I should really re-read Dale Carnegie—it's been three decades. It's about being kind and decent to people, regardless of how "big" you are.

It can be hard. One thing that people at the highest level have in common is a lower tolerance for bullshit. Whether you're Mike Wilson, or Keanu Reeves, or Aaron Judge, you place a high value on your time because you are being pulled in a lot of different directions. People are frequently demanding your time. So if the ticket agent is causing you a minor inconvenience, it can make you cross. Even five minutes out of your day is valuable. Patience and tolerance is our code. *Don't be a dick, don't be a dick, don't be a dick.* Watch the facial expressions and body language. People are doing their best. And if they're not, that's no big deal either. People don't remember much, but this is what they do remember: how someone who is allegedly important treats them. If you think you are a VIP, chances are you aren't very V, and you aren't very I either. You're just a P. If you want to know the reason why expensive hotels are so expensive, it's not because the beds are any comfier. It's because they treat everyone like a VIP.

In Nate Silver's book, *The Signal and the Noise*, he relates an anecdote where he was in the Red Sox dugout to interview Dustin Pedroia. Pedroia said, "I'm getting ready for the *big-league ballgame,*" and walked off. Dick. I'd hazard a guess that Nate Silver's name is more recognizable than Pedroia's these days. Don't do this. You may not be able to make time for everyone, but you can at least be decent about it.

So anytime you see someone getting too big for their britches, remind them: Rule 62. Don't take yourself so damn seriously.

I AM GENERATION X

I WAS BORN IN 1974, which was a bad year all around. People have different opinions on this, but most demographers say that all people born between 1965 and 1981 are members of Generation X. Being born in 1974 means I am pretty much smack in the middle of it.

Generation Xers are a cynical bunch. I am friends with a bunch of Xers on Facebook, and people like to trade memes about how we were the last generation allowed to play outside until dark. This is true. I rode my bike, drank from a garden hose, was a latchkey kid, and got into all kinds of trouble—without the grown-ups knowing. Some people might interpret this as freedom—as if we were raised by libertarian Boomers who had a laissez-faire attitude towards parenting and figured that we would flourish if left to our own devices.

Nothing could be further from the truth.

The reality is that we were abandoned by our Boomer parents, the most self-absorbed generation in the history of the world, who were spending a lot of time finding themselves and hooking up and not spending much time parenting. Boomer parents didn't go to Little

League games, spelling bees, school plays, or graduations. To say that Xers have frosty relationships with their parents is an understatement. Many of them are estranged, not on speaking terms, or express open hostility. The abandonment has continued into adulthood. About eight years ago I talked to a local woman about my age, who expressed bewilderment and anguish about the fact that her Boomer parents had less than zero interest in spending time with their grandchildren. What were they doing? Watching TV. The result of this is that as Generation X matures and ages into their 70s, they are going to be some mean, tough old birds. And conservative as hell, too. The "things were different when I was a kid" impulse is strongest in Generation X.

The result of this is that Generation X is a generation that is almost completely detached from politics—instead, focusing on their careers and families. I don't have the statistics at my command, but I can tell you that Generation X is severely underrepresented in Congress, which is filled will Millennials and Boomers, who all want to change the world. Xers just want to be left alone. It is highly likely—no, probable—that we will never have a Generation X president. There is simply nobody in our generation who cares enough to try.

I think this sentiment is shared by a lot of Xers—there is a lot of stuff I did growing up that today would land me in jail. For a period of time, I was going to public parks in the middle of the night with a bunch of other guys dressed as ninjas to frighten the lovebirds making out in the parking lot. Parents co-signed this, tacitly. This continued until we messed with the wrong car and a guy jumped out and chased us into the woods with an axe. I'm sure by now the statute of limitations has expired, but yes, I would have gone to jail. I also hacked into the school's phone system and changed all the teachers' outgoing messages to burp and fart noises. I ended up down at the police station for that one. But they let me go—just kids screwing around. The headmaster of the school made me do community service. People didn't take things so seriously back then. Which was a good thing! Now, we have zero tolerance for this sort of behavior, and a minor transgression committed by a 14-year-old can affect their employment prospects 30 years later. To me, our present society is dystopian.

Like I said, I was a latchkey kid. I lost my virginity six days after my 16th birthday with a girl who was 19. My mom was at work or something. She came home and was none the wiser. I think about this sometimes. Without parental supervision of any kind, we were basically adults. We were free to make our own decisions and our own mistakes, living with the consequences. Today, children are so carefully monitored that they would never have an hour of unstructured free time alone with a member of the opposite sex. You see this in the polling data—sex among adolescents has gone way down. So has drinking. The days of *Sixteen Candles*-style raging parties are long gone. The John Hughes movies of the 80s are pretty instructive—kids were living in their own world, and the adults were like the teachers in the Charlie Brown cartoons, going *wah wah wah wah wah*.

Parents today attempt to truncate bad outcomes. Nobody wants their kid to end up dead or in jail. Nobody wants their kid to be precluded from going to college for something they did on social media. Generation X may have been abandoned, but we had a much, much lower incidence of mental illness. I'm not saying anything that everyone doesn't already know. Millennials had far less freedom, and Zoomers even less than that. Being trapped in your bedroom with only a mobile phone doesn't sound like a recipe for sound mental health. Xers are a very emotionally healthy generation, and it's because of the freedoms that we enjoyed. I rode my bike all over creation. I got a car as soon as I turned 16, and within a week I was driving out of state, unbeknown to my mom. The car was a source of great personal freedom, especially for going out with girls. Kids don't date nowadays, and they don't drive either. Just alone in the bedroom with the phone.

The funny thing about the Millennials and the Zoomers is that the helicopter parenting continued into adulthood. They had Parents' Weekend at my college—nobody came. When I was at Lehman, I was having a discussion with a woman from HR—she said that Lehman's competitors were having Parents' Day on Wall Street. Lehman elected not to do that—that is where they drew the line. You're 25 years old, and your mom and dad are showing up to Wall Street? How embarrassing. And that's another crucial difference—Xers were embarrassed by their parents. The Millennials are best friends with their parents. I see this on Instagram—some 28-year-old woman will take a selfie with her mom and caption it *#bestfriends*. What? Unthinkable. At no point in my life was I best friends with either of my parents. I don't even know how to compute that. The best I've been able to achieve is some sort of détente.

As I write, we're getting down to tag ends in Season 20 of *American Idol*, and the clear frontrunner is an 18-year-old Hawaiian kid named Iam Tongi. Tongi is a 350-pound Pacific Islander, typically clad in a T-shirt, shorts, and sandals—just a sweetheart of a guy. You might have seen his audition—it went viral. He sang in tribute to his father, Rodney, who passed away two months earlier. The song he chose was "Monsters," by James Blunt. I have never seen this in an *American Idol* audition—two of the judges started to cry. I was crying, sitting on the couch, watching. The song was beautiful, but that's not why I was crying. I was crying because I was jealous of the relationship that Iam Tongi had with his father.

I treasure my childhood—I treasure the freedoms that I had. But I long for something resembling a normal relationship with my parents. My father was something of an amateur stock trader—when I told him that I got a job at Lehman Brothers, I begged him to come to New York and see the trading floor. He would have loved it. He never came. When my first book was released, he sent me a one-sentence email. Nothing about the second or third books. When I texted him that I published my first column at Bloomberg, he sent me a picture of a lizard. I haven't spoken to him in years.

What I would give to be a Millennial, and for my life to be complete.

A STUDENTS WORK FOR C STUDENTS

YOU KNOW HOW the saying goes: *A students work for C students. B students work for the government.*

Although, there has been some grade inflation in recent years, so maybe now the A students work for B students, and B+ students work for the government.

I was a terrible student growing up. I had the highest SAT scores in my class, yet finished with a class rank of 38 out of about 440. I had the third-highest SAT scores in my college class, yet finished with a class rank of 91 out of 222. I simply didn't give a flying fuck about school.

For starters, I had an aversion to what I thought was "kissing ass." Teachers were authority figures, and I wouldn't be caught dead asking for help. It was a point of pride. I was going to do it myself, or I wasn't going to do it at all. I don't know where I got this idea—that having anything other than an adversarial relationship with a teacher was tantamount to kissing ass. In college, I never—never—went to office hours. What I failed to understand—which should have been obvious to someone who was allegedly smart—was that you go to school to learn and that you should take advantage of all the opportunities you have in front of you. I simply wasn't that interested in learning, other than what I could get by osmosis in class in between naps. I would do the homework and hand it in out of duty—not because I was terribly interested in learning anything. This was a massive missed opportunity. I'd be a lot better informed today if I put in the work in school. Sure, I did intermittently. I worked hard at the subjects I liked. I took a creative writing class one semester in college, and poured endless hours into it—and got an A. I simply couldn't see how Chemistry 2 was going to make me a better person or influence my future employment possibilities. So I got an F.

You could sum this up neatly by saying I was smart and lazy. Let me tell you about smart, lazy people—those are the people who grow up to become wealthy. Those are the people in positions of great responsibility. Elon Musk does not strike me as the kind of guy who got a 4.0. Maybe he did—if he did, he did so effortlessly. You see, a lot of what passes for good grades in educational institutions is really obedience—follow the rules, hand in the assignments, participate in class, don't be a douche, and you get an A. The neurodivergent people who question why we're learning this stuff in the first place generally don't.

Class was a time for me to catch up on my sleep. In college, I was practically nocturnal. I'd be up all night, screwing around, procrastinating on papers, and then the next day I'd be face down on the desk, drooling. Let's just say I was not doing well on my class participation score. On one occasion, I was sitting in the front of the room, and fell so sound asleep that I fell out of my chair onto the floor. The professor tried to catch me. I actually had close to a 100 average in that class and missed out on an A+ because of the class participation grade. Like I said, smart and lazy.

Smart and lazy people tend to be entrepreneurial. They don't function well in large organizations. They're not obedient. Sorry to generalize, but girls generally do better in school than boys (this is a fact), and it is partially because of obedience. They follow the rules. I had an English professor my freshman year of college who prized obedience. She gave As to the cadets that sat up straight and asked questions. I got a C in that class. Ironically, she actually came to my book signing for *Street Freak* years later. I wondered if she remembered giving me a C, and I wondered if she recognized the irony that her C English student went onto get a book published by a Big 5 publisher. This whole episode should serve to demonstrate that school is fucking stupid.

But school is not necessarily stupid. Let me put it this way: you get out of it what you put into it. If you go through the motions and hand in the homework and do passably well on the tests, you'll get a diploma, but you won't have learned much. If you put in 100% and form relationships with your professors and spend time in the library and pursue enrichment outside the classroom, it will have been an excellent investment. As is true in most of life, people generally do the minimum, because they have lazy brains, which I think is one of the points that Daniel Kahneman was trying to make. We like to turn our brains off. But whether you're in school or not, you should constantly be learning new things. And I'm not talking about some *Jeopardy!* contestant who sits around and reads books about Italian operas. I'm talking about doing something completely new, like playing guitar, or starting a hedge fund, or opening a bike shop. There is no better way to stretch your brain than to do something completely different. Even if it fails, it will have been worthwhile.

Funny thing about *Jeopardy!* contestants. They are unquestionably smart people. Amy Schneider got a 1600 on her SATs, for starters. One of my ex-girlfriends actually appeared on *Jeopardy!*—she wasn't too shabby, either. But these people are part of a class of people I would call A students—they did the homework and aced the tests and were the teachers' pets. The sole exception to this—the sole exception—was James Holzhauer, the professional gambler who almost broke the game. You don't see many rich people go on *Jeopardy!* Why would they? The money is inconsequential. You would only do it to gratify your ego. But the real reason you don't see rich people on *Jeopardy!* is because the rich people are the C students—the smart and lazy people. They never bothered to learn the Italian operas, because it had no bearing on their lives. You might call them uncultured heels. Well, they are rich uncultured heels. *Jeopardy!* contestants also lean liberal—Ken Jennings almost didn't become host for some old tweets that were even too far left for the show's producers. You get a lot of academics on *Jeopardy!*, and a lot of librarians. Not too many doers. Amy Schneider tweeted this when she went on that epic run on the show, amassing millions of dollars: "Some of you may have heard, but I quit my day job yesterday!" A person with a 1600 on their SATs has a day job? If you got a 1600 on your SATs and you are a W-2 employee, something has gone very, very wrong in your life.

My wife hates it when I write about her, but here goes, and I'll deal with the consequences later. She is very, very smart. Smarter than me, in fact. She has three IQ points on me. We have both written books. I asked my nephew recently who he thought was smarter, me or my wife. He said that she was the "book smart" one, and I was the "street smart" one. Boy, is that ever true. She is the academic, I am the entrepreneur. She is the valedictorian, I am the C student. It may seem like I am painting this picture of her as a useless intellectual, but she is pretty savvy at times, and relative to a lot of academics she is definitely a doer. But she didn't trade for nine years, she doesn't gamble, and she doesn't play poker. She will occasionally take calculated risks. The upshot is that we actually make a pretty good team. I encourage her to take more risks, and she saves me from my own worst instincts. That's why we've been married for (checks notes) 27 years.

I have regrets. If I could do it all over again, I would have studied harder. Not because I care about the grades, but because I simply didn't learn shit when I was in school. And now I'm ignorant. And my academic wife knows everything, and it is embarrassing. But I have other skills. In any negotiation (like for a house), I will get the best of it. I've done a million transactions in my life, and I know how to extract the most value from the other side. That is a skill that comes in handy—quite often. But you haven't lived until you've been on academic probation.

LEGACY

MESSENGER BOY: The Thessalonian you're fighting—he is the biggest man I've ever seen. I wouldn't want to fight him.

ACHILLES: That's why no one will remember your name.

THAT SCENE IS from the movie *Troy*, of course. Not a bad movie. I watched it in the Galaxy theater in Guttenberg, New Jersey, in 2004. The movie theater had an organ. One of the few cool things about living in Hudson County.

Why do I write? For a whole bunch of reasons. The main reason is because it is therapeutic. If I wasn't writing, I would go nuts. Simple as that. Writing is how I stay sane. I have Bipolar 1, and to manage it, I take medication, get plenty of sleep—and write.

Another reason I write is for money. Sure, I write a newsletter for free, but the last iteration of that newsletter turned into a book which I sold for money. And maybe some people read the book who hadn't been introduced to me before, and maybe they subscribed to my paid newsletter, *The Daily Dirtnap*, or bought one of my other products. It is good marketing. So there is a business purpose to it, too.

But one big reason I write is because I want to create a body of work that will outlive me. That's why books are so important—if I were to die tomorrow, people would be reading them for years to come. I don't have children, so I won't be survived by my genetic material, but I will be survived by my ideas. And maybe 100 years from now, one of my books will be sitting among the dusty tomes in the reserves in some library somewhere, and some kid will pick it up and read about Wall Street in the 2000s, in its ugliest and most exciting time.

That's actually a pretty important idea—creating something that will outlive you. The vast majority of people don't. They go to work and put part A into slot B for eight hours a day, come home, drink a beer or ten, go to bed, and do it all over again the next day. Or the white-collar equivalent of that. Lots of people work on Wall Street. How many of them become famous? And that's the funny thing about fame on Wall Street, because Wall Street is a place where you can become rich without becoming famous, which is the best of both worlds. I know billionaires whose names you have never heard. And they don't make the billionaires' lists, because they are flying below the radar. Amazing. But occasionally you have a guy like Bill Ackman who wants to become part of the public discourse. If he just managed a fund and did well, we would probably applaud him, but now we get to read all his horrible takes and shitty opinions. This is a person who is seeking attention and adulation. Or, you just get so big and successful that it's impossible to fly below the radar anymore. Bill Gross, Steve Cohen, and Stan Druckenmiller are all examples. But a TV interview with Stan is as rare as an arctic fox. He has nothing to prove to anybody. Stan will be remembered for being the greatest of all time. He's in Cooperstown. I will be remembered for my books and newsletters. What will you be remembered for?

The vast majority of people don't have these sorts of ambitions. Or, they have different ambitions. If they're a good father, and they pass away, and years later, their offspring are posting on Facebook about how much they miss their father, that is enough. One of the reasons I don't have kids is because I had enough self-awareness to know that

I would be a terrible father. Maybe you disagree. No, it's true. There is no shared tradition of good parenting in my family. You're good at parenting, you should be a parent. I'm good at writing, I should be a writer.

There has been some controversy in recent years about e-books. You had tech venture capitalist Marc Andreessen telling people to go out and buy physical copies of their favorite books, pronto. There was the Roald Dahl controversy and the James Bond controversy, when both were republished with all the "sensitive" material removed or altered, and one of the dangers of e-books is that someone at some point in the future might decide that what you wrote is politically incorrect and edit it. Maybe machines will do it automatically. That might happen to my novel *All the Evil of This World* someday. But the nice thing about e-books (and print-on-demand books, and audiobooks) is that they can literally live forever. Physical books can go out of print, and good luck finding one. An author friend here in Myrtle Beach is trying to figure out ways to get another print run of his first book. Yet as long as Amazon stays in business—or whoever buys Amazon, or whoever buys whoever buys Amazon—those books will live forever. And if Amazon and its kind all disappear, e-books and audio are not hard to back-up and distribute. That's cool! The hardcovers of *Street Freak* are hard to come by these days, but you can always get the Kindle version. My earlier essay collection, *Those Bastards*, will live forever. So will the book you're holding in your hands. But my newsletter might not. Substack might hit the delete button someday. You never know.

I hate the word "content." I prefer "literature." But let's roll with *content* for a minute. I try to create content that will hold up across the decades. Back when I was publishing *Street Freak* in 2011, the imprint was focusing all of its effort on a memoir written by Levi Johnston—who? Levi Johnston was the boyfriend of Sarah Palin's daughter. The title of the book was *Deer in the Headlights*—a great title. But it was utter dreck. And it was stale the moment it was published. The imprint wasted all of its marketing resources on that politically-motivated vanity project and starved *Street Freak* of resources. I don't know how many copies of Levi Johnston's book sold, but I gather that *Street Freak* sold multiples of it. Pull up *Deer in the Headlights* on Amazon. It probably has an Amazon sales rank of 3,243,643,493. Nobody even gives a shit about Sarah Palin anymore, and hasn't since that Lisa Ann portrayal on PornHub.

In the early days of *Those Bastards*, the book had a stratospheric sales rank and was even ranked #1 in Essays for a time. You want to know what is usually ranked highest in essays? C.S. Lewis, of course, with his wide Christian appeal, but also Joan Didion's *Slouching Towards Bethlehem*. Some of the best nonfiction ever written in history, written in the 1960s, and still selling thousands of copies today. If you want to know what I want, that's what I want. Joan Didion died not too long ago, and her books are still going to be selling 50 years from now. Bill Bennett sold several millions copies of *The Book of Virtues* in the 1990s, the proceeds of which he deposited into high-limit slot machines, and one of the bestselling books of that era has all but disappeared from view 30 years later. If you've read any Robert Pirsig, you know about the concepts of static quality and dynamic quality. Bennett's book did not have much in the way of static quality.

TV is ephemeral. People are already forgetting about Tucker Carlson. But not in entertainment—*Seinfeld* ran for nine years, and the stars of that show will be coasting off of that for the rest of their lives. TV and movies (and music) are a whole different animal. If you can capture people's imagination, they will remember you forever. Look at me. *Ocean's Eleven* is 24 years old and I am still quoting that movie. I'd like the kind of fame where I don't have to go on TV very much. I'm not an entertainer, at least, not in that way.

You should leave your mark on the world, in one way or another. Jim Bob Duggar left his mark on the world, in a sense. So did Henry Ford. So did Michael Lewis. So did Larry Fink, in a malignant sort of way. But which of these people will we be talking about in the year 2100? That is the question that needs to be answered.

SINNERS AND SAINTS

I CHEATED ON A girlfriend once, in high school. And she loved me to pieces. It was a tragedy. I sat next to—I think the most accurate description is, a *hussy*—at the back of the bus on the way home from some marching band competition. It started out as cuddling, but soon I was going from first to third on a hit-and-run. I wasn't thinking about my girlfriend at the time. I was thinking about the pleasures of the flesh.

After I returned home, the guilt set in. This relationship that I was in was pretty long term by high-school standards—about three or four months—and everyone knew we were together. Hot Stranger on the bus knew we were together, and she clearly didn't care. I couldn't be certain that she'd keep the secret, so I broke up with my girlfriend pre-emptively, because I couldn't handle the shame. After that, I had no girlfriend and no Hot Stranger, either. But I felt like ending the relationship was the only honorable thing to do.

I think most people intuitively understand right and wrong. There is a small percentage of people—you might call them psychopaths—who just don't care. Bloomberg did a piece on psychopathy on Wall Street years ago. It was a low blow, but there is a reason the term *grinfuck* exists on Wall Street. I'm grinning as I'm fucking you over. But yes, most people know right and wrong, and do their best, but ultimately give in to sin, because the temptations are just too great. Would you cheat on a spouse with Hot Stranger if you knew, with 100% certainty, that you would not be caught? Would you get a prostitute? Would you do drugs, if you knew there were no repercussions?

Opinions differ on drugs. Some people treat their body like an amusement park. Why do puritans believe drugs to be wrong? Because you're trying to find God by taking a shortcut. The long way around requires prayer and mindfulness and devotion. The easy way is to sniff blow. We don't deserve the pleasures we get from drugs, and that is the point.

Most people are good people with specific moral failings. They are not perfect—none of us are. If you cheat with Hot Stranger and you experience remorse, you are probably going to heaven. If you cheat with Hot Stranger and you do not experience remorse, you are probably going to hell. Really what we are talking about is selfishness: *A promise is only binding until something better comes along. I'm going to do whatever the hell I want and screw everyone else.*

But there are all kinds of ways to be bad. The church-going housewife may be in a committed relationship, but engage in character assassination. She may lie. She may gossip. She may spread rumors and undermine people's credibility. That has never been my particular vice, but for some people, I guess it feels good while you're doing it. You diminish someone else's standing to enhance your own. Some people like to create drama.

Some people steal. I have never spent much time with people who do this. You can say what you want about Wall Street people, but they tend to exhibit cash-register honesty. They may be scumbags in every other aspect of their lives, but they will not steal money. And that is something. I did run into a small number of instances in which people were not cash-register honest on Wall Street, but I will save that for some later book when everyone involved is dead.

Some people may not do illegal drugs, but they will drink too much alcohol. One thing I've found about alcohol (and also pot, since that is mostly legal now) is that it serves as a sort of psychological crutch. Get home from work, pour yourself a drink. Get home from work, pour yourself a drink. Pretty soon you need a drink when you get home at night or you are going to be plenty grumpy. The only substance I am dependent on at the moment is ZYN, the tobacco-free nicotine pouches. I picked up this habit back in 2020 and I've never looked back. Nicotine, on its own, separated from the carcinogens in tobacco, is mostly harmless. And I've found that it sharpens my thinking. I have one in right now, as I write. It's not entirely harmless, though—it can raise your blood pressure and harden your arteries. In the grand scheme of vices, this is about as small as it gets, and I have no intention of quitting anytime soon.

So what makes a good person? Obeying the Ten Commandments? Is dang-it-all-to-heck Mike Pence, a family man in a faithful marriage, a good person? I believe he is. But I think the Jared Dillian of 20 years ago would have thought that Mike Pence was a stiff extraordinaire, and I would have preferred to live a colorful life with more excitement. I am not too much into excitement these days. If I were to die in the year 2053, at the age of 79, I would hope that someone at my funeral would say that I was a devoted husband. Actually, that happened recently—I heard that a friend of a friend of a friend referred to me as a devoted husband. And it is true. That is a reputation I would like to cultivate. You get older, and you get smarter, and you start to do the math on this stuff, and you figure out that 15 seconds of bliss is not worth a lifetime of regret. The risk/reward is atrocious. Wisdom that I did not have in the back of the bus at 15 years old.

I spend a lot of time thinking about how to be a good person these days. When I make mistakes, they are typically errors of omission rather than commission. I'm a bit self-absorbed (we all are), so I might not recognize when someone is doing something nice for me and forget to thank them. Or I might make a stupid Twitter comment that I will later regret. Little stuff. I think the definition of progress is when the bad shit that you do gets smaller and less consequential over time. These days, if I inadvertently ghost someone over text, I am wracked with guilt. I continue to make mistakes. It's progress, not perfection. I'm sure that there's at least one person out there who thinks I'm an asshole because of some slight that I didn't even know I did. But if these are the sorts of things you worry about nowadays, I think the gates of heaven are wide open.

Unlike a lot of people, I do not believe that my political beliefs make me a good person. I don't think voting Democratic or Republican makes you a good person. But Democrats and Republicans tend to view the other side as evil. I think we can have different opinions on things like abortion without being characterized as sinners or saints. I don't view the opposing political party as bad people. I view them as misguided people. People generally believe what they believe because of who they are and where they were when growing up, with a little bit of genetics thrown in. I draw the line at Communism—the people who are real, actual hard-core communists are bad people. They are destroyers, filled with hatred. Outside of that, we can have a difference of opinion on anything, and still remain friends.

Does charity work make you a good person? It depends what your motivations are. If you are attention-seeking, it does not necessarily make you a good person. I endowed a scholarship at my high school, and there was lots of splashy PR around it, and while the scholarship will undoubtedly do good (and already has), it was an exercise in ego gratification. But I've made contributions in other areas that I've taken great pains to keep secret. There is that old saying that if you do a good deed and you go around and tell everyone about it, then the good deed was nullified. I always like looking up at those donor walls in art museums and seeing "Anonymous" listed there. That person has the right idea.

The goal here is to get into heaven, right? I mean, if there were no such thing as hell, then what is the point of being good? Clearly, you don't have to donate a ton of money to get into heaven. And you won't go to hell if you work on Wall Street. You just have to be a good person, right? Well, it is a little more complicated than that. It's not quite about altruism or selflessness, but it's close.

WINNING

I WILL TALK A little bit about how I got a job on Wall Street.
At the time, I was getting my MBA at the University of San Francisco. Funny thing about that program. The education was first-class. Couldn't have been any better. But its reputation, as a business school, was... not so great? I think, at the time, it was ranked 170th out of all MBA programs in the country—well into the third tier. I went there because Stanford and Berkeley were incompatible with my Coast Guard work schedule. At USF, I could do all the classes at night. But what I quickly learned was that not all MBA programs are created alike, and at the lower-ranked ones, your likelihood of getting a job on Wall Street was slim to none.

I was undeterred. I exploited every single contact I had, set up informational interviews in New York, and made several trips out East to visit with these people. Not all of these meetings were successful. But my message seemed to be resonating at Lehman, which liked the idea of a scrappy Coast Guard guy becoming a trader. I make it sound easy, but this was not easy. I was working a full-time job, another part-time job (on the options exchange), taking three classes at once, doing all the job search prep and flying out for interviews. I was sleeping two hours a night. But I had what you might call a killer instinct—failure was not an option. I took everything I had and bet it all on myself. It would be one of two big risks I would take in my lifetime, and it paid off.

I have had about 10-12 interns over the years, and I have taught a lot of college students, and occasionally I have smart interns or smart college students, but the one thing that absolutely cannot be taught is the killer instinct. You either have it or you don't. You either have the insatiable desire to succeed, or you don't. For every person who has the killer instinct, there are a hundred who are complacent. *I have a job, three squares, a roof over my head, life is good.* They have enough. Then there is the rare breed of cat for whom it is never enough. They will sacrifice their social lives, their fun, their health, their sanity, in order to achieve their goals. Not many people are willing to make those sacrifices. That is why there are winners and losers.

And I'm not specifically referring to Wall Street. Read this blurb about the writer Michael Crichton, which I found from the Twitter account @TrungTPhan:

> Michael Crichton: One of the biggest cultural influences in the 1990s, Crichton scored the trifecta of having the #1 book, film, and TV show in the same year. He did it twice in 1995 with *ER* (TV), *Congo* (Film), and *The Lost World* (book). Oh, and again in 1996 with *ER* (TV), *Twister* (film), and *Airframe* (book). Crichton died in 2008, but his work remains popular, and he's sold over 200 million books. While getting a Harvard Medical School degree, Crichton would frequently write 10,000 words a day and published multiple novels under a pseudonym before graduating (he never practiced medicine). Steven Spielberg—who adapted Crichton's book *Jurassic Park* to film—said that Crichton was known for doing 18-hour work days for weeks on end until a project was done.

That is one first-class motor. Does that make you feel lazy? I hope it does. By the way, the typical book is 85,000 words, so this is writing a book in 8.5 days. For comparison, I write about 3,000–4,000 words a day across all my ventures, and people think that I'm a writing juggernaut.

There is an ongoing debate about whether hard work or talent is responsible for someone's success. I'm going to go with hard work eight times out of ten. For a period of about 12 years in the 1990s and 2000s, I read virtually every investment book that was available on Amazon. As I write, I have them all on a shelf next to me. I was reading constantly. Nobody told me to do it. And so I found that I had a lot more intellectual depth than most of the people I was working with at Lehman. Funny thing about Wall Street. On Wall Street, knowledge is power. If you're the only guy on the equities trading floor that knows how a treasury bond auction works, you are going to become pretty valuable once one of them goes pear-shaped. I think about all the back- and middle-office people who have every resource at their disposal, all the computing power, all the market data, and mechanically do the same VLOOKUPs on spreadsheets every day, without once cracking a book for the SIE or the Series 7. Without getting a subscription to *Barron's*. Without subscribing to any newsletters. Without reading any books. And they wonder, perhaps out loud, why they are sitting there doing VLOOKUPs all day when the traders and salespeople are making multiple seven figures on the trading floor. Perhaps it is because they are lucky, but perhaps it is because they did the work. These kids lack the killer instinct. And it doesn't take much in the way of political skills— you just have to go down to the trading floor and make a nuisance of yourself until they give you the job. The squeaky wheel gets the grease. If you don't squeak, no grease. It's not as if there's much in the way of risk. The worst they can do is say no!

I am a baseball fan, so I will pass along some baseball anecdotes. Here in Myrtle Beach, we have the single-A Cubs affiliate, the Myrtle Beach Pelicans. A few years back we had a couple of future professional ballplayers at the club: Ian Happ, who went on to play with the Cubs, and Gleyber Torres, who went on to play with the Yankees. Ian Happ worked his ass off. Not being physically gifted, he worked out constantly, doing drills, spending time in the batting cage, lifting weights—and it paid off. He is now a valued member of the Cubs. Gleyber Torres was physically gifted, a natural athlete, but was lazy, and spent most of his time sitting around. Torres now plays second base for the Yankees, but in spite of his physical gifts, is a thoroughly average hitter and is prone to mental errors, both defensively and on the basepaths. Say what you want about Roger Clemens, but that guy had a first-class motor. His workouts were legendary. When Andy Pettitte visited his ranch to work out in the offseason, he spent the first few days puking.

Back in 2016, Randi Zuckerberg laid out the entrepreneur's dilemma. You have a list of five things, and you only get to choose three. I have altered it somewhat for our purposes.

1. Work
2. Sleep
3. Friends/Family
4. Fitness
5. Fun.

I choose work, sleep, and fun. I don't spend much time with friends or family, and I don't do much in the way of fitness. I always make sure I get enough sleep—sleep is important. And I make time for fun, which usually involves music. And I work all the damn time.

I think a lot of Wall Street people choose work, fitness, and family. They get up at 3:30 a.m. to work out in the gym, they put in a 12-hour workday, and they come home to spend a few hours with the kids. Rinse and repeat.

By the way, if you're only putting in an eight-to-ten-hour day, then you don't get to say you choose work, because everyone puts in an eight-to-ten-hour day. It is what you do with those extra hours that is important. I'm not saying that my choices are prescriptive—everyone has different priorities—I'm only saying that if work doesn't make your top three list, then you're not going to be the CEO. You're not even going to get a job on the trading floor. Spit in one hand and wish in the other, and see which one fills up first. In my career, I have occasionally been outsmarted, but I have never been outworked.

I don't particularly care if someone doesn't want to put in the effort. That is a choice, and like we discussed above, people have different priorities. But then you lose your ability to complain that you're not rich or successful. If you want to chug along and make your $x a year and raise your kids and watch your football on the weekends, there is no dishonor in that. More beer for me.

The most important decision we will ever make is what to do with the next 24 hours.

THE BEST DAYS ARE AHEAD

I WENT TO A Coast Guard retirement ceremony recently. I have to tell you, the military really does it right, with all the pomp and circumstance and speechifying and shadowboxes and awards and fancy medals. In contrast, when I told my boss at Lehman that I was leaving after seven years, he said "Okay," and I walked out the door.

Anyway, the guy retiring was a very dear friend—we were roommates on our first tour of duty on a Coast Guard cutter out of Washington state. The best of times, the worst of times. We were very close. He went on to be an aviator and I went on to be an agitator. He had an incredible career, going to the East Coast and the West Coast and the Gulf Coast and the North and South Pole, and a lot of stuff in between. At the end, he was running HITRON, which is where they hook up machine guns and sniper rifles to helicopters to stop drug-runners in speedboats—the elite airborne fighting unit of the Coast Guard. Real *Top Gun* stuff. And he looked the part, with his white T-shirt and aviator sunglasses, a throwback to Miramar in the 80s.

So I went up to him before the ceremony, and I asked him, "What are you going to do next?" He said, "I have no idea." I was stunned. My friend could walk into any executive job in the corporate world, having led hundreds of people in high-intensity environments—and, not to mention, he is one of the nicest, most charismatic guys I know. I've never met a person in the world who didn't like him. Me, I make enemies without even trying. So with those kinds of skills, not to mention 3,900 hours of being a stud pilot, now is the time to cash in.

And then I started to think about it. After being Iceman for 27 years, what do you do as a second act that could possibly be better than the first act? And the second act really must be better than the first. Because your best days must always be ahead of you, rather than behind you.

There are a lot of people in the world whose best days are behind them. Professional athletes, for instance. I met a guy in Myrtle Beach who used to pitch for the Orioles. In fact, he was the visiting pitcher for the last game at old Yankee Stadium. I had this guy on for a full two hours of my radio show. You would not believe the stories. And better than the stories on the air were the stories that he was telling me in commercial breaks. He has stories to last a lifetime. You want to know what he is doing now? He is a roofer.

Before the class warriors pull an arrow from their quiver, there is absolutely nothing wrong with being a roofer. It is an honorable profession. People need roofs to keep the rain out. But all that glory is in the past, or sitting on the mantle. What is there to look forward to?

There must always be something to look forward to.

I will tell you a story. When my first book *Street Freak* came out in 2011, there was a big rush of publicity and attention and people were blowing up my phone, and I got to go on TV and all that, and then after a few months, things settled down and my life went back to normal. And then I started to think, *I am never going to top that*. That was the pinnacle of my life, and it is all downhill from here. I became depressed. Not clinical depression, mind you, but existential depression. I was a mess. I couldn't stand the idea that I might never be able to top that achievement. So I bought a motorcycle, knowing full well how dangerous motorcycles were. I didn't care if I got greased by a Dodge Ram on the highway. What was the point? There was nothing to look forward to.

It is a good thing that I didn't get greased by a Dodge Ram on the highway, because as it turns out, there has been a lot to look forward to. Five more books, for starters, a radio show, speaking gigs, an MFA, a gig as an op-ed columnist, lots of money, and a whole bunch of other stuff. It's funny—I was talking to my literary agent about a year ago, and he remarked how I've continued to build my career after *Street Freak*, the implication being that there are a lot of authors who write books and end up being one-hit wonders. And you know what? The best is yet to come. Wait until my next book comes out—that is going to be huge. And you know what else? Even after that, my best days will still be ahead of me. Because when your best days are behind you, that is incomprehensible demoralization and death. That is sitting down at the VFW drinking at 11 a.m., waiting to die.

This happens to Wall Street guys all the time. You see, Wall Street practices ageism to an extent unseen in any other industry in the world. You get to be about 47, you have all this knowledge and all these relationships, and they blow you out because you are too expensive and they can replace you with someone who is 22. Then what? Sitting down at the country club drinking at 11 a.m. There aren't too many traders and salespeople who have a second act that is better than the first. It's like being a professional athlete. You're performing at a high level for two-and-a-half decades, and next thing you know, you're cold-calling your college roommate for Northwestern Mutual. It's fucking depressing. If I had advice to anyone working on Wall Street, it would be this:

1. Save your money.
2. Make a plan for what to do when the game of musical chairs stops.

And just for the record, the second act doesn't have to be greed and glory or cash and prizes. The second act might be learning how to play guitar, and gigging at the local restaurant in town. It might be spending most of your time at your favorite charity. It might be going back to school, like I did. But you need something to get you out of bed in the morning. As I was getting to the end of my MFA program, my wife said to me, "You are going to need a new challenge." I didn't know what that challenge was going to be. As it turns out, I am writing a ton of short stories and trying to get them published. I am doing some other things, too. I am getting back in the gym after a three-year hiatus—that gives me purpose also. I did have an existential crisis, like my wife predicted, but it only lasted about three weeks.

If you don't have something to look forward to, you might as well fucking die.

And you know what, you can see it when it happens. I'm sure you know someone who hit a professional dead end, who didn't keep growing and finding new challenges, and they were drinking at the country club at 11 a.m., and next thing you know, dirtnap. That happens to people after they retire, a lot. They're at the top of their game until age 65, and then at age 66 they're divorced, because their spouse didn't realize what an a-hole they were until they were sitting on the couch all day. At 70, they're dead. My wife's grandfather is 102 years old, and just gave up playing golf last year. At age 100, he played 27 holes of golf and walked the course. He has a woodworking shop, and will make 300-odd toys for kids every Christmas. His wife died about five years ago. He still has a reason to get out of bed in the morning. That guy is going to live to be 130, and remember I said that when he does. The best days are ahead of you—even when you're 101. More than anything, that is the key to longevity.

Arthur Brooks has written about this a lot—what do you do when you are in professional decline? Trading is a young man's game. Sports are a young man's game. But even after you age out of those careers, you have so much wisdom and experience to offer the world.

As Ellis Boyd Redding once said, "Get busy living, or get busy dying."

RESTRAINT

Back in 2011, I was tapping away at my desk at *The Daily Dirtnap* headquarters, when I got an email from one of my subscribers at a large hedge fund:

"How do I get off this thing?"

The name wasn't familiar to me. Nonetheless, I told him that I was happy to unsubscribe him and took him off the list. Then he sent me this:

"Goodbye, and bad luck."

It was one of those emails where you sit there, stunned, staring at your computer for 15 minutes. *Bad luck?* He could have called me a lot of things: *dipshit*, *jerkoff*, *ass-wipe*—no. Wishing somebody bad luck is about one of the most devastating burns in history. Savage.

I was like, *who the fuck is this guy?* So I googled him.

Oh.

The guy was former Vice Chairman of the Fed.

So here's what probably happened. In retirement, he was in some emeritus role at this hedge fund to pick up a couple of bucks. In comes me, 37-year-old newsletter writer, shitting on the Fed all the time. He probably got sick of me after a while, and put me in my place.

Except: now I will always remember him as a giant douche.

Before he sent that email, I had no idea he was a douche. Now I think he is a douche. He's dead, now, and I still think he is a douche. You know what they say: *Better to remain silent and appear a douche, than to open your mouth and remove all doubt.*

My man did not exercise a great deal of restraint that day. Let me tell you something. Every single time—*every single time*—I have sent an email in anger, I have regretted it. Every time. Batting 1.000. And let me tell you something else. As a financial newsletter writer, there are lots of opportunities to lose your cool and send an email in anger. The vast majority of my subscribers are happy warriors, but I do have some malcontents. People will fire off insults at me from time to time. The challenge is to handle them with grace and dignity.

There is another saying: *People don't remember what you said. People remember the way you made them feel.* I'm a writer, and also a funny writer, and my wit can be a neutron bomb. I've been told by many people that they thought it was hilarious when some rando would mess with me on Twitter and I'd hang 'em high in a quote tweet. I don't do that anymore. I have the ability to do that, but nuclear weapons aren't meant to be used. They're a deterrent. I'm also practicing restraint, which is an underappreciated virtue. Another thing people don't realize: when you lose your cool, you lose the argument.

So I have lots of opportunities to practice the underappreciated virtue of restraint on a daily basis. Sometimes with my wife. Anyhow, we are building a house and the big dumb bank decides they're going to withhold part of a draw to the general contractor. Basically, there were some cost overruns and they were withholding the amount of the cost overruns. Except there's nothing about that in the loan agreement. That's what I told them, in an email—we signed a contract. I was firm, but polite, and eventually they backed down. There's an essay in here about not trusting banks, but the bigger point is that if I flamed on them, there probably would have been a different, unfavorable result.

Like in 2008, when I first started *The Daily Dirtnap*. I was wound pretty tight back then. I was in a hurry to get a professional liability insurance policy in place (to insure me in case of slander or libel), and the insurance agent wasn't moving fast enough, so I flamed on him. He responded in a way that conveyed nothing but disappointment. I got what I wanted—but he was not cool to me after that. That guy still thinks I am an asshole. If anyone ever asked him, hey, do you know Jared Dillian? He would say: *That guy is a flaming asshole*. I really don't want to go around leaving a trail of people who think I am an asshole. I did that enough when I was in college.

It's not just emails. We all have that filter that prevents us from saying what we really want to say. If you asked anyone who knows me, they would probably tell you that I don't have much of a filter. I sure have been working on it. My best friend freshman year in college was a guy who had no filter whatsoever—he would say anything to anybody. That was a quality I admired—brutal, unvarnished honesty. Back then, for me to be nice to someone I didn't like felt like I was telling a little lie. Me and my fucking principles. As an adult, you learn to go around to get around, and you're polite and decent to everyone you come into contact with—even people you don't particularly like.

One of the things about working on a trading floor pre-2010 is that there was a lot of yelling. Lots and lots of yelling. And I was the biggest yeller of them all. We'd all scream at each other all day, and then go have a beer and laugh about it. Except one time, I unleashed my fury on a young analyst who was just trying to do his job. From my vantage point, he was screwing up. So I let him know about it. He never spoke to me again. At the time, I thought he was a cherry, but in hindsight, he was just a lot more civilized than I was. He is part of the long trail of people who think I am an asshole. In any event, a bank trading floor is like a wax museum today, to the point where people whisper. It's bizarre.

When I first started the newsletter, I had rented a small, windowless office in an executive office suite on 3rd Avenue. I rather liked the office manager. She was nice, and cute. One day I'm sitting in there doing my thing, and she abruptly opens the door and tells me that my rent is going up. That was the last thing I wanted to hear—money was tight in the early days. I don't recall exactly what I said, but I snapped at her. I bit her head off. And then I sat in my office, sulking, filled with regret.

Fuck. Now I have to go apologize. So I drag my ass down to her office, poke my head in, and apologize for being an asshole. And then something magical happens. She says, "You know, Jared, people around here really like you." I will never forget it. The point here is that if you are an asshole to someone, and don't practice restraint, you can unfuck the situation if you make yourself vulnerable.

Restraint of pen and tongue. The key thing to do is pause, rather than react. If you get a provocative email, write a draft and stick it in your drafts folder. Go home and sleep on it. When you get to work the next morning, 98 times out of 100 you will decide not to send the email. If someone says something provocative to you in person, pause, and think about it before you react. I was a trader, and I will always have trader in my DNA. My instinct is to react—not think. It has taken 15 years of training to unlearn this behavior. Think. Be deliberative. These things don't come easy to ex-traders.

Every interaction you have with someone is an opportunity to make their day better. I forget that sometimes, being wound up in my own shit. And remember what they always say: *Don't sweat the small stuff.*

Everything is small stuff.

TIME MANAGEMENT

People seem to think that I have accomplished a lot. I mean, sure. Here are some of the things I have done in the last few years:

- Finished grad school
- Written a daily newsletter
- Written a weekly newsletter
- Written two monthly newsletters
- Hosted a radio show
- Published six books, with a seventh coming
- Written a bunch of essays
- Written a bunch of short stories
- Played racquetball
- Had several speaking engagements each year
- Had several DJ gigs each year
- Was a dad to seven cats
- Built a house
- Did a small amount of philanthropy work
- Taught at the university level.

Here is another thing I did:

- Gained 30 pounds.

Here is a thing I did not do:

- Watch TV, movies, Netflix, or play video games.

So you can kind of see where this is going. There are 24 hours in the day. You're asleep for eight of them. How you allocate your time, on a daily basis, is the most important decision you will make in your life.

A couple of other notes:

- I don't have kids
- I don't have much of a social life
- I don't have much in the way of family or family obligations.

I got married when I was 23 years old. Back then, at age 23, my wife and I decided that we never wanted to have kids. I don't particularly like kids, but beyond that, we wanted to focus on our careers. I can tell you that I might have only been able to do one or two things on that list if I had kids. Pretty much all my friends have kids—and they aren't able to accomplish much professionally unless they have a lot of resources and a lot of help and a lot of resources to buy help.

Having kids is a sacrifice for sure—you're accepting that you'll have a lower earnings potential and lower promotion potential and everything that goes along with it. I was not much in the mood to make the sacrifice. People tell me that I am missing out on a lot, the joy you experience when you look in a child's eyes, and all that. Sounds like a bunch of crap to me. All the parents I know spent the first five years dealing with poop and pee and screaming, and the next ten years dealing with insolence. I think the whole kids thing is a giant cult, and the people in the cult want you to join the cult, like some kind of malignant pyramid scheme. No,

I will never be proud of my imaginary son for hitting a Little League home run. I will never be disappointed in him, either.

So I have lots of time to do other stuff. This is my typical day:

06:30: Alarm goes off.
07:30: Out the door to work.
08:15: Sitting at my desk.
11:30: Lunch.
12:00: Sitting at my desk.
15:30: Leave for the gym.
17:30: Home from the gym.
18:00: Eat dinner.
18:30: Sitting on the couch, writing, with baseball on TV.
22:00: Bedtime for bonzo.

As you can see, I get a full eight hours of sleep. Sleep is actually the key to my productivity—without it, I'm a banana slug. So if you add up all the hours in this schedule, you will see that I spend about 10-11 hours actually working, which doesn't seem like a lot. Well, I'm not scrolling through Facebook. I know a lot of finance people spend a huge amount of time on Twitter—I don't. I'll lope in every once in a while with a smart-ass comment, but it's not a huge time sink for me. When I'm working, I'm working hard, and I'm typing relentlessly, and you can accomplish a lot by working 10-11 hours a day.

I'll tell you a big-time suck for a lot of people: taking a dump. I have never understood how some people can spend a half hour, even an hour, sitting on the toilet. In the old days you would bring a magazine; today you bring your phone. I don't know if my body is engineered differently than everyone else's, but it literally takes me 60 seconds to crap. I drop trou, sit on the can, take a smash, wipe, stand up, and pull up my pants. One minute, and then I am back to work. A half hour every day over 365 days is 182 hours. Over 40 years, that's 7,000 hours. You can write books—books plural—in 7,000 hours. You think I'm joking about this, but I'm not. If you want a quick and easy way to ramp up your productivity, shit with alacrity, shit with a purpose. And it's the principle of the thing. My guess is that someone who spends an hour dropping the kids off at the pool doesn't really act with a lot of urgency in other areas of their life. Also: I never masturbated at work. Roughing up the suspect in the office is a bad idea, for a whole bunch of reasons.

I wasn't born with my time management ability. I learned it in the military. My nine-year Coast Guard career wasn't good for much—I pretty much had to unlearn everything once I got to the private sector—but the one thing it taught me was time management. When you are a cadet at a service academy, you have a million things thrown at you. First of all, you're taking 18 credits at a time—one semester, I took 22. You have to keep your uniform in tip-top shape, polishing brass, shining shoes, and ironing shirts. This can take as much as an hour a day. You are required to do sports of some kind. There is a whole bunch of military B.S. that you have to deal with. You accomplish more in one day than most college students accomplish in a week. So I have the U.S. government to thank for that.

For me, time management is an obsession. If I ever finish one task, and find myself staring off into space for even a minute, I say to myself, *get moving, fatass,* and then I am on to something else. You might say that I am efficient, which would be an understatement. There isn't a minute wasted in the day—it is all for a purpose. I don't fuck around. But I'm not Superman. I'm not as successful as some people, and it makes me reflect on what I am doing wrong, or what I could be doing better. Maybe I work hard, but I am working hard at the wrong things. Maybe my time is misallocated—maybe I should be spending time on other things. I never saw the benefit to going on TV, but maybe I should be hustling TV appearances. Maybe I should be doing more marketing. Who knows. I may be the hardest working man in the financial media business, but I am not the most successful person in the financial media business, so these are important questions to ask.

If you spent as much time thinking about time management as I did,

TIME MANAGEMENT

you would probably be pretty good at it. Because I think about it every second of the day. Do everything with a sense of urgency, as if your life depends on it. You will see results.

PERSEVERANCE

I HEARD A CRAZY story the other day. Someone told me that J.K. Rowling pitched *Harry Potter* to something like 45 publishers before Scholastic finally took a flyer. After ten publishers, you have a stiff upper lip. After 20, you're a tough cookie. After 30, you're a masochist. After 40, it's borderline mental illness. And yet she persevered.

My experience in publishing was entirely different. I was recruited to write *Street Freak*. A friend of mine was forwarding my Bloomberg notes to another literary agent friend, and when Lehman went tits up, the literary agent approached me about writing the book. I actually turned him down—I didn't want all the drama. Six months went by, and he reached out again, pressuring me to do it. I reluctantly agreed. Of course, that book launched my career in ways that I could not have imagined.

But that is not how it usually goes for authors.

Most authors have a tough time even getting an agent. They send out hundreds of queries. Most of them go unreturned. And even after you get an agent, and you submit the book proposal or whatever, there's still no guarantee that you're going to get published. And to think, I didn't have to go through any of this. The book came to me. This never happens. So it distorted my view of what the publishing industry is like, because when I wrote my second book, *All the Evil of This World*, I couldn't find a publisher, and ended up doing this hybrid self/traditional publishing thing with my literary agency.

Success has come easy to me, in a lot of ways. But not in all ways. Certainly not in athletics. I had this conversation with one of my racquetball buddies the other day: If I am winning 13-8 or something like that, I have this voice in my head that says, *lose*. This guy will score seven points and come back and beat me. And then I lose, ignominiously—the guy scores seven points and comes back and beats me. I expect failure, and I get failure—I am simply not a good competitor. So I told my friend this, a successful architect who's genetically engineered to be a racquetball player—he can scratch his knees without bending over—and he said, "Well, you're a good competitor in the game of life." Which is true. My story of getting a job on Wall Street is pretty similar to J.K. Rowling's experience trying to get *Harry Potter* published. I kissed a lot of frogs, and I was humiliated multiple times. Lots of doors closed before the one at Lehman finally opened. I remember being in my office at Coast Guard Intelligence, talking on the phone to Alan Augarten, head of equity derivatives at Prudential Securities. He gave me the bullet to the brain. I pleaded with him to take me on, pulling out all the stops. He was adamant—I was not going to work at Prudential. I hung up the phone, thinking that I would never get a job on Wall Street. Anyway, Prudential Securities was gone a couple of years later—good miss. Funny how things work out.

There is a genre of American movie that is about persisting in the face of unbelievable obstacles. The best in that genre? *The Pursuit of Happyness*. People have one of two reactions after watching that movie: they are demoralized by it, or they are inspired by it. I was the latter. Funny—*National Review* recently came out with a list of the top ten most conservative movies of all time, and this was at the top, and not because there is an ounce of conservative politics in the movie. There isn't. But working hard and achieving something is a conservative value, I guess, though it shouldn't be. One thing I will say about that movie—the rich, white-bread Dean Witter guys that Will Smith was working for as an intern were all very nice. A less capable director would have made them out to be villains, and set up an adversarial relationship between the employer and the employee. Wall Street people are nice, if they think you can help them make money. A little self-absorbed, but nice. When I was looking for a job, someone went out of their way to help me, and I've never forgotten it. Behind every successful person in finance, there is usually someone who went out of their way to help them get hired.

Lately I've been working on getting short stories published at literary magazines. Success is not coming easy to me this time. I've done the math. There are about 200 prominent literary magazines of varying quality, and each them might publish 10-20 stories a year. So there are about 2,000-4,000 short stories published in the U.S. every year. That may sound like a lot, until you consider that there are tens of thousands of MFAs, cranking out tens of thousands of stories, and the ones who have already been published have a leg up. There might only be 500 stories published by "emerging writers" every year. If there are 50,000 submissions, then your chances are 1 in 100. So far, so good—those are not the worst odds in the world. The feedback I usually get from these places is that my writing is excellent, but not a good "fit" for the magazine. Well, shit. Nothing I am going to write is going to be a good fit for these magazines. Lots of times, I am writing about rich and successful people. I am writing about very unsympathetic characters. I am operating under the philosophy that if I keep doing what I am doing, if I turn out great stories, then someone will notice someday, and take a risk. So far, I have had about 60 rejections. I will have hundreds more. I am past the "stiff upper lip" and "tough cookie" phases, and now I am onto "masochism." When disappointment turns into despondence and you think you're a failure, and you have no chance, all that is left is faith.

I don't tell many people this, but I had an English teacher in high school who you might have heard of. His name was Wally Lamb. Wally and I didn't see eye to eye in those days, but I will tell you his story. He'd be sitting there, at the front of the class, with a checkered shirt and a knit tie, squared at the bottom, telling us about all his rejections. Back in those days, you'd get a rejection letter—an actual letter—from a journal. He'd thumb-tack it up the to the bulletin board in the classroom. He had dozens of them. This was before he got his first book deal, and this was before his first book was one of the early selections for Oprah's Book Club. The guy fucking did a moonshot after that. So you can say whatever you want about Wally. *Right place, right time, lucky fucker,* all that, but the reality is that guy paid his dues. You can't say that he didn't. He went through the "borderline mental illness" stage of rejections. I've said this before here and there—you never want it to be easy. It was easy for me, and I got a stilted view of what the real world was like. I thought I was that talented. Yes, I am talented, but shit talented out your ass. There are a lot of talented people out there. Talent is nothing without work.

Just keep writing. Or, if you are in athlete, just keep playing. Or, if you are a banker, just keep banking. Etc. Just keep putting in the work, day in and day out, and people will notice, and you will get breaks. Or, you could quit. There is a place for quitting, but not after 60 rejections. Not after eight months. We must have hope or starve to death.

I am happy (or sad) to say that things continue to be easy for me. I spent eight months working on a book proposal for *No Worries*, and I was ready to go through the beauty contest of pitching it to publishers, when I got an email out of the blue from an editor at Harriman House. I had on my Twitter profile that I was working on a book, and he emailed me about it. After some back and forth, I had a book deal, the second one I've gotten without even trying. I love *No Worries*, and I think it is going to be a huge success, but it is not my ambition to be the best financial writer in the world. It is my ambition to be the best writer in the world. Like in any other industry, there are gatekeepers, and you have to get past the gatekeepers. I will say that getting published in one of the reputable lit mags is a big deal—if you get published in one of the top ones, there is a pretty good chance that it is going to lead to a book contract.

So I write. I am writing at the pool of a hotel in Miami. I write on the plane. I write in waiting rooms. I write when I get up. I write before bed. Every successful person has an unhealthy obsession with their work, which is broadly applicable to all industries. I eat, breathe, sleep writing. Someone out there eats, breathes, sleeps natural gas. Or eats, breathes, sleeps beer distribution. Or figure skating. Or cornhole. If you're talking to me, and I zone out in the middle of a conversation, there's a good chance I'm thinking of a story I'm working on.

I will be successful. You can timestamp me on it.

TIPPING

I LOVE TO TALK about tipping etiquette. Here's the way I look at it—if you have the means, you should be tipping far above and beyond what you believe is warranted for exceptional service. Someone who is waiting tables is poor, and you are rich. Karma dictates that you give an extra five or ten bucks to make their life a little easier. It's five or ten bucks. I'll tell you what—if someday you go bankrupt on account of not having five bucks, you can blame me.

But some people are self-centered and don't really believe in karma, so for those people, I will put this in real, practical terms that they can understand. If you tip people more, they will think you're a swell guy. All it costs to be a swell guy is five bucks. That's the best bargain in the world. Don't you want people to be happy to see you, instead of sad to see you? Now, I suppose if you are traveling and in a restaurant somewhere in Seattle or something, and you are certain you will never go back to that restaurant ever again, then you don't care. But you still should care, because it's shitty karma to stiff people, which gets us back to the first paragraph. But if there is a local place that you go to all the time, you had better be tipping 30% at minimum. Otherwise, when you walk in, they will say, *here comes the cheap fuck*.

In general, service is very, very good in the Myrtle Beach area. I drink gross amounts of iced tea with meals, so the server is filling up my iced tea four to five times during dinner. They are very attentive. Or, here's a thought—maybe they are attentive because they know they are getting an outstanding tip. And it's not about the money—it's about the gesture. Five bucks doesn't make a difference in anybody's life—but if you are nice to people, they will be nice to you back. I have given 50% tips. I have given 100% tips. Had lunch today, came out to $17, threw down a 20 and a five and left. Better than waiting another ten minutes for the waitress to make change so I can get $2 back—that's not a very good use of my time. Remember, don't sweat the small stuff—everything is small stuff.

There are different cultural attitudes towards tipping. In Connecticut, people will get out the tip calculator to give you exactly 18%, because you are not getting a penny more than you deserve. In Myrtle Beach, the redneck in a tank top on vacation with his four sugar-bombed, hyperactive kids will take the four ones out of his pocket on a $70 check and call it a day. In Miami, they just grat you 20%, and half the time people forget and leave another tip on top of that (I've done this). New York City generally has good tippers—say what you want about bankers and hedge fund guys, but they typically have pretty good attitudes towards money.

What if the service is terrible? That happens, sometimes. In those cases, I tip 20%, which I view as kind of a floor on wages for wait staff. I wouldn't dream of leaving less than that. I'm pretty easygoing about service, but my one pet peeve is when I want to leave and get in the car and Kayla forgets to bring the check, leaving me sitting there like an impatient chump. And yes, if you name your daughter Kayla, she will grow up to be a waitress in Myrtle Beach. They are all named Kayla.

I tip valets $10, if I'm driving my POS Toyota. If I am driving my Corvette, I tip $20—before and after. You are entrusting a $50,000 piece of machinery to some college flunky in the hopes that it doesn't come back with any scratches or dents. Three dollars isn't going to cut it. I especially appreciate the hustle of valets. I've stayed at the Four Seasons in Atlanta a few times, and those guys sprint to get your car when you give them the ticket. But to this day, I'm a little sniffy about giving my bags to the porter—I'm an able-bodied guy, ex-military, with blue-collar sensibilities: I can carry my own bags. I went to a fancy hotel in Miami Beach last week—no choice, I had to surrender my bags. The porter got $8 out of me. I wasn't pissed about the money, it's just a stupid system, which results in me waiting longer for my stuff, and surrendering my backpack with my laptop, which literally has my entire life in it. Maybe I'll feel differently when I'm a codger and walking with a cane.

I have opinions on tip jars. Lots of times, someone will walk into a Dunkin' Donuts, buy a coffee for $4.38, pay with a five, and drop 62 cents into the tip jar. They do this every day, and over the course of two weeks, they have put $6.20 into the tip jar. I have a suggestion. Put nothing in the tip jar, and then once a month, put a 20 in the tip jar. You'll see an attitude adjustment in a hurry. I've been going to the same Dunkin' Donuts for years, and for years I did this, dropping 20s in the tip jar, and I always got big smiles and nice chats out of the cashier. It works out to be about the same amount of money, but there's a huge psychological difference between a small, frequent reward, and a large infrequent (and random) reward. I'm sure B.F. Skinner did an experiment on this. Anyway, for the last two years, the cashier at Dunkin' has been a grumpy old lady, and the $20 bills didn't seem to produce a change in demeanor, so I stopped doing it.

Which brings me to Starbucks. For years, Starbucks had a cash tip jar—now, you pay with a credit card, and there are suggested tips: 15, 20, and 25%. I have feelings about this—I'll pay a 20% tip for someone who spends 45 minutes waiting on my table, but for pouring a cup of coffee and sliding it across the counter? I disapprove. This is part of a larger trend where every store has these credit card kiosk-things, and everyone expects a tip. As much as I hate it, I usually leave a tip, under the philosophy that you should not sweat the small stuff, and everything is small stuff.

I got married when I was 23, and I was unaware that you were supposed to tip the wedding DJ. I stiffed the guy. Such a heel I am. Of course, my wife wasn't a big fan of the music, because he played "The

Humpty Dance." Too lowbrow. I fucking love "The Humpty Dance," and I'll eat up all your crackers and your licorice. But also, I gave the dude a list of music ahead of time, and he played none of it and went rogue. Anyway, just as a word of warning to all the fiancés and fiancées out there—the bride will never be happy with the music. My advice is to let the bride pick the DJ, because then she'll be responsible for the decision. For the record, being a wedding DJ is the worst job in the world, jukeboxing the "Chicken Dance" and the "Macarena," dealing with an avalanche of requests and a pissed-off bridezilla, so you had better tip these guys—big.

I am a big fan of random acts of kindness. Lunch comes out to $36, drop down a hunge, and walk out. It will be fun the next time you see that person, but it's fun even if you don't. You can walk out knowing that you made someone's day. Which is really what it's all about, right? Spreading happiness wherever you go, as opposed to spreading misery wherever you go. Think of it this way—if you save $5 on a tip and you go out to eat twice a week, that's $520 a year. Do that for 40 years, and that's $20,000. So when you retire, you can have an extra 20 grand and be a miserable SOB, or you can be a nice person. That's all it costs you to be a nice person over an entire lifetime—$20,000. I'm sure there are some people reading this who make that in a week.

Also, make sure you tip extra at Hooters. Not because you're trying to get a date, but because the whole thing is kind of demeaning.

REGRETS

You want to know what grinds my gears? When people say they have no regrets.

What? Who has no regrets? I have a ton of regrets. I regret things that I said, I regret things that I didn't say, I regret things that I did, I regret things that I didn't do, and I regret causing psychic pain to people totally by accident. My life has been a series of one fuck-up after another, leaving a bunch of damaged and broken relationships in my wake. I don't understand when people say that they have no regrets. Are they psychos or something? Have they lived flawless, unblemished lives? Do they not care about the people they've steamrolled along the way?

Exhibit A out of 5,000 exhibits in my life: I broke up with a girl in high school. That wasn't the issue. It was how I did it. Later, I ran into her at the ten-year reunion, and she wouldn't talk to me. I liked her, personally, and I would like her to talk to me, so this causes me pain. Actions that I took when I was 15 years old cause me pain today. There was another guy, in college, that I ratted out for getting some cuddle time underneath the altar in the dorm chapel. I could see him from my window. I mean, it was absurdly bad behavior, but crucially, it was none of my business. Anyway, I ran into that guy at the 25-year reunion, and he wouldn't talk to me either. There are probably a hundred people that I've crossed paths with in my life that won't talk to me. And I think most people would consider me to be fairly well liked.

Having said that, the goal isn't for everyone to like you, because that's an impossible task. You can't please everyone. People unsubscribe from my newsletter all the time. I'm not everyone's particular brand of vodka, and that's fine. And the more successful you get, the more haters you will have—this is just human nature.

I think the purpose of regrets is so you don't make the same dumb mistake twice. It's okay to make a dumb mistake—two of the same genus or species is stupid. I've made a host of personal and professional mistakes. They cause me pain and discomfort, and the purpose of the pain and discomfort is to make me learn, and then I don't make the same mistake again. I'm sure you've heard the phrase, "The definition of insanity is doing the same thing over and over again and expecting a different result." The people who make these types of mistakes fall into a specific category: addicts. Get drunk and fuck your boss's wife. *I have no idea how that happened!* Get drunk and crash your car. *I have no idea how that happened!* Get drunk and make out with your best friend's boyfriend in the closet. *I have no idea how that happened!* The one thing that defines addicts is the failure to learn from their mistakes—until one day, when they figure it out. Or they never do. Addiction fits the definition of insanity.

When I was at Bloomberg, I wrote an op-ed about a commodity ETF, and I did some sloppy research, and the head of the ETF issuer wrote in all pissed off, and I had to issue a correction. In the grand scheme of human wickedness, this was not a big deal, but it was embarrassing, and I vowed to never do it again. And I didn't. Back in the early 2010s, I used to get political in *The Daily Dirtnap*, and I pissed off a bunch of people, and lost some subscribers. Good subscribers. That caused me to re-evaluate my priorities, and I never did it again. Life is a continuous process of trial and error, getting feedback along the way. Some people think that if you're making everyone mad, you must be doing something right. I don't share that belief. I guess it is true in some cases—Macron is raising the retirement age in France, and people are burning down the country. He is doing what is right, and unpopular. Maybe history will view him more kindly in 20 years, or maybe not. In Macron's case, he doesn't have much in the way of blue-collar sensibilities. Only Nixon could go to China, etc.

There is a corny saying: *The past is history, the future's a mystery, so that's why we live in the present—it's a gift.* I have regrets, but I don't dwell on them. And you get enough distance between you and the things you messed up, and maybe you can get to the point where you can laugh about them after a while. And after that, you can get to the point where you can use your story to help someone else going through the same thing. We don't dwell on the past, we learn from it. There is nothing in the past but pain. Don't go back there. Which is maybe what people mean when they say they have no regrets—that they are living in the present. But I doubt it. I think those people are dickheads.

This is a thing that I do. I live in fear of future regret, so I try not to do things that will cause me regret in the future. One aspect of this is that I treat every phone call, every meeting, every interaction as if that is the last time I will see or hear that person alive. Dumb example: I called my wife this morning and told her that my flight was canceled. I told her I loved her. She told me she loved me. But I don't treat our goodbyes as routine or commonplace. I think to myself that if this ended up being the last time I ever talked to her, that I would remember those words forever. I don't just do this with my wife—I do this with everyone. Every phone call might be the last call. You talk to one of your buddies on the phone, you don't hear from him for a few years, and then you found out that he's dead. Then you rewind and think about that last interaction—was it positive? If it was not, you will have regret. I wrote a short story about a couple that got into a fight, and then the husband got into his car and was killed in an accident. Imagine the guilt! You never want to be in that position.

And yet I continue to make mistakes, both acts of omission and commission. The key is that they really are mistakes, just dumb screwups—I really don't have a malicious bone in my body. And the crazy thing is that at the age of 49, I keep making mistakes—you think I would have stopped by now. I just keep coming up with new and creative ways to fuck up. It's super frustrating. And even at the age of 49, I don't know how to handle all situations. Experience counts for a lot, but it's not everything, and I can tell you that I am not in possession of the best people skills in the world, and I am very jealous of people who are. There are situations which absolutely baffle me, and that's why I'm a writer, not an admiral or a CEO.

Regrets are my superpower. I have them, but instead of pretending I don't have them, I use them for good. If you're going through some shit right now, there is a 100% chance that someone you know has gone through the exact same thing. And his or her willingness to talk about his or her experience will make a difference in your life. The most valuable thing that we each have is our story—the things we did well, the things we did poorly. All of human experience is one human being talking to another human being. If we're not talking, we're sunk.

HAPPINESS

AFTER 20-PLUS ESSAYS, we are finally getting down to the core of what this is all about.

How do you live a happy life?

It's actually not as hard as you think.

Deep, meaningful relationships make you happy. Porn does not. Sure, it does for 15 seconds, but then you are back to square one.

Work and achievements make you happy. Crack does not. Sure, it does for 15 seconds, but then you are back to square one.

A relationship with your higher power makes you happy. Video games do not. Etc.

That's pretty much it. There are a few things that will give you lasting happiness, and everything else will give you transitory happiness. Material things will make you happy for a time, but that wears off, and then they end up in the landfill. That's not to say that material things don't have their place, because they do. I get annoyed with people who eschew all material possessions, saying that they want to live a spiritual life. Not everyone can be Gandhi. Buy a nice car if it makes you happy, with the knowledge that you will need another car someday.

This is the point at which I bring up addiction. People can become addicted to all sorts of things: alcohol, drugs, sex, and gambling are the big ones. I mentioned crack for a reason. I know some people who have used crack, and they say that the high is so powerful, the first time they try it they add up all their money and figure out what it would take for them to be high all the time until they die. I've never tried crack, and I don't want to. It's not a drug that people do recreationally, in take-it-or-leave-it fashion. I do know some people who have tried cocaine, and said, *nope, not for me*. They are not addicts.

Addicts are God's chosen people, and I'll tell you why. They are in pursuit of a high which approximates that produced by a genuine spiritual experience. Except they are fooled—no matter how much alcohol or drugs they consume, they are unable to attain it. They are trying to find God—they are just looking in the wrong place. This is why 12-step programs work as well as they do—they supplant the high produced by drugs with the high produced by a relationship with a higher power, replacing transitory happiness with true happiness. It's really that simple. For people who enter 12-step programs with preconceived notions about religion or spirituality, this can be very, very difficult.

I'll go further. The biggest study ever done on happiness was recently completed at Harvard University. It was a 70-year longitudinal study on a Harvard graduating class that measured every aspect of their lives: their careers, their spouses, their kids—even the length of their scrotums. Everything. They were trying to find out what made people happy. They did find one thing. You know what all the unhappy people had in common? Alcohol. Those that had above-average consumption of alcohol were far less happy than their peers. How about them apples.

It's funny: alcohol prohibition was considered one of the most grievous errors in public policy—and also an infringement of personal liberty—but, sometimes, I understand why they did it. It is estimated that 90% of crimes are committed while people are under the influence of alcohol or drugs. The abolitionists thought they could get rid of 90% of crime, until the law of unintended consequences kicked in.

We are stuck with drugs and alcohol, at least until we get central bank digital currencies, and that, my friends, is a discussion for another day. Prohibition is not the answer—people must be free to make bad decisions.

One thing I have constantly tried to emphasize in these essays is the importance of professional accomplishments. Not everyone shares this view—a lot of clock-punchers out there. I would say that the vast majority of people understand the importance of deep, meaningful relationships with family and friends—I can probably name ten guys off the top of my head who don't take their jobs particularly seriously, but are shot out of a cannon at 4 p.m. to go spend time with their kids. That has its place, too, but I can tell you that nothing compares to the feeling of doing something, building something, or winning something, then standing back and saying: *I did that*. When I graduated in June of 2023, I won the award for being the best writer in my graduating MFA class. Still buzzing three months later.

I always go back to the funeral. Some people's lives will be measured by their achievements ("great men") and some people's lives will be measured by their relationships ("good men"). It is possible to have both. And it is possible to have the third leg of the stool as well—a relationship with God. Some people will chafe at the mention of God in this essay. Let me tell you that you don't have to believe in God to have a relationship with God, as nonsensical as that sounds. This is everything you need to know about God: there is one, and it isn't you. I have had mixed experiences with organized religion, and I haven't been to church since 2010, mostly because I don't like the behavior of other people in church. But I have a relationship with a higher power today, whereas I didn't 20 years ago. It has made all the difference.

I will add that doing quote unquote "bad" things will decrease your happiness. I call this the "sneaky scumbag" phenomenon. If you ever find yourself doing sneaky scumbag things, like getting a prostitute, or stealing, or engaging in character assassination, what you will experience is a drop in your self-esteem. You will like yourself less, and your happiness will be diminished. We all know the difference between right and wrong, and you're only as sick as your secrets. Which is essentially what my novel *All the Evil of This World* was about—seven people with seven very sick secrets. I had to write that book to get it out of my system, and now I don't have to write about it anymore. I can tell you, you could hire a private investigator to follow me around, and they would not find anything interesting, except for the occasional lunch at Hooters.

I can't seem to find the chart at the moment, but I saw recently that happiness, in the aggregate, is declining in the U.S. We can all guess at the causes. Social media? Maybe. Isolation and loneliness? Maybe. An increase in drug use? Maybe that too. Maybe it's all of these things and more. I can only tell you what works for me: relationships, achievement, spirituality. Maybe you have another solution. Maybe whacking off six times a day makes you happy—whatever floats your boat. I'd write a book on it, but I don't have enough material. I don't even have enough material for a 10,000-word article. It's really simple. Love other people, love yourself, love God. Two out of three is pretty good. Most people don't even get one.

THE PURPOSE OF THE BODY

You may find this hard to believe, but when I was in my 20s, I was a brick house. Planet Fitness would have referred to me as a *lunk*. I spent hours in the gym, running, playing sports, gobbling creatine and egg whites until I resembled Luke Voit. I was so statuesque, I had designs of running off and joining the porn industry.

Then I turned 30, and everything changed.

I found that I was so consumed with work that even though I may have had the time to work out, I didn't have the will to work out. Lehman Brothers stole my mojo. So my V-shaped torso turned into a cylinder. My weight bounced around, but at that point in my life, I had the determination to eat salads for a few months and take the pounds off.

Then I turned 40, and everything changed.

When I was 40, I tore my ACL and meniscus, and I found that, as a result, I gave less of a shit what I looked like. I was still going to the gym, playing racquetball pretty regularly, and I still paid attention to what I ate.

Then the pandemic hit, and all fucks went out the window.

I will tell you what I have learned over the years: I learned that the only sensible purpose of the body is to carry around the brain.

I know a guy who is beyond obsessive about what he puts into his body. Eating only spinach and chicken, never any carbs, no soda, no dessert, no chips, no ice cream, no processed food. The obsession borders on neurosis. Any free time is spent in the gym or running. Unsurprisingly, the guy is a brick house, coming up on 50 years old. Actually, I probably know 20 people like this.

By contrast, I am not too obsessive about what I put in my body. I get burgers from Cook Out, roast beef sandwiches from Arby's, and I put queso on my Chipotle. I eat salads more as a carbon offset. I don't have much in the way of physical activity other than the occasional racquetball game. I do not look like a brick house—I look like chewed bubblegum.

Do I care? I'd be lying if I said I didn't. I don't like what I see when I look in the mirror, especially with the knowledge of what I have been and could be now. That's vanity talking, though, and vanity equals pride, which is one of the seven deadly sins. When you're young, you want to be Peter North, and then you grow up and your worth isn't measured in hammer curls or your hammer, but in intellect, and your intellectual contribution to society. I could lift heavy things when I was 26—I picked them up and put them down. That did not get me a job at Lehman, it did not get me a successful newsletter, and it did not get me a bunch of books. In fact, it's not good for much of anything, except for hanging around in bars, and that has never been an aspiration of mine.

I look at this in terms of absolute advantage. Those with good bodies should use their bodies, and those with good brains should use their brains. Athletes, for sure, should eat chicken and spinach and spend hours in the gym. Their livelihood depends on it. Mine does not. In fact, it takes me away from the things that provide me with a source of income, and the things that give me joy. Working out is pure drudgery—I would be doing it out of duty, and I don't do things out of duty. In fact, I don't do anything I don't want to do. I do the mental math on the amount of physical and mental energy I'd have to expend to look like my friend, and the time it would take away from the things I like to do, and it just doesn't make sense.

So I just laid out the argument for being a fat fuck. What are the counter-arguments?

Well, hard work and effort is a virtue. So if you spend a lot of time and effort on your body, you are virtuous. But that's not the only kind of virtue. If I spend 16 hours a day writing, or investment banking, or painting, that is also a virtue. So that argument doesn't hold water. Hard work of any kind is virtuous.

So, if you eat right and exercise, you will live longer. Not precisely. There is a correlation between diet and exercise and longevity, but it is not a strong correlation. You have elite athletes who die at 38 and fat smokers who live to 100. Diet and exercise does not guarantee longevity. If it did, then I might feel differently about it. If I knew I could definitely live an extra ten years by eating right and exercising, I would probably do it. Or maybe not! Maybe the joy of eating cheesesteaks outweighs the benefit of the years added to my life. There are trade-offs in everything we do. People make this choice all the time—they continue to smoke, even though they know it will kill them eventually. In their calculation, it is worth it. It is a rational decision.

One argument I hear a lot (from my brother, in particular), is that if you're physically fit, you'll be mentally fit as well. It is a known fact that exercise is one of the best antidepressants around. I don't fundamentally disagree. When I exercise, I always feel better. But if the argument is that I will perform at a higher level mentally if I am physically fit, I dispute that claim. I mean, for God's sake, take a look at Vitalik Buterin, the Ethereum creator. Jeff Bezos is now a brick house, but crucially, it wasn't until after he stepped down as CEO. There are plenty of out-of-shape weaklings who are billionaires. Ever see that picture of Elon Musk with his shirt off? It's just not all that important—in fact, it doesn't matter at all. I will concede one point—when I was finishing up my MFA, and I hadn't exercised in three years, I was getting a little bit strung out. Some occasional exercise would have done me some good.

Or maybe the argument is that you want to be healthier, longer. You want to be mobile and active well into your 70s and 80s. Well, Stephen Hawking was able to accomplish a whole lot with one muscle in his cheek. I don't need to be downhill skiing when I'm 75, and I generally view things like that with some skepticism. That's not your role in life anymore. You're not Bode Miller, you're a sagacious old man, and you're supposed to sit in a chair and dispense wisdom. My grandfather on my mother's side didn't have his mid-life crisis until his 60s. He got a divorce, bought a plane, a sailboat, and a motorcycle, and built a cabin in Vermont with his bare hands. I thought that was pretty cool at the time, but in retrospect, it was clear he was running from something.

I just don't think the body is all that important. It's flesh, it decays, and all of us will be underground, someday, getting chewed apart by insect larvae. It's like that scene in *Casino Royale* where Mads Mikkelsen is torturing Daniel Craig by hitting him in the nuts with a rope. "You have taken good care of your body, Mr. Bond—such a waste." In the universe of investments, it's not a very good investment. It's like an option that decays. You can fluff it up as much as you like, but eventually it is going to expire worthless. All I really care about is that my clothes fit and I don't get so fat I have to start shopping at Haggar. And I don't think other people's bodies are that important, either. Now, I am not one of those "it's what's on the inside that matters" people, because frequently people's insides match their outsides. As much as we deny it, we are all a tiny bit shallow. But you wouldn't go spouse-shopping among vapid Instagram models—that's not the best way to find a life partner.

The only sensible purpose of the body is to carry around the brain. It's the brain that counts—it's who you are, and your body is not who you are. It's just a vessel. Your intellect, your character, your capacity for love is what is important. And this isn't left-wing body-positivity talking. If I could wave a magic wand and not be fat, I would do it. But one of the things we're learning in the age of semaglutides is that genetics is responsible for at least 50% of how you look. If I could look like one person in the world, it would be Rafael Nadal. Until then, I will have to watch my churlish figure.

SLEEP IS MY SUPERPOWER

I USED TO BE so dumb when I was a kid.
 True story. Back in 1999–2000, I was a pretty busy guy. I was working a full-time job as a LTJG in the Coast Guard, I was going to grad school part-time, and I had a part-time job on the floor of the Pacific Options Exchange. This was my typical day: I'd get up at 3:45 to drive to San Francisco for my trading floor job, I'd work there until about noon, then I'd head back to my Coast Guard job to work from 1 p.m. until 10 p.m. Then I'd come home and study until one or two in the morning. Then I'd go to bed and do it all over again. For a period of a little more than a year, I was averaging two hours of sleep a night. I'd catch up a little bit on the weekends.

You dumb dummy. I mean, it all worked out in the end—I got a job on Wall Street, and the rest is history. But that was a really unhealthy thing to do. And towards the end of that period of time, I was delirious from lack of sleep, just going insane. I have distinct memories of standing on the trading floor, looking up at the screens, and having no idea what the hell was going on because I was so sleep-deprived. But there were no ill effects on my health, at least none that manifested immediately. I have the usual stories about pulling all-nighters in college, including one time when I pulled two all-nighters in a row, but that was just bad time management. And the military in general is not good for sleep. I'd be at sea, standing one-in-three watches on the bridge, getting up at 2:45 a.m. to stand the 4 a.m.–8 a.m. watch, then working a full day. From age 18 to 32, I got practically no sleep at all.

That changed in 2006 when I was diagnosed with bipolar disorder. My doctors stressed to me the importance of getting a full night of sleep—lack of sleep can trigger a manic episode. So I slept. And the interesting thing is that, once I started getting sleep, I went from being a minimally competent trader to being a stud trader. When I started getting sleep, everything in my life got better. These days, I get eight, sometimes nine hours of sleep a night. It is my superpower.

Oftentimes, someone will say to me, "You do so many things—when do you sleep?" This always makes me smile. I do so many things because I sleep so much—it makes me a million times more productive. I would say that my productivity drops 10% if I get seven hours of sleep a night, 30% if I get six hours of sleep and 50% if I get five hours of sleep. Less than four hours of sleep, and I am practically useless. People have been studying this, and they've found that a lack of sleep is highly correlated to all sorts of health problems, including things you would never think had anything to do with sleep. People are a bit obsessed with longevity these days; well, one simple way to live longer is to go the fuck to sleep. Lack of sleep makes everything worse.

In the United States, we have a workaholic culture where people routinely under-sleep—investment bankers and such. I recently heard a story where a junior banker was told by a managing director that he could "sleep when he's dead." I don't have a problem with the workaholic culture, but we'd all be vastly more productive if we got a good night's sleep every night. But there are trade-offs in everything we do. If you sleep two extra hours a night, that is two fewer hours you have to do other things. Frequently that means exercise. The number of Wall Street guys that get up at 3:30 in the morning to work out is uncountably infinite. You have to work out, right? I've done these calculations, and in my estimation, you'll get more longevity out of sleeping than exercise. Not that both aren't important, but sleep is more important. "Well, I have kids." Heard that one before, too. Let me tell you something—it has been almost two decades since I stayed up to watch a late-night show. Who watches these things? On average, I am in bed by 9:30 p.m.

I don't think I've made my case convincingly enough. I do a lot of different things, as you know. None of this is possible without sleep. A friend of mine goes to Burning Man every year, and asked me if I would come next year. So I asked him: When do you sleep? He says, *oh, I sleep.* But is it noisy? *There is house music playing 24 hours a day,* he says. *Your tent is rattling. You can feel the vibrations through your sleeping bag.* This doesn't sound like a very good idea to me. He offered me a slot to DJ at his camp, but I don't think spending a week in the desert with no sleep is really worth it. Too old for that shit.

Also, sleeping is fun! When I was in my 20s, I viewed sleeping as a waste of time. I wanted to be awake all the time, experiencing life. I really thought I would sleep when I was dead. Now, I don't consider sleeping to be a waste of time at all—I get some of my best ideas when I am asleep. A couple of months ago, I dreamed up an idea for a short story, got up the next morning, and started writing. I get a lot of ideas from dreams. I even get investment ideas from dreams. Also, dreaming is a blast, you get to do all kinds of things in your imagination that you can't do in real life. And most of those dreams occur in the one to two hours of REM sleep, right before you wake up—that's where I do all my good thinking as a creative. Nothing worse than having your alarm go off at 3:30 a.m., right in the middle of stage-four sleep, and you have no idea where you are. Dreaming is your subconscious trying to solve problems in the middle of the night. There is a whole science around dream analysis, and while I don't put too much stock in this, I do think that dreaming is when you allow yourself to think about things you wouldn't allow yourself to think about when you are awake.

I should also add that any program of exercise should be accompanied by a program of sleep, especially weightlifting. You can lift weights all you want, but you are not going to get any stronger if you don't sleep and allow your muscles to heal. I lifted weights for four years at the Academy, and didn't get much stronger. The only time I got stronger was went I went home for a long weekend and slept ten hours in a night, then I'd go back to school and add ten pounds to my bench press. I should also add that drugs and alcohol are terrible for sleep. You might get drunk and pass out, but you're not really sleeping—you'll be exhausted the next day. Cocaine sounds like fun (never tried it), but the idea of not sleeping for a few days doesn't agree with me. I am currently writing this on a plane to Los Angeles. Got up at 2:45 this morning to catch the early-bird shuttle to Charlotte, and I can tell you that I'm going to be in bed at 7 p.m. tonight, West Coast time, so I can catch up on my sleep. I am as fastidious about sleep as some people are about diet and exercise. They may be physically healthy, but I am mentally healthy.

And that's another thing—if you are prone to stress and anxiety, your stress and anxiety are going to be amplified a hundredfold if you are not getting enough sleep. I'm like everyone else—when I get in bed, my mind is racing, worrying about shit I have to do or stressing about this or that. It takes me about a half hour to fall asleep. But sleeping is like ctrl-alt-del on my brain—I wake up the following morning rebooted, and the stress is gone. It's the best possible thing that you can do for your mental health. But, of course, all the ding-dongs are focused on their physical health, while sleeping four hours a night. What is more important? How you answer this question says a lot about your outlook on life, and your priorities.

Every once in a while, you hear about these jerks who say that they only need two hours of sleep a night. You know who used to say that? Eliot Spitzer. He'd be running around Central Park at three in the morning. He was not Superman—he was just an idiot. We are not different. Nobody needs less sleep. If someone tells me that they're getting four hours or less of sleep a night, and that's all they need, I fundamentally distrust them. They're lying to you, and they're lying to themselves.

We all have demands on our time. Sleep always seems to be the last priority for people because they don't see the benefits of it. They'll muddle through on two hours less than they need. When was the last time you got a full eight hours of sleep. Years ago? Do you remember how good it felt? You can feel that way all the time. Colbert sucks, anyway.

THE GOODNESS OF PEOPLE

I DON'T KNOW IF you've ever had this happen to you: You're walking into a building, someone holds the door for you, and then they turn and look at you, all irritated, and say *you're welcome*, and walk off in a huff. Maybe you were lost in thought and didn't say thank you, maybe you're from New York, where people aren't especially polite, maybe you were going to say it but they interrupted you, and now this person is going to sit down at their computer and log onto Facebook and write about how terrible people are and how the world is going to hell.

So, for starters, impolite people are not bad people. Politeness has to do with social norms, which vary in different parts of the country, and sure, someone who is impolite might be a bit self-absorbed, but self-absorbed people still go to heaven. The point of me bringing this up is that what a lot of people think of as "good" and "bad" have nothing to do with goodness or badness. It's just disagreements between people. The guy at work who you think is a scumbag is probably not a scumbag. He probably has no idea that he screwed you over.

That's not to say that there aren't bad people, or at least people with moral failings. Let me tell you something: I could have written about a lot more misbehavior in *Street Freak* than I actually did. People doing bad things, or even illegal things. I'm not in the business of ruining people's lives, and I didn't want people to get hurt by the book—even people I personally disliked. So I poked fun at their foibles and their eccentricities and left it at that. If you're a trader, or a sales trader, you have lots of opportunities, every day, to be bad. People make these calculations all the time, about what they expect to gain and how often, and what they expect to lose and how often. There are rules on Wall Street, but no ethics. There are ethics in the CFA program, but it is all arcane bullshit.

But yeah, I have met a handful of morally challenged people in my life. And when I say morally challenged, I am referring to people who will hurt someone on purpose. There are degrees. Someone who sleeps with a co-worker is morally challenged, but it is a weakness of the flesh. You don't end up in bed with someone completely by accident, but one thing leads to another, and—you can see how it goes. I put character assassination on another level of badness. When you engage in this behavior, you're trying to destroy another person. Some people dedicate their entire lives to the destruction of another person. Some people have dedicated their entire lives to the destruction of Trump, which is pretty nuts if you think about it. Some people get paid good money to sit in front of a computer every day and attempt to destroy Trump. He's probably the least sympathetic character in the galactic supercluster, but he's still a human being. No empathy.

Which brings me to Twitter. Twitter is a vicious place. It's really not the greatest design for a social media platform, where Rando Calrissian building model airplanes and pouring money into OnlyFans can just reach out and ruin your day. It doesn't matter who you are—anyone with over 10,000 followers has experienced hate online. Oftentimes it has nothing to do with politics—it could be about your personal appearance. People tell me I'm fat all the time. You might have a difference of opinion on the bond market, and people take it personally, and call you a fraud, grifter, or worse. Women seem to think they have a bad time of it online, but I'm not so sure they have it worse than men. What strikes me about this is how many people there are out there who are willing to attack someone without provocation. What is the definition of a good person? Don't hurt people and don't take their stuff. After a while, you start to think everyone is a turd, and you have a warped view of human nature. But as human beings, we focus on the bad people more than the good people—for every turd, there are a thousand people who support you completely. If you want to know which people have the most pessimistic outlook on human nature, it is cops. They deal with turds all the time, so they think everyone is a turd, when in fact that is not the case.

In fact, the vast majority of people are good. There are good drug addicts. There are good prostitutes. I even believe that some murderers are good. Don't believe me? Ever see *The Shawshank Redemption*? Of course you have. Red was a murderer. It wasn't mentioned in the film, but it was in the novella that it was based on. I believe that some people make mistakes, even big mistakes. I believe that some people have lapses in judgment. I believe that some people have moral failings and low impulse control. I also believe that these people can feel remorse and experience regret, and do penance. If you find that you're consumed with hatred of another person, and you're actually taking time out of your day to do harm to them, then you've given in to the Dark Side.

A special word about infidelity: A few paragraphs ago I excused it. Infidelity is violence—violence to the institution of marriage. It is the ultimate betrayal of trust. Marriages can survive strip clubs and carousing and such, but they frequently can't survive an emotional betrayal. My experience with this is that infidelity doesn't usually happen when the marriage is going well. It usually happens when the marriage is already going poorly, and oftentimes people use this as an easy (but traumatic) way to end the marriage. My suggestion is: If you're not happy in the marriage, then tell your spouse that you're not happy. You then have three options: end the marriage, fix the marriage, or limp along with a sucky marriage. The third option is the worst, obviously. The fourth option, to blow it to smithereens by getting some strange, is not a good option. You might go to hell if you cheat on your spouse. Just saying. But the worst hell would be to get away with it.

I spend a lot of time thinking about what it means to be a good person, and trying to be a good person. Let me tell you, it does not come easy to me, but it's one of those things that, if you work at it, you get better. The guy who does not return any of your calls and text messages is not a bad person. He's just jammed up in his own shit, and one day, he'll regret it, or he won't. He's just on a different path. The thing with trying to be a good person is that you're still going to piss people off—it's inevitable. But these are simply differences between people, and have nothing to do with right or wrong. I'm sure there are some people out there who think I'm a bad person, for some perceived slight, or something else, real or imagined. Not much I can do about it. Christianity tells us to love our neighbor—even when our neighbor isn't following the script we have for him in our heads. The key here is forgiveness, and another way of saying that is: be gentle with people.

Don't get me wrong, I still lock my car and my house. There are some creepy-crawlies out there. There are people out there with nothing to lose, who will hurt people just to hurt people. That's why we live in our gated communities with our ADT and motion-sensing lights. But the vast majority of people are not like that. People are good. I believe in the goodness of people. And even so, I am always surprised when someone does something nice for me.

THE HUSTLERS

I HAVE WORKED WITH over a dozen interns over the years, and the vast majority of them—save one or two—were hustlers. And I hired them because they were hustlers. I did not always hire the smartest kids, I did not always hire the kids with the best grades, I hired the kids that were hard-working and ambitious. *Poor, smart, and determined*, as Ace Greenberg, CEO of Bear Stearns, would have said. They have all far outperformed what would have been expected from a graduate of Coastal Carolina University. There are traders and portfolio managers and analysts and investment bankers among them, and huge successes outside of finance as well.

But here's the thing about hustle—you can't teach it. You either have it, or you don't.

I'm not kidding. I can pull strings and help them make connections, but whether they get the job or not is ultimately up to them. There is that quote about leading a horse to water. Absolutely true. You have to want it. Some people want to want it, which is not good enough. You have to want it with every cell in your body. You have to ache for success.

I am worried that we, as a country, are losing our capacity for hustle. California contemplated imposing a 32-hour workweek (while getting paid for 40). The UAW labor union is asking for the same thing. Much has been written about Zoomers and Millennials opting for free time instead of pay or perks, working fewer hours in the office. There were quite a few nights I worked late on the trading floor at Lehman, ordering sesame chicken off of Seamless, even though the markets closed at 4 p.m. There was no reason I had to be there—I loved my job and I was researching trades to put on. The bankers were pulling 20-hour days, either by will or by thrill. They didn't have to be there—they had the option of quitting and becoming a lunch-pail guy at any moment. This sort of thing doesn't exist anymore—go to a trading floor at 4 p.m., and you could fire a cannon and not hit anyone. Lots of places are taking off Friday afternoons, or Friday altogether. Some places are taking off Monday and Friday. Sure, this is because of the pandemic, and there was something that happened in our collective psychology where we decided we didn't give a fuck. Giving a fuck, and working, is a necessary condition for producing wealth.

Not to get all financey on you, but people like to say that the stock market returns 10% a year, so you should log onto vanguard.com and buy some index funds and get your 10% over the course of your investing career. Why does the market return 10%, on average? Because it returned 10% a year for the last 100 years. I guess past performance is a predictor of future results. But what if the conditions that were present for the last 100 years, aren't present for the next 100 years? What conditions are those? The rule of law, property rights, and tax collections that have averaged around 20% of GDP. All of that could disappear. But there is more. Output is a function of hours worked, productivity, and effort. It is the effort part that I am concerned about. What are the economic consequences of people simply not trying as hard? What are the economic consequences of a lack of hustle? If you knock one percentage point off GDP, and we're growing at 2% a year (at best), then it's hard to see how those 10% equity returns will continue in the future, without debt, and we don't have much capacity to add any more of that. If we want to get richer as a society, we have to work harder, work longer, or work more productively. If we're not willing to do that, then we will stagnate. Like Europe, whose stocks have returned essentially zero over the last 15 years. Europe values leisure over productivity. We are going down the same path.

There have been two periods in history where the stock market returned zero for an extended period of time—1928 to 1946, and 1968 to 1982. I forgot to mention 2000 to 2011. The first period was a result of a depression after a huge stock market bubble, and the second was a result of high inflation and interest rates following a smaller stock market bubble. So you can look at it in terms of working off the excesses of overinvestment and malinvestment. But there is another model. What if, during those time periods, people simply weren't working as hard? If you go back and read some primary source material about the Depression, it wasn't simply as if some exogenous economic shitstorm suddenly hit the U.S. and unemployment went to 25%. There are two sides to the story, and the other side of the story is that New Deal economic programs and entitlements destroyed the work ethic of the country and actually contributed to unemployment, and lots of people weren't super interested in working. The good news is that these things go in cycles, and post-WWII, America started hustling again. The 70s were also not known for hustling. What I am suggesting is that there are some powerful trends in social psychology that we don't fully understand, and they have huge implications for economics. I'll cut to the chase—I think we are at the beginning of one of those decade-long zero return periods for stocks, a decade filled with economic misery.

Get to work, fuckers.

I will say that hustling does not come naturally to me. If you go in my high school yearbook, you will see that my greatest ambition as a senior was to work for the government and cop a retirement check after 20 years. What changed? I read Mariam Naficy's *The Fast Track*, and when I got to the page where it showed what kind of money people in banking were making, my jaw about hit the floor. It said I could make $600,000 to $800,000 in five to seven years. I hadn't thought of myself as a person who was motivated by money, but at that exact moment, I was. Now, I had an intellectual interest in capital markets anyway, but the prospect of almost a million dollars didn't hurt. I did an outrageous amount of hustling. I was shameless. Nowadays, the kids like to cold email people—I was cold-calling people. Smiling and dialing. Taking trips out to New York for informational interviews. I was a bulldog. And if you want a job on Wall Street, you have to be a bulldog.

Want to know another activity that requires a lot of hustle? Book publicity. In the old days, publishers would spend a boatload of money to send you on a 96-city book tour to promote your book. Gone forever. They might have one person who will package up and mail out books for reviewers. You have to do everything else yourself. You have to be shameless. You have to bulldog it. Again, this does not come naturally to me. With *All the Evil of This World*, I had 100 galleys printed and sent out. Almost nobody helped. Kept bulldogging. Kept hustling. In spite of all that, the book sold reasonably well, given the subject matter. I did the hustle of all hustles for *No Worries*. And for my next book, I am going to be hustling you. *You will get an email from me with a pitch to buy the book*. And you had better buy it. Bulldog. Shameless.

Hustling is about doing whatever it takes to get what you want. Which means: you have to put your own interests above those of other people. For those of us who are naturally altruistic, this is an uncomfortable position to be in. There are some jobs out there that require you to hustle. Real estate agents. Interdealer brokers. Strippers. Imagine working in a strip club, asking guys for lap dances, and getting turned down 100 times every night. Imagine what the rejection feels like, the first time. Imagine brokering variance swaps and getting hung up on 30 times in a row. Keep pushing, keep fighting. There are plenty of jobs out there where you don't have to hustle at all. I used to have one of those jobs—it was soul-destroying. I like being in a position where I constantly have to advocate for myself and my own interests.

Like I said, hustling cannot be taught. But it can be part of the culture.

Lots of people don't like the fact that a few million people crossed the southern border into the United States. Guess what—those people are hustlers! They had to hustle through jungles and deserts to get here, dodging alligators and drug runners. They will make fine Americans. I would prefer that there was a mechanism to get these people into the country legally, so it doesn't make a mockery of our national sovereignty, but that is a separate issue. Anyone who wants to come here and hustle is okay by me. There are a lot of people here who have no interest in hustling who I'd like to put on a raft to Cuba.

In America, there are virtually no limits to your success. It seems as though fewer and fewer people are taking advantage of that. Just don't be surprised when someone who is smart and ambitious turns out to be smart and ambitious.

THE CREATORS

M OST PEOPLE LEAD a life of doing stupid syntactic stuff that other people tell them to do. I'm sure you remember the TPS reports from *Office Space*. Filling out forms, forms, and more forms, putting part A into slot B, you're a cog in the machine, and then you go home and have beers and watch some shows. This is, literally, 99% of the population. And it's not just confined to low- or mid-wage jobs. Investment bankers fall into this category, as do most consultants. Whether you're an admin in a doctor's office or you're cranking on spreadsheets, you're simply making the donuts.

Very few of these people have the capacity to create. I'm not talking about creativity in an organizational capacity, where you dream up a fancy bond covenant for a new issue, in a corporate structure where it's all laid out for you—I'm talking about real unstructured create-it-from-nothing achievement, which is an entirely different animal. Writing books and painting paintings, but also creating a business from scratch with a radical new idea. You have people who rise to the highest levels of government, the military, and corporate America, and yes, those are achievements, but not in a creative sense. It takes skill to navigate the politics of an organization. But they are not creators. So few people in this country have created anything worthwhile. When they leave this earth, there will be nothing to remember them by.

Take books, for example. How many times have you heard someone say, "I have always wanted to write a book." Let me tell you how to write a book. Turn on the computer, open Microsoft Word, and start typing. There is no secret. Yes, I have some talent in writing, but the difference between me, with six books, and you, with none, is that I actually fucking did it. I did the hard thing. There is nothing special about writing a book—lots of people have done it. I have people send me their janky self-published books with Fisher-Price covers and ghastly formatting, and you know what? They're still books. They did it. They created something from scratch and offered it to the world. So what if only their fifth-grade teacher and step uncle-in-law read it? It's still creating. The foregoing is also true for any work of art or music.

The same applies to business. As I am fond of saying, you just do the hard thing. You solve one problem, then another problem, then another problem, and at the end of it you have a big pile of money. This is scary to some people, because most people aren't problem solvers, they're just good at doing the stupid syntactic thing they've been doing for years. I ran into an old friend last night who is thinking of starting a motorcycle-repair business. He knows how to fix motorcycles. He knows nothing about business, but he will figure it out. "Figure it out" are three very powerful words. Let's say you wanted to open a bar. Well, you would have to find a location, remodel it, get a liquor license, order furniture, hire staff, all that shit. Nobody knows how to do these things other than people who have opened bars before. You just figure it out. You wanted to know what I did before I started *The Daily Dirtnap*? I looked up every financial newsletter I could find, and wrote to the editors, asking them about their business, what they liked, what they didn't like, what kinds of problems I could run into, etc. Some of them wrote back and said that I should abandon all hope, that I had zero shot at success, which served as a powerful motivator. But the point is, I did the hard thing. I figured it out. There is no secret formula—you just have to do it.

You hear the word *grifter* being thrown around a lot these days, especially on Twitter. What does it mean? A grifter is someone who is selling a secret formula to people who want a shortcut, like most crypto guys, real estate speculators, gurus, furus, yogis, and some priests. People find shortcuts to be irresistible. *Follow these seven easy steps.* Anyone who has subscribed to my newsletter will know that I have never said it is easy. In fact, if you're doing it right, it's really hard, and you have your ass in a jam about two-thirds of the time. Always beware of someone selling easy solutions, because there are no easy solutions. There is only the hard way, the way filled with pain and struggle.

I get hate mail from time to time, or at least unkind mail. These people come from all walks of life, but they have one thing in common: they have never known actual achievement. If you have never known actual achievement, then you can be critical of the achievements of others. These people are fucking turd burglars. I actually sat down to write an entire essay on this two months ago—the mark of a good person is a man who allows himself to experience joy at someone else's achievement. There are seven deadly sins, but envy is the worst of them. I mean, this is basically the entire premise of *Atlas Shrugged*. I outgrew that book a long time ago, but if you zoom out, you will see that society is perpetually engaged in a pitched battle between people who can, and people who can't or won't. Entire nations have been destroyed by envy. A 100 million people have been killed by envy. On a smaller scale, it's DMs from randos telling me that my wife is uglier than a dog (this happened) and that I can peddle my grift in hell (this also happened). The definition of a turd burglar is the person who hates success. They are everywhere. They are in finance, they are in law, they are in academia, and they are in government. If you become successful, there will be a horde of people who want to take you down. That's human nature, it's ugly, and I come face to face with it every day.

Usually, when I talk like this I get accused of being an elitist, which is a funny thing to call someone who grew up in a 1,200-square-foot house on a $10,000 income. I am not unique—there are people like me everywhere, people who grew up under difficult circumstances who overcame great obstacles to achieve success. These people tend not to be very sympathetic to other people's bullshit excuses as to why they can't do something. They are the last true conservatives, not the faux populists like Tucker Carlson, the "men of the people" (unless those people approach their table at Per Se, at which point they will call the maître d' to have them removed). Nobody talks about personal responsibility anymore, not since the early 1990s. Let's bring it back. Let's reintroduce the idea that where you are today is the sum total of all the decisions you have made in your life, good and bad, and you are responsible for them. You are in control of the choices you will make in the future, too.

People spend way too much time thinking about politics. Politicians are destroyers, not creators. The most well-known creator today is Elon Musk, and as you have probably noticed, he is up to his ass in alligators. Elon is flawed—most great people are, in one way or another, but one of the most disheartening things I've seen online in the last ten years was the gaggle of otherwise right-thinking finance people who participated in $TSLAQ, the anti-Tesla hashtag on Twitter. They tweeted about Elon and Tesla for years, trying to destroy him. Imagine spending that much time and energy trying to take down another human being. Those are turd burglars, right there. Terrible people. Oh, I know the motivation—Elon was a fraud, and they were protecting the small investor in the name of truth, justice, and the American way (salutes flag). No, they were taking up about 80% of their brain space with hatred of another person. Screw those people. Life being what it is, I don't like everyone, but I have never, ever rooted for someone else to fail.

Creating is an act of love—love of self, love of man, love of man's achievements. I spend my time thinking about how to spread joy. I have selfish motivations, sure—I want to sell a lot of subscriptions and books. But isn't that what capitalism is about? Each working for our own benefit, which results in benefit for others? I don't waste a second thinking about the opinions of achievement-less people. When you write a book, then I will listen to your opinions on how to write a book. Funny, people who write books don't criticize other people's books. Ever. Wonder why.

PROCRASTINATION

I THOUGHT ABOUT WRITING this essay later, but I guess I might as well do it now.

Procrastination will destroy your dreams one day at a time.

I was a terrible procrastinator in college. If I had a paper to write, it was getting done at 3 a.m. the night before it was due. There was no other acceptable time. I'd come back from dinner and wander the halls, shooting the shit with the other cadets, and then I'd settle down at about 11 p.m. with my Mac Classic and a Mountain Dew, and oh, let me play some video games first. Three hours later, I'd be like, *fuck, I have to get this done*, and then I'd shit out some froggish leavings and hand in what was essentially a first draft, and get a B on it. Then I'd be a zombie the next day. In one computer science class, I basically did no work the entire semester, and then pulled two consecutive all-nighters to study for the final. I got a C. My grade-point average in college was 3.03, far below what I could have accomplished if I wasn't such a turd. One of my many regrets.

I don't procrastinate much these days. Much. When you write a newsletter with a daily deadline, you have to get after it. I dive in every morning at 8 a.m. and don't stop until it is finished. If you follow me on Twitter, you might notice that I don't tweet (or even look at Twitter) from 9-12 in the morning. After I am done with the newsletter, then I can come up for air. By the way, social media is the number one way in which people procrastinate. You can lose two hours doomscrolling through Twitter or Facebook or Instagram. Then you look up and wonder where the time went. I use social media much more judiciously than I have in the past. By the way, Jefferies economist David Zervos had a really cool theory about technology and social media: he said that in the early days of the internet, we had a huge productivity boom (*Look! I can order these plane tickets online!*), and as the internet progressed, and social media appeared on the scene, the internet became a huge productivity suck, as people spent hours and hours doomscrolling and looking at 48 photos of "Fun Dinner at Pam's."

I am very conscious of productivity sucks. A productivity suck is something that can lull you into a semi-conscious state, where your brain turns off and your mind wanders, like when you've quaffed three beers while watching ESPN and you start wondering what kind of dogs Sage Steele has, while looking at Alexis Ren on Instagram. I try to free my life of productivity sucks. It's funny, a few years back I bought one of those vintage video game systems, with 250 games from the 80s, and it was fun for a while, but after a few months I asked myself, *what am I doing here, down in my basement playing* Robotron *for three hours?* I haven't touched that thing in two years. Basically, the only time I am going to be playing video games is if I have absolutely nothing to do, and there is never a time when I have nothing to do. If I were playing video games, it would be because I am procrastinating on something else.

At the time of writing, I have a few ongoing items in my tickler:

- Write two more short stories for my short story collection, *Night Moves*.
- Continue writing essays for the essay collection you are reading right now.
- Get ready to move into my new house.

- Publicize the shit out of *No Worries*.
- Learn to play the guitar.
- Plus, ongoing stuff like the newsletter, the radio show, the class that I am teaching, petting the cats, and all the other miscellaneous crap.

So I pretty much always have shit to do. I could procrastinate, for sure. I could dick around with these last two short stories, they would never get done, and then I wouldn't have a book. I mean, lots of people do this. Have you ever met someone who said they were writing a book—for ten years? And it's never done? The best thing to do to those people is to ask them, "How's the book coming?" Makes them miserable. Keep asking. Make them experience shame. Maybe at some point they will get sick of people asking, and actually write the damn book. *Doers do. Talkers talk.* Nothing you haven't heard before.

Here's how procrastination will ruin your life: You will be lying on your deathbed, and you will regret not doing X or Y or Z. Because you screwed around and never did it. Now, this would be acceptable if instead of doing X or Y or Z, you were doing something equally worthwhile. Dumb example, but let's say instead of taking up painting, you decided to travel the world instead. That would be equally worthwhile. But that's not how people usually spend their time—they spend it in front of the TV or computer, growing lichens under their armpits. I have never heard the story where someone is lying on their deathbed, and they're completely satisfied with all the time they spent watching *Jetsons* reruns.

Look. It's a gorgeous day in South Carolina right now. Seventy-five and sunny, no humidity. I could be going for a walk. I could be enjoying a cigar on the back porch. I could be sitting in the bar, outside, at Frank's Outback. All of those things would be fun. But I haven't written an essay in about a week, and as much as I find writing essays pleasurable, there is an end to my means: I have an audience that I want to keep happy so that hopefully they will pre-order my book. Or maybe this essay will get traction and I'll get more subscribers and I'll be writing for even more people next time. It is work. So I'm sitting here on the couch with my cat Wendy, tapping away on the most beautiful day of the year. Fucked-up priorities? Some people are driven to create, some people are driven to succeed, and some people are driven to be idle. That's the way I look at it.

Honestly, the one thing that I procrastinate on is taking time off. I am always procrastinating on vacations. The last big vacation I took was to Greece in 2021. The best vacation ever. You'd think I would take more of them. I took a short four-day vacation to Miami in August. Stayed at the Faena and spared no expense—it was an amazing trip. I could definitely stand to take more vacations, but it is tough to take time away from the newsletter, and I just get busy with shit, so I never do. But the thing about the vacations is that I remember the vacations—I don't remember all the days I spent grinding away at my desk. He who makes the most memories wins. So clearly, I am deficient in this regard. And I have no idea when my next vacation will be—it's a sprint until the book comes out in January, then I'm moving into the new house in February, and it will be a few months before we get settled. At least I live someplace nice.

How do you stop procrastinating? You just do the thing. There's no tips or tricks. I can tell you that, when I got my MBA, I worked way ahead of schedule. I was weeks ahead in class. Probably because I was super excited about the stuff I was learning. Probably because I had a bit more maturity. Also, perhaps, because I was motivated by money. I was determined to get a 4.0 because I thought it would get me a job. I was right—it did help get me a job. When something isn't enjoyable, you tend to procrastinate on it. If you have a list of shit to do, you tend to do the enjoyable things first, and leave the annoying ones for later. Later sometimes means never. And then you're stuck. Just stop being a shitbird and do the fucking thing, already. How's that for advice?

TARDIVE DYSKINESIA

I AM KNOWN AS a mental health advocate. I give speeches sometimes, but mostly I just write.

Normally, when you think of someone with mental illness, you think of someone sitting in the dark, looking out the window, feeling blue. At least, those are the depictions you see in the commercials for antidepressants. I'm not a big fan of those commercials, because they really understate the suffering that people go through. People with various types of mental illness struggle to get dressed and get in the car and go to work in the morning. They put on a brave face and power through, when they are going through an indescribable amount of pain. There are a lot of courageous people out there.

I am doing well these days. I have had a pretty good run, since graduation. I was an absolute mess in May 2023, having paranoid delusions about how someone or something would sabotage my degree. I've been good since then.

But here's an aspect of mental illness that people don't spend a lot of time thinking about—dealing with the effects of the medication. For example. Prolonged use of various atypical antipsychotics can result in tardive dyskinesia, which is uncontrollable shaking of the hands and twitching of the facial muscles. I have this—it hasn't spread to my face yet, but my hands shake. It comes and goes. Sometimes, I will pick up a glass in a restaurant and I'll be spilling water all over the table. Sometimes, I struggle to put a forkful of food in my mouth, because my hands are shaking so badly. About ten years ago, I joined a slow-pitch softball league. I used to be one hell of a pitcher in slow-pitch softball. Couldn't do it—had the shakes. Walked six people in a row, and switched places with the shortstop. It was benign for a number of years, but it's gotten to the point where it's starting to be noticeable in social settings. People will ask about it—*are you nervous or something?*—and then I'll explain the cause, and it will be awkward for everyone. It sucks.

That's not the only side effect, either. The other big one is weight gain. I am—count 'em—70 pounds heavier than when I started taking the meds. And my cholesterol shot up, too, which is another symptom. Sure, I'm not super conscientious about my diet, but I actually eat a normal amount of food. And I do the intermittent fasting thing, too— no help. I actually took Ozempic for a while last year, and lost 25 pounds, but it got expensive, and I quit, and the weight went back on. I give up. This is also irritating because every dickhead has diet advice—*keto, paleo, do this, do that,* and I'm like, listen, it's not going to help. Everyone has opinions. And there are sexual side effects, too, and let's just say the meds don't make your johnson bigger.

So here is the thing. They are starting to come out with some new bipolar meds that don't have the metabolic or sexual side effects, or the tardive dyskinesia. I have tried them. They just don't work for me. They actually make my bipolar disorder worse. Latuda, Vraylar, there are others. I have tried everything. I'm on one of these medieval meds that's about two steps up from Haldol. Well, at least it is generic—it costs me about $20 a month.

So you might be wondering why a lot of bipolar (or depressed) people don't take their meds, even though they work. This is pretty much the reason—they turn you into a fat eunuch. So would I rather be fucking crazy, or a fat eunuch? Most people go for fucking crazy. Of course, that is a bad decision—that is how people end up dead or in jail. But yeah, one of these days, my face is going to start twitching, which is not really optimal when you're a public figure. They actually recently came out with meds to stop the tardive dyskinesia, but then you're on meds on top of meds, and who wants that?

There is a saying that you should be gentle with people, because you don't know what kind of burdens they are carrying. That is a pretty good saying. Sixteen and a half percent of the population is on psych meds of one kind or another, basically one in six people. They are all dealing with these side effects. Also, finding the right meds that work is a challenge. I had the best doctors in the world, who pretty much got it right on the first try. For most people, they're dealing with psychiatrists of varying levels of competence, and it's a process of trial and error, and let me tell you—switching from one medication to another in rapid succession will really fuck you up. You might ask, why are so many people on medication? I'm not really sure I have the answer to that question. Clearly there are more stressors. Being online doesn't help. Isolation doesn't help. Lack of community and friends doesn't help. For me, it's purely a case of bad genetics. I signed up for 23&Me and downloaded my genetic code and plugged it into Promethease and found out that yup, I won the genetic shit lottery. Anyway, I'm not an expert on this stuff, so I'm just going to shut up about it.

But I have to tell you—the medications I am on: lithium and risperidone—are miracle drugs. There is no other way to describe it. I don't get high off of them. It's not like an antidepressant, which has stimulative qualities. I just don't think crazy stuff. Here's an interesting stat for you—lots and lots of writers are bipolar. There was a study done years ago, that found that four out of five poets were bipolar. Four out of five! There is a clear link between creativity and bipolar illness, and it's well-known in scientific literature. Kay Redfield Jamison did some work on this years ago, and identified a number of well-known writers were bipolar. So let me tell you something else—when I am off the meds, my writing is fucking amazing, just mad genius. I read some of the stuff I wrote 20 years ago, before I was diagnosed, and it was pure fluid intelligence. I'd love to go back there, but I can't. Again: I'll end up dead or in jail. So every night, I gulp down a bunch of pills and sleep for eight hours, and I go into work, and I write my mediocre drivel every day. But I am alive.

And that's what's at stake. For someone who's never experienced suicidal thoughts, it is probably difficult to comprehend how they could happen. I'll explain it: I think about it pretty much all the time. Enough so that I have to lie about it from time to time. I have a pretty good relationship with my psychiatrist at this point—I've been seeing him for 15 years. I'll be struggling, and he'll ask me if I have suicidal ideation, and I'll admit it: *Yeah, but I'm not going to actually do it.* He knows the drill. He'll increase the dosage and I'll power through and come out the other side. A less experienced doc would pick up the bat phone and call an ambulance to whisk me off to the land of plastic spoons. Anyway, I have seen a bunch of people commit suicide over the years, and I see what it does to their friends and families, so it's not something I really want to do. But when things get really bad, you forget.

Life is good. I have very few complaints. I actually consider mental illness a blessing. I mean, would I like to be a ripped, 185-pound stud, raking like an All-Star, partying like a rock star, and hammering like a porn star? You bet I would. But that was not the hand I was dealt. There's something unique and special about my brain—it doesn't work in some ways, and it works really well in other ways. I wouldn't trade places with anyone. I definitely wouldn't trade places with Elon Musk—that guy is off his meds for sure.

ASMR AND CRINGE MEMORIES

Have you ever been listening to music, and you get goose bumps, and the hair stands up on the back of your neck, and you feel euphoric?

There is such a thing as ASMR, which stands for autonomous sensory meridian response. Here is a short bit from Wikipedia:

> An autonomous sensory meridian response (ASMR) is a tingling sensation that usually begins on the scalp and moves down the back of the neck and upper spine. A pleasant form of paresthesia, it has been compared with auditory-tactile synesthesia and may overlap with frisson. ASMR is a subjective experience of "low-grade euphoria" characterized by "a combination of positive feelings and a distinct static-like tingling sensation on the skin." It is most commonly triggered by specific auditory or visual stimuli, and less commonly by intentional attention control.

I've had this a number of times in my life, almost always related to music. Eleven years ago, I was driving to work in the morning, down Highway 501, when Eric Prydz's "2Night" came on my iPod. There was something about the way the sun was shining, my mood, the weather, and the piano riffs in that song that all came together and conspired to make me feel joy. I started to cry, spontaneously. A few weeks later I listened to the song again, to try to trigger the same response. Didn't happen. Now, when I listen to the song, I think it is kind of cheesy. Because Eric Prydz is cheesy. You know what song does it to me every time, though? Mat Zo's "Superman," which I played live at a party in 2012. Back then, Mat Zo was playing some of the most beautiful uplifting trance around. Now he plays electro house. He later told people that while he was writing all this beautiful music, he was suicidal, and if he ever started producing uplifting trance again, you should probably check him into a hospital.

Just listened to it again. ASMR.

Then, on the other side of the spectrum, you have cringe memories. These are things you did in the past that you regret, except they bubble to the surface from time to time, when you least expect it. I wrote a whole piece on regrets—I have done a lot of dumb shit in my life, and I continue to do dumb shit. I did stuff when I was 15 that makes me cringe today. I have done stuff last week that makes me cringe today. Cringe memories are the worst—you'll be in the shower in the morning, and for some inexplicable reason you'll think about the girlfriend you ghosted in high school because you were too much of a coward to break up with her properly. And you crushed her. It was a mistake, you regret it, but the memory keeps bubbling to the surface. You should not regret the past, nor wish to shut the door on it, but wouldn't it be nice if we could forget it, if each day was a tabula rasa and we could start fresh, instead of having to deal with the wreckage? Even if you make amends to these people, the memory persists. I was puttering around the house the other day and I had four cringe memories, one after another. I had to sit down for a moment.

Here is what it comes down to—I want to have more ASMR and

fewer cringe memories. I had a therapist who once told me to write down five things that bring me joy. The first one was easy—music. Then the cats. What after that? Writing brings me joy—about 10% of the time. When I am really rolling, when the words are flowing, and I know I have written a masterpiece, it brings me joy. The other 90% of the time, it is a slog. (This piece falls into the 90%.) The point was to do more things that bring you joy and less things that don't, like alcohol and drugs and sex. Lots of people confuse ASMR with sex, or having an orgasm. They are two different things. An orgasm lasts a few seconds—the joy from ASMR lasts forever. I still think about that time in the car in 2012.

So I wanted to tell you about something that happened recently that gave me ASMR. Marching band was a big part of my life in high school, probably the best and most indelible influence on my perfectionism and work ethic. For the past few years, I have been helping my high school marching band in myriad ways, sometimes financially. I was back at the school a couple of years ago, and saw some of the uniforms hanging on the wall, and I asked, *how old are these uniforms?* And the band director says, *they're 20 years old, and we don't even use them anymore. We make digital prints every year.* I made a mental note of that and went back to writing newsletters in South Carolina.

Over the past year or so, the development folks and I have been working on a design for new uniforms for the marching band. And let me tell you, they are hot. So freaking cool. So I donated the money, without hesitation, and flew back up to Connecticut to watch them at their band competition. Before they took the field, we had all the kids gather round, and I announced to the band that they were all getting new uniforms. Pandemonium. The kids were going nuts. The head of school told me that it was the best thing he'd seen in weeks.

And there it was—ASMR. Goosebumps and all. I will never forget it. I will never forget the looks on those kids' faces, the band director, the night sky, the drumlines warming up in the distance—I will always remember those details.

ASMR AND CRINGE MEMORIES

Giving brings me ASMR. When I discovered that, the world opened up. It should have been on the list of things that brought me joy, but I hadn't discovered it yet. If you could feel joy by pushing a button, how many times are you going to push the button? I will probably never be rich enough to donate a wing of MoMa. I will probably never be rich enough to have a building named after me. But I will do what I can.

I have a theory on helping people in general—it's not for the people who need it, it's for the people who want it. Giving should be not too different from investing—you want a rate of return. Of course, it's senseless to expect a financial rate of return, but you don't want to be pouring money down a black hole, either. I'm not a fan of giving that temporarily alleviates one's suffering; I'm a fan of the kind of giving that changes the course of someone's life. There is too much of the former and not enough of the latter.

As for the cringe memories, we all have them. I was a black-belt asshole for about 14 years of my life. Tons of regrets. The good news is that they are fleeting. I don't live in the past. I think cringe memories exist as a reminder not to be a dickhead in the future. I think we need these reminders. But I tell you what, I sure would like less of them. One of my favorite cringe memories: the Lehman holiday party in December 2005 (of course). This was in my drinking days, and my object was to get to the party as fast as possible so I could load up on free beer and wine before anyone else got there. I was about eight glasses of wine deep when I bumped into a female equity research analyst that I recruited to the firm the previous year. She looked not unlike Taylor Swift. So I'm drunk, and ranting, and sweating, when I realize that I have sloshed wine all over her fancy shoes. And I look up at her, and the look of contempt that she gave me—I will never forget. And I never saw her again. She probably still thinks I'm a drunk idiot. A small thing, but a moment of complete and utter humiliation. That one has stuck with me for 20 years—I'll never forget that look.

Yeesh. Let's not do that anymore. Speaking of which, I bet 90% of people's cringe memories come from when they're drunk. So there is an easy solution to that. Even with the 10% left over, I still have plenty of fuck-ups. No, let's focus on the things that bring us joy. What are the things that bring you joy?

Let's do more of that.

INTELLIGENCE

I BELIEVE THAT OUR brains are like filters: they stand in the way of our souls—essentially infinite intelligence—and the world around us. Those of us with really good filters are considered "dumb." Those of us with really bad filters are considered "smart." The brain is just an organ. We can have good hearts, good lungs, or good brains. I have a good brain with a Mr. Magoo body. We are all differently abled.

And I truly believe that—that isn't just hokey bullshit. I really do believe that we are all differently abled. I got a good brain, a brain that is good with writing and math and music, but you know what it's not good at? Spatial relationships. When I look at a car engine, I see a tangled mess of tubes and pipes. I have no idea how it works. I can write books, I can trade derivatives, but I cannot fix a car. Someone four standard deviations below me in IQ can fix a car. So I don't spent a lot of time or energy looking down on people who I consider to be dumb, because we are all good at different things.

I'll go further on this, about the spatial intelligence. If you've ever taken an in-person IQ test as a kid, you know that they give you those blocks with the triangles on them that you're supposed to form shapes with in a certain amount of time. Man, I was terrible at that. I simply can't think in 3D. I could never be an engineer, or a general contractor. I cannot fly a helicopter. When I was qualifying as deck watch officer on the ship, I had to draw a schematic of the fire main. I found it to be the hardest part of the qualification process. So the funny part about this is that my IQ is X, but my performance on spatial intelligence is X - 30, which means that my performance on the rest of the exam must be X + 30—truly exceptional. But I can't put IKEA furniture together. It also means that I am uniquely suited to trade delta-one instruments, because trading volatility means that you have to think in three dimensions. When Lehman jammed me in index arbitrage in 2001 they were actually doing me a favor, though I didn't realize it at the time.

I did well on the SATs, both in math and verbal. Actually, my best test result was the GREs, which I took in 1995. If I were to take them today, I would probably get an 800 on the verbal, and significantly lower on the math. Though, I always had a beef with the reading comprehension part of the verbal SATs. They had you reading an impenetrable fog of academic drivel, stuff from the Sokol bullshit generator, and while I suppose this is appropriate for a test of scholastic aptitude, in real life nobody reads this stuff. I didn't do as well on the GMATs. I was one of the first people to take the test on the computer, and I took it ice cold, while I was in the Coast Guard, in between deployments. It was more than good enough to get me into business school. Anyhow, these are not really tests of scholastic aptitude, except to the extent you remember your geometry from eighth grade—but intelligence tests. Nobody is using them anymore, which is the dumbest thing out of all dumb things.

There have been some debates about IQ in recent years, and its usefulness. I think IQ is a decent measure of intelligence, but it does not capture all kinds of intelligence. Specifically, emotional intelligence, something I'm a bit challenged in. But IQ is a statistical measure, and it follows a normal distribution. Most people know this already, but in case you don't: mean IQ is 100, and one standard deviation is 15. Someone with an IQ of 145 is three standard deviations above the mean, which is

INTELLIGENCE

pretty rare—about one in a thousand people. The highest recorded IQ is about 200, which is *Good Will Hunting* levels of intelligence. I read a story about a guy with a 200 IQ once—he has not been successful. In fact, there seems to be a "sweet spot" in intelligence—successful people in a variety of fields tend to cluster between 130 and 145 IQ. I don't know why this is—maybe there is such a thing as being too smart for your own good. I have met some highly intelligent people in my life—I went to the most notorious gifted and talented camp in the world. Let's just say that the vast majority of them are not in a position to donate back to the program.

I think we place a bit too much emphasis on how smart people are, and not enough on their character. I did a bit of social engineering in my college personal finance class this semester: I put in the syllabus that if a student completed all the assignments and handed them in on time, then they would get no lower than a C, regardless of how well they did on the exams. There are three students in the class whose performance on the exams are so poor that they would be in a position to get a D or an F, but they're being rewarded for their conscientiousness. My view is that someone who shows up and puts in the work deserves to get a middling grade, at a minimum. Of course, the students who do all the assignments tend to get the high grades, and the students who don't hand things in on time tend to get the low grades, but then you have the grinders, the kids who try hard in spite of their weaker intellects. This is the way.

Intelligence doesn't count for everything. Look at the case of Vivek Ramaswamy—high intelligence without virtue. I have taught a lot of students over the years, and I have had a lot of interns, and I can tell you that the correlation between intelligence and success is pretty weak. Over the course of these essays, we have talked a lot about what it takes to be successful. I think the first precondition for being successful is wanting to be successful. Wanting it more than sex or food. The successful ones have an obsession to learn and grow. The unsuccessful ones are complacent. Of course, when you have someone who is smart and driven, that is a deadly combination. With our God-given talents, and this organ we call a brain, we each have a certain amount of potential. The question is: are you realizing your potential? This is something I think about a lot—have I realized my potential? A lot of times, I don't think I have—but more will be revealed.

About the gifted and talented camp—it was called CTY: Center for Talented Youth. I knew a girl there, aged 14, who got a 1600 on her SATs in seventh grade, who was working for NASA. Knew a guy who published his first academic paper in computer science at age 14. There was a nine-year-old there, taking probability and statistics. Mind-bogglingly intelligent people, and I was clearly in the bottom half. The vast majority of these kids went on to Ivy League schools. I was probably the only one to go to a service academy, and my MBA program was ranked pretty far down. The point of telling you this is that for most of my adult life, I have been on the outside of this academic elite, looking in. I don't have the pedigree, so I am partial to people who don't have the pedigree. The scrappers. The hungry. The poor, smart, and determined. I think a lot of these people who went to Ivy League schools are assholes, because they've been told how smart they are over the course of their entire lives. No humility, and as you know, humility is a very important quality when you're managing money.

Some people will dispute me on this, but while I was at Lehman, I heard that the firm had an informal policy of not hiring anyone from Harvard. Allegedly, these folks from Harvard would be at the firm for three months and would be telling everyone how to do their jobs. A big part of intelligence is knowing what you don't know. I'll tell you what two things are a dime a dozen—smarts, and good looks. Patience, tolerance, kindness, and character are commodities in shorter supply. When I was a kid, I used to think that being smart was enough. Now, I know it's not even the beginning of the beginning.

PESSIMISM

L ITTLE-KNOWN FACT ABOUT me—I have actually hiked a decent part of the Appalachian Trail, about 15 years ago. I went from the Pennsylvania/New Jersey border to the Massachusetts/Vermont border. It is a tragedy that the only decent book about the Appalachian trail was written by a dillweed who couldn't hack it and tapped out after less than a month. Then they made a movie about it. Terrible. The dillweed, Bill Bryson, is an amazing writer—but a pussy.

Anyhow, once you spend some time on the Appalachian Trail, it is expected that you will acquire a trail name. People will no longer refer to you by your first name, but by your trail name. It is something that happens organically; you can't name yourself, like George Costanza with "T-Bone." So I had spent a few weeks on the trail and I didn't yet have a trail name, and I was getting a little tweaked. I was hiking with this guy named Terry, from Winnipeg, who looked a bit like David Cross, and he mentioned that there must be a shelter up ahead, and I was doing my usual Eeyore thing, saying, *no way, that's at least another five miles from here.* And he said, "Pessimist. That's your trail name: Pessimist." And it stuck.

I have always been a bit on the dour side. Quick note: "dour" is pronounced like "sewer," not "sour." The more you know. I generally think the worst possible thing is going to happen at any moment in time. Last week my cat Uma was getting surgery. In my mind, I was writing her obituary. But her surgery ended up having the best possible outcome, as it always does. The way I look at this is that if you always think the worst thing is going to happen, then you are never disappointed. I am the master of catastrophic thinking.

I will also add that there is a cult of optimism in financial Twitter. The guys who think that the stock market always goes up. I mean, it does, over time, but you can have some pretty big drawdowns in between, and there are guys who make a living trying to trade the drawdowns. This is how I invest my personal money: when the stock market is going up, I'm flat, but when the market crashes, I'm killing it. My wife knows me by now; if she hears that the stock market had a big down day, she'll say to me, "You had a good day today, didn't you?" And I just smile. It doesn't mean that I'm short, or buying puts, but there are a lot of different idiosyncratic ways to express a trade that gains from disorder.

Here is the way I look at it. I don't want my financial fortunes to be correlated to the rest of my life. If we have a recession, a lot of bad things might happen: you might get fired, take a pay cut, your house will be worth less, your business will shit the bed, there is a risk of bankruptcy—literally everything in your life will get worse, so why would you want to compound that by leveraging up your life savings to the business cycle and the vagaries of the stock market? At a minimum, you would want your portfolio to be uncorrelated to the economy, and ideally, you would like it to be a hedge. Wouldn't you like to be happy in a recession, instead of sad in a recession, or at least, not miserable? Why do we do this thing where we truck along for ten years and then, whammo, everyone gets cut in half? Wouldn't you want to spare yourself that stress? That's no fun. You get these stupid reporters who write stupid pieces about how rich people are so dumb, because they invest in hedge funds, and everyone knows hedge funds don't beat the S&P 500, neener neener. It's not about returns, you stupid fucking

Columbia J-school graduate, it's about *risk-adjusted returns*, and the depth and length of drawdowns, and it's about not having your entire life correlated in one big ball of risk. My portfolio is a hedge on my life. If we get a recession, my business is going to suck, and I want something to offset my business sucking. Not too hard to figure out if you take one second to think about it.

The optimists like to talk about how awesome everything is, because… we have iPhones, or something? Let's talk about the myriad ways in which things are worse than they were 25 years ago. Governments globally are much more authoritarian. Press freedom, social freedom, and overall economic freedom have declined. International trade is vanishing. There are more wars, and there is the possibility of many more. Birth rates have dropped dramatically. Drug use and overdoses have skyrocketed. Suicides have gone parabolic. The number of people experiencing depression or anxiety has risen dramatically. Political polarization only runs in one direction. Crime is up. People live in fear of saying or doing the wrong thing. And crucially, life expectancy is lower—the ultimate measure of prosperity is going tapioca. Really, the only way in which things are better than they were 25 years ago is that we can order a taco from our phone. Admittedly, this is pretty incredible, but now people spend so much time staring at their phones that they don't even interact with each other. I would not characterize this as progress. The peak of civilization came in 1999, and we are never going back. Reason and enlightenment have diminished. Barbarism has returned. You know, there was a period of time known as the Dark Ages when reason and enlightenment disappeared completely, civilization receded, and we returned to might makes right. There is nothing that says that can't happen again. It is also worth pointing out that the Dark Ages lasted about 500 years. Things are pretty terrible right now, and they're getting worse at a near-exponential rate.

Now, I don't dwell on these things. If I sat around and thought of how terrible things are, I'd be miserable. I'd like to point out that I'm not, in fact, miserable. I do my thing, I make money, I write books, and pursue my own happiness. I am a very happy guy. And I encourage you to do the same. I would also like to point out that I have a very low opinion of the doomers, the blogs and websites and newsletters that are constantly predicting market crashes and societal collapse. That's nothing but pornography. Some of it is very good pornography, but let's just say I stopped reading *ZeroHedge* or *Drudge* many years ago. It turns you into an asshole, and makes you not a lot of fun to be around. Also, even as a pessimist, I acknowledge that things often work out for the best. But sometimes they don't. There is nothing saying they have to.

I knew 1998 was the top. I was living in San Francisco at the time, in the middle of the tech bubble. Purple Yahoo! taxicabs roaming the city. Complete donuts making haystacks of cash on the P. Coast. Dot com billboards everywhere. People were throwing money at each other. And everyone was so damn happy. Lou Bega and Venga Boys were my jam. People were eating tiramisu at baseball games. We were so free, you could do cartwheels down the sidewalk wearing assless chaps and nobody would look sideways at you. When I say that I knew that 1998 was the top, I *knew* it. And I was very worried as to what would follow. Two years later, 9/11 happened, and that cemented it. Civilization has been in freefall ever since. Yes, *but but but AI and EVs and SpaceX and blockchain* and so on. Just because we are experiencing technological progress, does not mean we are experiencing social or political progress. In fact, the anomaly here is that we are experiencing technological progress in the midst of all this shit. And people take it for granted, that technological progress goes in one direction. Sure, it has, for 130 years. But it doesn't have to. And in most parts of the world, it doesn't exist. If there were someday an existential threat to capitalism in the United States, my suggestion would be that you sell your stupid index funds. We are always one election away.

HARDER THAN IT LOOKS

I DON'T REMEMBER THE details, but a few years back Tom Cruise got semi-canceled for saying that filming *The Edge of Tomorrow* was like fighting in Afghanistan. What ensued was a dogpile from political commentators and celebrities alike. I have a pinhead Coast Guard Academy classmate who is usually the first to get his knickers in a knot about comments like these.

I thought about it, and I was like, *you know, he is probably right*. I mean, aside from the part where you can get killed.

I'm not sure if you ever saw that movie, but there are numerous, extensive battle scenes in terrible conditions, including lots of rain and mud. Undoubtedly it was one of the most physically demanding things he has ever done, from the guy who once stood on the wing of a plane as it took off, and rode a motorcycle off a cliff. Could you or I be a movie star? Not a chance. I certainly couldn't. First of all, I don't have any facial expressions, which automatically disqualifies me from acting, but I would look like a complete donkey trying to do fight scenes. No amount of magic beans or camera tricks in the world would get me to look like

Tom Cruise, Keanu Reeves, or Christian Bale. My guess is that acting is really fucking hard, probably a lot harder than you think it is.

But we look at these movie stars and we think, *wow, they must have it so easy*. Red carpets and TV interviews and the Academy Awards. It must be such a charmed life. Wrong. First of all, any male celebrity has dozens of stalkers, some of them dangerous, and female celebrities have thousands. There are a lot of crazy people out there. Every time you step outside your house, Imelda in her muumuu is going to want a selfie. I think that any celebrity would tell you that fame is not all it's cracked up to be. Not to mention the actual mechanics of filming a movie, including doing 150 mind-numbing takes on a single scene until you get it exactly right. Honestly, it doesn't sound like a lot of fun. And if you want to talk about harsh conditions, Leonardo DiCaprio essentially won an Academy Award for *The Revenant* for spending days swimming in freezing water in the Canadian Rockies. I pass.

Tom Brady stepped in it once, saying "I almost look at a football season like I'm going away on deployment for the military. And it's like: 'Man, here I go again.'" Pinheads got up in arms about that one, too. *How dare you!* My guess is that being a quarterback of a professional football team is probably pretty hard, even with the offensive line protection that Brady gets and the favorable treatment from the refs. It's fucking arduous. Try getting shithoused in the back by a 260-pound linebacker. Even if that only happens ten times a season, that is ten times too many. Brady was no physical specimen, but these guys are working out all the time. And you're probably physically destroyed after playing 60 minutes on the gridiron. I simply don't have what it takes, and you don't, either. When Tom Brady says that playing football is like deploying in the military, first of all, it's an offhand comment, so calm down, and second of all, I take him at his word. My guess is that it is equally hard, though in different ways, and without the risk of getting killed. Though that almost happened last season, with Damar Hamlin almost taking a dirtnap on the field after being hit in the chest with a helmet. No thanks. Playing football is a lot harder than it looks.

You know what else is a lot harder than it looks? Working on Wall Street. To the outside observer, it probably looks like a bunch of rich white guys throwing money at each other. First of all, there is no more money. Check the headlines about layoffs on Wall Street last year, with bonuses going down the poop chute. People are getting zeroed. I'm not kidding when I say that it is practically more remunerative to drive a UPS truck than to be a trader. Maybe there was a time in the late 90s when it was rich guys throwing money at each other, but those days are loooooong gone, never to return. If you do it, it's because you love it.

But what is there to love? Compliance is absolutely suffocating. It's not much of an exaggeration to say that you can go to jail for accidentally pushing the wrong button on your keyboard. To say that the culture has changed is an understatement. In the mid-2000s you could have an open conversation about licking balls on the trading floor. Now, you had better have a very strong filter. Not saying that this new civility is a bad thing, but living in fear that you might say the wrong thing is no bueno. But most of all, the fun part of the business—thinking of ways to make money—is pretty much gone. The Volcker Rule, the prohibitions on proprietary trading, killed that. I like to say that traders are no longer traders—not the swashbuckling risk-takers that they once were. They are now finance workers, lunch-pail types, going in to make the donuts every day. There used to be real glamour associated with the job. Dropping 100,000 shares of XYZ into an algo and staring it all day is hardly glamorous. I haven't even brought up office politics and the psychopathy associated with it. Conclusion: it's not a lot of fun, it's a lot harder than it looks, and it pays less than ever. And everyone hates you.

The solution here is to take a walk in someone else's shoes. People dump on teachers these days, but that's not an easy job, and speaking of compliance bullshit and hassle, that job is worse than ever. Before you criticize teachers, maybe try out teaching? My guess is that you would suck at it. I teach at the university level, and I think I do a pretty good job (and I do, as evidenced by my course evaluations), but it's not easy. I'm teaching one class, and it wipes me out. There are lecturers teaching five classes at a time. That's a lot of time in class, and an inordinate amount of grading. It's an 18 hour-a-day job, if you're doing it right. I would not want to be a construction worker. I would not want to be a cop. I would not want to be a soldier. I would not want to be a cowboy. I would not want to be a biker. I would not want to be an Indian chief. Actually, that's the Village People. Nobody's job is harder than anyone else's.

Except for government jobs!

I will add one last thing. If you were the type of person to get offended by Tom Cruise's comment or Tom Brady's comment, let's have a few words. You *chose* to be offended. That's right, it was your choice. The world is filled with shitty opinions. They are all over Facebook, Twitter, TV, and radio. When I encounter an opinion that I find distasteful, I simply keep on scrolling, or change the channel. I do not react, because I am not an animal. Animals react. Human beings can theoretically control their emotions. Speaking of shitty opinions, it is pretty much my job to spread thousands of shitty opinions across the internet. I can't possibly expect someone to agree with all six million words that I have written. I would hope that one sentence would not cause someone to fly off the handle and rage quit the newsletter. The appropriate response is to strike when the iron is cold, and have a thoughtful and reasoned conversation about it. You might be pleasantly surprised by how it goes.

GREATNESS

WHAT, EXACTLY, DO you contribute to the world?

Lots of people go to work and come home. Good enough. A trader might have an infinitesimal contribution to market liquidity. A house flipper might, after great effort, provide someone with a home. A teacher might change the course of someone's life. A doctor might save someone's life. An engineer might design a road or a bridge. A journalist might inform the public.

Those are all worthwhile contributions. But what, exactly, do you contribute to this world? I mean, aside from your job and your genetic material.

Elon Musk and I disagree on this point. I don't necessarily think that having kids, on balance, is a positive contribution to the world. Depending on your parenting abilities, it might be a negative contribution to the world! Just because you can put part A into slot B, commingling drops of semen with clots of blood, does not confer any special abilities. We can all do it. You had four kids—so what? I will be impressed if they all contribute something to the world.

So we do the jobs that we do, and we have the kids that we have, but did we leave the world better than we found it? Or did we merely—exist?

Here are some ways in which we can make a lasting contribution above and beyond our lunch pail job and our DNA:

1. You can invent something that will improve people's lives.
3. You can endow a scholarship.
4. You can write a book.
5. You can record music.
6. You can build a building.
7. You can perform important academic research, advancing human knowledge.
8. You can develop a lifesaving medicine.
9. You can work with one alcoholic, addict, or mentally ill person and turn their life around.

What I'm driving at here is making a contribution that will endure long after you are gone. I'll go further and say that all lives do not matter—some matter more than others. Someone who merely consumes and never produces has lower moral status than someone who produces more than they consume. This is the crux of my morality, and this is the crux of your morality, too—you just don't realize it. No tears are shed when a career criminal is murdered. But when Matthew Perry dies—an entertainer who figured prominently in a show that entertained millions of people and will be enjoyed for decades—there is an outpouring of grief. All lives are not equal.

What I'm further driving at here is the concept of greatness—agree or disagree, like or dislike, Elon Musk is a great man. Agree or disagree, like or dislike, James Patterson is a great man. Pat Sajak is a great man. And so on. And the great thing about greatness is that we can all aspire to be great.

Years ago, when bitcoin was bubbling up, I did a podcast with Marty Bent, who had the *Tales from the Crypt* podcast. It was the strangest podcast I have ever done—he came to my office building in Myrtle Beach in the middle of the night with a small recording device, and we recorded it in my spare office. Subsequently, Marty got involved in politics of the right-wing variety, has had some appearances on *InfoWars*, and renamed his newsletter *Truth for the Commoner*.

I thought about that for a while. Who would aspire to be a commoner? Believe it or not, people do—their self-image is tied up in being an Average Joe. Like pretty much everyone who belongs to the UAW, or any other union. The thing I philosophically disagree with about collective bargaining is that it should be individual bargaining—*hey, I work harder and faster than all these other stiffs, so I should get paid more.* That's how it is on Wall Street, and a lot of other places. There is no room for greatness in a union. There is plenty of room for greatness in finance, tech, or elsewhere. It's about trying to be the best, which is a lesson that we are taught in tee-ball, but we forget as adults, when we work our 9-to-5 lunch-pail jobs.

We gave the middle finger to a king 250 years ago, and Americans in general don't have high opinions of monarchy, but here is the funny thing about royalty—these families have been groomed for leadership for decades. By virtue of work or effort or ingenuity, they are nobody special, and yet they are great—I think the one thing we learned from the Prince Harry debacle is that some people are cut out for that job, and some are not. When the royals are in the news about one thing or another, a lot of Americans are like, *who the fuck cares?* It is actually pretty important.

You also don't have to have money to be great. Dumb example, but true example: Mother Theresa. Lasting impact. Great writers are poor. Lasting impact. You don't have to donate a $150 million building to Princeton to be great. I frown on that sort of thing, anyway—you're helping the people who don't need help. That's more about ego gratification than anything. John Paulson donated a bunch of money to Harvard years ago, and Malcolm Gladwell, who never tweets, went on a tear on Twitter about what an idiot he was. It's Paulson's money, and he can do what he wants with it, and it's not really our place to say how he disposes of it, but gee whiz—he could have potentially helped a lot of people, if he'd wanted to.

In the hierarchy of greatness, inventors are at the top. Light bulbs. Cell phones. The internet. Talking about making billions of people's lives better over a period of centuries. There is this ongoing debate on internet memes about who was better: Edison or Tesla. The difference between them was that Edison was profit-motivated, while Nikola Tesla was not. I don't think there is anything wrong with inventing something and profiting from it—I don't think it makes your contribution any less noble. I present as evidence the pharmaceutical companies. Immunotherapy drugs cure cancer. With the billions spent in R&D and the length of the FDA approval process, nobody is going to do this for free. And nobody is going to do it at cost. It kills me when politicians go after the pharmaceutical companies and their lifesaving drugs. Remember when Jimmy Carter got brain cancer, and then… he suddenly got better? This wouldn't have been possible even ten years before. If you invent something, you get to be stupendously rich, and it does not detract one ounce from your greatness.

So how do you strive for greatness, if you are not blessed with raw intelligence, business acumen, or artistic ability? The answer is simple. Absent these qualities, you simply show kindness to everyone you meet. Not everyone can be great, in the traditional sense. We can't all be Thomas Edison or Matthew Perry or Elon Musk. I know my limitations: I'm smart, but not that smart. Here's the answer: you want to live your life in such a way that a lot of people show up at your funeral. That's pretty much it. I had a good friend in Myrtle Beach commit suicide about seven years ago. Three hundred and fifty people at the service, with overflow out onto the sidewalk. That hit me right between the eyes. He was part of Myrtle Beach's upper class, working in commercial real estate, but people from all walks of life showed up to that service, and that is because he was cheerful and outgoing and kind to everyone he met. I never heard him say anything bad about anyone. Let me say that again: I never heard him say anything bad about anyone.

Greatness comes in all different shapes and sizes. There are billions of people in this world. The vast majority will not be remembered when they pass. Great people are remembered, and talked about, and revered for years to come.

YOU ONLY DIE ONCE

O BVIOUSLY, THE TITLE of this essay is a play on YOLO—You Only Live Once. YOLO is like carpe diem for idiots, basically an excuse for people to do dumb shit, like YOLOing GameStop call options. My cats are smarter than the YOLO people.

Dying is one of the most important things we will ever do, and we spend precisely zero time thinking about it. We as Americans, I mean. Americans are not terribly introspective about death. And then, once it happens, we spend a few hundred bucks on cremation and end up in an urn on the piano or scattered across San Luis Obispo. I do not understand the obsessive focus on cremation these days. As recently as 2010, 54% of people opted for burial, and 40% for cremation. Now, 37% opt for burial, and 57% for cremation. I guess the other 6% go for the woodchipper. Not much need for people to embalm the goner these days. I guess there are financial reasons for cremation, but the economy wasn't so great in 2010, so who knows.

I don't want to be cremated. Let me back up a minute—a few years ago, I wrote out a very detailed set of instructions for my wife to follow when I die, and sealed it up in an envelope and put it in her file cabinet. I said that I wanted a full burial, and not just a full burial, but the most expensive casket possible, with Bose speakers in it and a full wet bar. Also, I'm not an organ donor. Yes, I realize I am an asshole for not being an organ donor. I am a little squeamish about people harvesting my organs when I die. I'm fully aware that I won't need them when I'm dead. It's just a silly superstition. I also said that I want a copy of all my books in the casket with me, along with the cremated remains of all my cats, except for the ones that are still alive, of course.

I want a lot of fucking people to show up for my funeral. A lot. I'm not an anthropologist, so I'm not sure which cultures hire mourners for funerals, but I would totally hire mourners. I've been to some big funerals, and I've been to some small funerals, and I can tell you that the small funerals are fucking depressing. You have probably heard the saying, possibly attributable to Rudy Giuliani: "Weddings are optional, funerals are mandatory." Sage words. I'm not a wedding crasher, I'm a wedding bailer. But I will make every possible effort to show up to a funeral, even if it means flying across the country at great expense. Usually it doesn't require that—you only have to go a little bit out of your way. I went to a memorial service in Myrtle Beach about two months ago—it was about five miles up the road. What struck me was how the family told me how awesome it was that I was there. And then I thought about some of my friends who couldn't be bothered to get off the couch to pay their respects. The funeral is where you find out who your friends are.

Some people say they want their funeral to be a big fucking party. Like, you don't want people to be sad, you want them to be happy, and celebrate your life. I get where they're coming from, but I'm pretty sure I want people to be sad at my funeral. Devastated, actually. Of course, that is dependent on the cause of death. Dying suddenly is easy on you, but hard on the survivors. Dying slowly is hard on you, but easier on the survivors. I once wrote that I really wanted to get cancer, and that's why. I can shoulder the burden of pain and discomfort—I don't want to put that on others. There is no worse death than one that is random. You go to Tanger Outlets to get some boxer briefs from the Under Armour store, and you get strafed by a mass shooter. You die in a fire. Or you just get killed in a plain vanilla car accident, something that kills 35,000 people a year. Nope, I want to get stage-four cancer of the anus. I mean, things can't get any worse for my anus than they already are.

You have to think about this stuff, though. Cleaning up the mess after someone dies can be incredibly time-consuming, compounded by grief. If you are the type of person with 14 different bank accounts, eight different credit cards, 27 different subscriptions, including a monthly payment to AdultFriendFinder, you are going to make a lot of work for your significant other when you pass. That's one of the good things about cancer—you have a bunch of time to get organized. My mother is the most organized person in the world. I know where she keeps her papers, and I can be done with the process in a day or two. My finances are significantly more complex, but I left instructions for my wife in that sealed envelope. It's never a good idea to hide money, so you should probably let your wife know about that account in the Caymans. And for the love of God, make sure your spouse knows where the life insurance papers are. I saw a *60 Minutes* piece a few years ago about how life insurers don't really go out of their way to pay claims unless someone bothers to send them a death certificate. I'm a capitalist, but I hate insurance companies. I think that is perfectly acceptable.

But most people don't think about this stuff. Earth to ding-dong—you're not going to live forever, and not only are you not going to live forever, you might die tomorrow. Here's one for you—I knew a guy who got into a blowout fight with his wife and then went out for a night ride on a moped and was killed by a drunk driver. The last words his wife ever spoke to him were *fuck you*, or something to that effect. Talk about guilt. As I wrote about in "Regrets," one thing I think about a lot is that anytime I see someone, or talk to them on the phone, it might be the last time we ever speak, which is an argument for treating people with love and tolerance at all times. I had a very good friend commit suicide in 2019, and I did the rewind thing—I thought back to the last time I talked to him and what I said, replaying every word. If you've ever lost someone close to you, you do the rewind thing. This is why married couples always say "I love you" when they hang up the phone. It's boilerplate, but you do it just in case. I would love for the last words I ever spoke to my wife were "I love you." Right? Right.

To be perfectly honest, I didn't think about any of this stuff when I was 22. Everyone knows that 22-year-olds are invincible. Live hard, die young, leave a smoking crater—that was my philosophy. Not my philosophy at the moment. Never pass up a bathroom. Never trust a fart. Never waste a woody. These are the words I now live by. I went to the movies about three weeks ago and the woman behind the counter gave me the senior discount. Do I really look 60? I must. Well, I look pretty good for 60. My uncle James, a brilliant orthopedic surgeon, told me that statistically, people die in their 50s more than in their 60s. If you can make it to 60 without getting heart disease or cancer, you're in the clear. He ended up getting pancreatic cancer at age 58 (and survived). I am 51. If I really want to get depressed, I think about the fact that I may be about 60% of the way through my life. That's why I live like there is no tomorrow—and you should, too.

EVERY SINNER HAS A FUTURE

Back in January 2007, I found myself at a crossroads—I was at a spiritual retreat at a convent in New Jersey. I was coming to terms with a decade of bad behavior, awful, terrible, no-good things I had done, and I was sitting off in the corner of the room by myself, contemplating these transgressions, when one of the wise old men of the retreat came over to me and asked what was wrong.

I told him.

He said, "Every saint has a past, every sinner has a future," and walked off, leaving me to my thoughts.

Let's start with criminals. First of all, I will say that plenty of criminals are good people, and plenty of people who have never committed a crime are bad people. The law doesn't specify "good" or "bad" behavior—it only delineates behavior that is prohibited. Is someone who drives drunk a bad person? What about the person who cheats on his spouse? Cheating on your spouse isn't against the law, but it might make you a worse person than the person who has two extra drinks at the bar and gets popped for a broken taillight on the way home. I don't attach any moral significance to breaking the law, in most cases. I mean, sure, murdering someone is bad and also is against the law. But cops often call lawbreakers "the bad guys," and I don't think that breaking the law necessarily means that you're bad. The prisons are full of deadbeat dads who fell behind on their child support, locked up with the rapists and murderers, along with the scofflaws who were busted with an ounce of weed.

I'll go further and say that I'd rather hire someone with a criminal record than someone with a low credit score. The guy with the DUI is labeled a bad guy for one single lapse of judgment over the entirety of his life. The guy with a 560 credit score has demonstrated a repeated pattern of being a slob, day in and day out, week in and week out, over the entirety of his life. More data points. I keep going back to the example of the DUI, which in the grand scheme of human wickedness is pretty small beer. What about more serious offenses? The thief, the wife-beater, the con man, the pederast? Are any of these people redeemable? Can they find redemption, if they try hard enough?

Every saint has a past, every sinner has a future.

The truth is that everyone is capable of redemption—everyone—and this is one of the central tenets of Christianity. None of us is without sin, not Nelson Mandela, not Ruth Bader Ginsburg, not Ronald Reagan, not Ayn Rand. In fact, the person you hold up as your ideal, the historical figures that we all have reverence for, are very complicated people, and probably sin more in a week than you do in a year. Every once in a while, in the news, there will be a fall from grace. Matt Lauer, for example. A few years ago, I watched the video of Matt Lauer systematically dismembering Paula Deen on TV for her use of a racial epithet decades ago. Matt Lauer, of course, was not without sin, and if you watch that video today, and you see Matt Lauer's righteous indignation, and then you understand it in the context of what happened afterwards, you suddenly have an understanding of that piece of scripture that says *he who is without sin, cast the first stone*. I don't go on Twitter and start calling people scumbags and saying that they should go to jail. Even actual scumbags. Because I'm not perfect. I just can't summon that level of righteous indignation, not for anybody or any reason. Because there but for the grace of God go I.

Being a good person does not come naturally to me. It takes effort. But I try. If I didn't try, I'd be calling people a fuckhead in emails about ten times a day. Some people don't try. Charlie Munger said that envy is the worst of the seven deadly sins, because you don't get to have any fun at it. But really, all sins are born from sloth, the state of not giving a fuck. "Fuck it" are two very powerful words, and by extension most of our problems come from the use of "fuck it." *I don't care.* You should care. Look—we can have disagreements about how to help people in need. Some people prefer supply-side solutions, and some people prefer demand-side solutions. But indifference to human suffering is, well, bad. There are the people who want to save the world, the ones out marching in the streets. If you want to save the world, you start by helping one person, and that person helps another person, and so on. But most people don't want to get down in the muck with other people's problems. It's too attractive to think about human suffering in the abstract, and go march in the street. As you can tell, I take a very dim view of marching in the street.

Back in 2016, I published my book *All the Evil of This World*, an episodic novel about seven characters involved in an options trade related to the 3Com/Palm spinoff. There was an underlying message in that book, and almost nobody got it. The title *All the Evil of This World* is ironic—our sex addictions, our drug addictions, our infidelities are all very pedestrian, and not evil at all. It was a story of seven good people whose lives were completely and utterly out of control. It was a big in-joke that nobody got. Most people read that book, had righteous indignation, and wrote Amazon reviews about all these degenerates doing bad things, without having even a moment of introspection over the myriad ways in which they, themselves, were bad. We all have secrets. I will say that again—we all have secrets. Some are sicker than others. But the average jabroni who read the book got to the chapter about the hookers and blow, and said, *HE IS BAD, I AM GOOD,* and reinforced his sense of superiority. Completely missed the point. It wasn't just a book about a trade—it was a deeply philosophical book about morality itself. And that is why, to this day, it remains my favorite thing I have ever written. At age 51, I would have toned it down a little, so it's probably good that I wrote it at age 42.

When a bad person does bad things, atones for them, makes restitution, does good things and becomes a good person, we have a word for this—it is called a miracle. Sam Bankman-Fried is depraved, and there isn't a lot of evidence that he is too remorseful about his gigantic fraud. He may be one day. The best thing for SBF would be to serve the time imposed on him, rehabilitate, get released, and devote the balance of his life to helping people in similar circumstances. We are all in possession of one very valuable asset—our story, and how we can use it to benefit others. When I tell you my story, the account of my sins and my restitution, you identify with it, and you can see how redemption is possible. SBF doesn't realize it yet, but one day he will be capable of doing much good in the world—by helping just one other person. And that person will help another person, etc. We could have a conversation about the criminal justice system, about how it doesn't really help people rehabilitate, how criminals usually just end up being groomed into being even worse criminals, but a few years behind bars gives people a lot of time for introspection.

As you can probably guess, I am not a fan of the death penalty, for a billion reasons, and the interesting thing about the death penalty as a political issue is that the people who proclaim so loudly that government is incapable of doing anything capably and efficiently, will make an exception when it comes to executing criminals. Anyone, literally anyone, is capable of rehabilitation. But it's not for the people who need it; it's for the people who want it. I have seen miracles performed countless times. I am a miracle. I had a future, and I took advantage of it.

THE ROAD
TO HELL

MY WIFE TELLS the story of periodically flying out to Kenya for her archaeological research. She would inevitably be seated next to some missionary from a megachurch in Texas, flying to Nairobi with a group of sloe-eyed, blond-haired, hopeful kids up to their eyeballs in self-importance, headed out to the countryside to build a school for the poor kids in Africa. This is the point at which my wife would usually put her AirPods in, knowing how this was going to turn out. The missionaries would indeed go to the countryside outside of Nairobi, build a ramshackle school with cinder blocks and whatever materials they could cobble together, stand back and marvel at their accomplishment, and head back to Danny Gokey country with the knowledge that they saved the world, and an Instagram timeline full of White Savior Barbie pictures with undernourished African children.

Then the school would become a goat-storage unit.

What the missionaries would not and did not consider was that they didn't provide anything in the way of compensation for a teacher to actually work at the school, so it just became a convenient place to keep goats. In fact, if you are on the outskirts of Nairobi and look out across the horizon, you will see dozens of such goat-storage units built by missionaries. I even heard of an instance where the Kenyans waited until the middle of the night to rebuild one of the schools before the concrete set while the Americans slept. The Kenyans take a dim view of all of this, and the high-BMI Americans in their jorts typically make an easy target for the muggers, scammers, and street criminals of Nairobi.

This is an instance where people set out to do good and end up not doing good. It is more common than you might think. It is said that the road to hell is paved with good intentions. Does that mean that all charity is bad, or misguided? Of course not. But there are certainly unintended consequences to charity. There are unintended consequences to all charity. The city of San Francisco, in handing out money and drug paraphernalia (and actual drugs), is trying to do good. They are trying to ease the burden of the homeless people in the city. But there are unintended consequences. Really what they are doing is incentivizing homelessness, and there is a lot of evidence that most of the homeless population in San Francisco is not even from San Francisco. They go there for the free stuff. Until San Francisco makes it inhospitable to be homeless, they will have a homeless problem. But that is mean. Locking up people for petty drug offenses is mean. So it's an endless doom-loop of altruism like the kind that you used to construct in Applesoft BASIC. Oftentimes, being mean to people is actually helping them out. In the 80s, there was a book about this—it was called *Toughlove*. A much longer discussion.

A few glaring examples of doing bad while trying to do good: the food stamp program. Twenty percent of food stamp benefits are obtained fraudulently, which amounts to tens of billions of dollars. And for those that are obtained legitimately, they provide a powerful disincentive to escape from indigence, because the benefits phase out when you reach a certain level of income. An economist would say that a food stamp beneficiary, on the cusp of earning more money, faces an implied marginal income tax rate of over 100%. Food stamps may temporarily ease one's financial burden, but they are trapping generations of people in poverty. The PPP loans during COVID were another example—hundreds of billions gone to fraud, and there isn't a lot of evidence that jobs would have been lost without the loans. This isn't an argument for Milei-style minarchism, as this is not a political essay, only to point out that when we set out to do good, we often do bad.

It happens on a micro level, too. Your brother-in-law has fallen on hard times and is asking for $25,000 to pay off some debt and get back on his feet. The reason he is coming to you is because he has exhausted all other possibilities. He's maxed out his credit cards, banks won't lend to him, and he's faced with asking you for money or getting triple-digit interest rates from a payday lender. *This time is different,* he says. Okay. If you help him, do it with your eyes open, and know that the 25 grand is a gift, not a loan, and it's effectively going to ruin your relationship with him, because you're going to want the money back, and he's going to be avoiding you. It's going to create some other ugly family dynamics, too, like envy and jealousy. If you just tell him to fuck off, he'll be butthurt about it for a few days, and then eventually go find another host. Being mean has its advantages. I run into this in teaching all the time. Deep down, students really want to be challenged. I get high marks from my students, and I do not give especially high grades.

So how does one perform acts of charity? First, recognize that much of charity creates dependence. I am not one for volunteering at the soup kitchen. Fill a void, make a turd. Where would these people be, without the existence of the soup kitchen? Confronted with the realities of their situation, they would have to scramble. People are resourceful. They will find ways to make money when their next meal depends on it. Democratic president Bill Clinton drastically cut welfare benefits in his first term. It was the zeitgeist at the time, the crack-addicted "welfare queens" that were mooching off taxpayer dollars—if you were around in the early 90s, you probably remember the prevailing mood. What happened when the welfare benefits disappeared? Did millions of people starve to death and get piled high into a giant pyramid in Nebraska? Not a single person. People are resourceful when they have to be.

I'll also add that any charity that is done by a third-party payer will always backfire. If you want to give food or money to a crack addict, that has an infinitely better chance of helping than the government taking money from you in the form of taxes and giving it to the crack addict. Of course, these programs have the best of intentions, which is why they fail. The only charity that ultimately works is done person to person. People have become skeptical of the giant nonprofits, the Wounded Warrior Projects and the ASPCAs, where a huge percentage of donations go to administration. If you want to help a Wounded Warrior, go help a wounded warrior. If you want to help cats, there are plenty of local organizations in your area. Nobody wants to get their hands dirty. I don't want to get my hands dirty. But that's what you have to do, if you want to do good.

There is an area dead-lifter who talks about the phenomenon of *naive intervention*. When you intervene naively in a system that you do not understand, you are bound to cause unintended consequences. Like the missionaries with their goat-storage units. They know nothing about Kenya and its people and culture. They think schools are needed, when what is actually needed is money for people to teach in schools. The government naively intervenes in things all the time. The Federal Reserve naively intervenes in things all the time. How do you think we got so much inflation? I mean sure, any newsletter writer could have told you that doing trillions of QE and holding rates at zero for ten years would have consequences. The Federal Reserve really does believe that it can plan an economy, something that is as intricate and beautiful as a spider web. We're veering back into minarchism here. We could talk about the unintended consequences of our interventions in Ukraine, too, which were based on the best of intentions.

My philosophy on charity is my philosophy on life in general—it's not for the people who need it, it's for the people who want it. I am an investor, and I think about charity much in the same way as investing—

where will the world get the highest rate of return? Hire the poor, smart, and determined. Lift up those who have hit bottom, and are willing to make profound changes in their lives. No person on earth has been attacked more than the queen of selfishness, Ayn Rand. Ayn Rand gave to charity, you know. You know what she gave to? Cats. I don't care what kind of person Beth Stern is in her personal life; in my book, she is an absolute saint. There is no naïve intervention in helping animals, they truly are grateful for it, and you will always be doing good.

LONELINESS

Sometimes, I get pretty lonely. I work by myself, for myself, in an office. There is nobody around. I am inundated with electronic communications: emails, texts, and tweets, but it's not the same, is it? We all crave human contact. I go out to lunch and eat by myself, and one of the reasons I go out to eat so much is because I crave human interaction—sitting in my office alone eating salad out of a Tupperware container does not appeal to me. I drive to and from work by myself. I'm alone from 7 a.m. to 5 p.m., and which point I go home to hang out with my wife and cats. I don't have much of a social circle—a few friends here and there. I don't go to church. I'm not involved in my community. I'm not involved in local politics. I have a short list of friends that I talk to every few days or so, including my brother, but that's about it.

When I lived in New York, it was a little different. I was on a trading floor surrounded by hundreds of people. I always went out for drinks after work. I don't miss being an ETF trader all that much, but I do miss the camaraderie, if you can call it that. Ten hours a day of jackassing around. Huge amounts of fun. I still keep in touch with all those mooks.

Loneliness can be debilitating. Loneliness can be deadly, when it turns into isolation. And one can experience isolation while being surrounded by friends and family. Here is how it goes: You drive to work alone. You sit at work alone. You don't talk to anyone. You drive home alone. You sit on your couch and watch your shows alone. You don't call anyone. You go to bed alone. I have seen people being driven to madness by isolation. I have seen people commit suicide from isolation. And the irony is—they were surrounded by people who loved them the entire time. In fact, complete isolation is usually the last step before suicide. When someone commits suicide, the reaction of family and friends is pretty much the same every time—*Gee, I had no idea he was going through that. All he had to do was call.*

In other words, loneliness, like a lot of things in life, is a choice.

I frame it like this: Some of us have big worlds. Some of us have small worlds. Some of us talk to a hundred people a day, are working on several different projects in parallel, have outside interests, participate in organized religion and civic organizations, and have a tough time fitting it all in. And some of us go to work and go home and watch our shows. Here's the thing: My life is enriched by other people—even people I personally dislike. More friends, more viewpoints, more perspectives make me a bigger person. If you're not exposed to viewpoints different from your own, you descend into despondence and depression—and sometimes hate. In my email inbox, I am exposed to hundreds of different opinions every day. But that's no substitute for sitting across the table with someone at lunch, talking about the demerits of Keynesian economics or something like that. I have friends here in Myrtle Beach I'd like to hang out with, but they're all preoccupied with their kids. And that's the thing about having kids—you're constantly going to little kid birthday parties and little kid soccer games and spelling bees and shit like that. Your kids have friends, then you become friends with the parents. I am friends with a couple that has ten cats, and the owners of the local cat café. Kind of the same thing.

If you are living in isolation, you start to believe your own bullshit. There is nobody to do a make-sense check on your ideas. If you come to believe that some compliance people at your office are monitoring your web-browsing activity, and that they're hatching a plot to get you fired from the company, there's nobody to tell you that it's all in your head and you're being ridiculous. All of us make up scary stories and believe them. If you don't have anyone to bounce them off of, you're going to go nuts. And people do go nuts. I make up scary stories sometimes, and when I do, I pick up the phone and call ten different people. If ten different people tell me I am nuts, I let it drop. If you don't have ten, five, or even one person to call, you're going to lose your mind. And I hate to bring this up, but you might kill yourself. There's a reason I keep bringing this up—this is where I was in the mid-2000s.

Bill Ackman is in the news these days. What is Bill Ackman up to? Well, he runs an enormous hedge fund comprised of highly concentrated bets, and he is currently engaged in a fight against antisemitism in higher education. He is pretty busy. He has a lot going on in his life. My guess is that he is talking to dozens of people a day, and doesn't really have a lot of time to make up scary stories and believe them. I don't have any strong opinions about Ackman—I don't care much for his investing style, and if I was a billionaire like him, I would probably mind my own business and fly to my condo in the Faena House and watch porn on my TV that is the size of a parking space. I don't have to have an opinion about everything (says the guy who writes opinions about everything). But the point is, Ackman has a very full life. His world is big. His Rolodex is fat. Then you have the guy who goes home and watches his shows. I'll give you three guesses who I want to be, and the first two don't count.

We all went through this in the pandemic. We had Zoom, but it wasn't quite the same. As I've said before, there is no substitute for being in the presence of another human being. The pandemic was tough on people, the poor bastards alone in their apartments in New York. It wasn't unlike solitary confinement, which is the worst punishment you can impose on someone in prison. When I saw Andy Dufresne spend two weeks in the hole in *The Shawshank Redemption*, I knew I wouldn't last ten minutes. And I'm an introvert. My experience with the pandemic was far less arduous—a 4,000-square-foot house with my wife and cats. Also, the lockdown didn't stay in place very long in a red state. But the pandemic was tough on some of my friends up north, and I was making mental health checks fairly frequently. Not to get into the politics of pandemics, but the lockdowns were terrible for people's mental health. They were terrible for a lot of things, but mental health is kind of my pet cause, so I really, really hope nobody is stupid enough to try that again.

I mentioned that I was an introvert. A lot of extroverts couldn't do what I do—sit alone in an office for eight hours a day. But on the introvert/extrovert axis, I am not as extreme as some introverts. Some people never leave their house. If I don't have one or two social engagements a week, I feel it. I love my wife, but if she is the only person I see over the course of a week, I get a little cagey. I have some close friends who read my stuff, and by this point they're probably laughing, because they know that in social gatherings, I don't have much to say. I don't talk. It's a running joke among my friends. Well, introverts have accomplished some pretty great things, too. The idea of running for office, gripping and grinning and smiling and dialing in some place like Rapid City, South Dakota, eating corn fritters, is not my idea of fun. The Myers-Briggs does not have a good reputation these days, but I am a classic INTJ, known as the "Mastermind," and the least common personality type. But I'm not a solid "I." I like my alone time, but I also like to be around people. Everyone else can do the talking.

Many people have observed that "kids these days" don't socialize much. They sit in their rooms with their phones and play imaginary games on Instagram, while the Generation Xers were out riding bikes and playing pickup football games and going on dates and getting to second base. Like a lot of Xers, I am very grateful for the childhood I had. Suicide and suicide attempts are up sharply among young people. It is one-to-one correlated with the invention of the smartphone, and it is because of isolation. We are more connected than ever, and yet we are further apart, one of the great ironies of the 21st century. And now, if a man approaches a woman in a bar, he is labeled a "creep." Apparently, the only acceptable way to get a date is on Bumble, which is where the actual creeps are. Much more to say on this, but we'll stop here.

THE NATURE OF EVIL

In the *Dungeons & Dragons* universe, your player character gets to pick an alignment, which is basically a core philosophy. You can pick from three definitions of good (lawful, neutral, and chaotic), three definitions of evil (lawful, neutral, and chaotic), and three definitions of neutral (lawful, chaotic, and true neutral). As a child, I always picked the lawful good character, usually paladins. As an adult, I would characterize myself as chaotic neutral—probably a bard or something like that.

You see the different variations of evil in the movies as well. You have lawful evil (Darth Vader), neutral evil (Bane), and chaotic evil (The Joker). But those aren't typically the types of evil we encounter in daily life. You don't see people vaporizing planets, threatening to blow up a city with a nuclear bomb, or breaking a pool cue in half and letting two guys fight it out. The evil that you see in the movies is actually sadism. And there are examples of sadism in real life, for sure—15% of the prison population is incarcerated for a murder conviction. Some bad dudes. But most of us do not come in contact with people who are sadists—people who experience joy in other people's pain. The types of evil you might find in daily life are like the people who engage in character assassination—a subtle whisper campaign to get someone denied pay or promotion. Those people will go to hell, too, along with the murderers.

I have arrived at my own definition of evil, which I think is the correct definition:

Hatred of the good for being good.

Let's use Jeff Bezos as a straw man. I think he is the second-richest person in the world, or something like that. I have run into people—seriously—who refuse to order off of Amazon because they "don't want to make Jeff Bezos any richer." This always makes me smile, because when you order something off of Amazon, you're making him poorer. For years, the retail business was being run at a loss, subsidized by the profitable cloud business. But beyond that, why not be happy for Jeff Bezos? He came up with a time-saving invention. You can sit in your air-conditioned house and order pretty much any item in existence, and save yourself an hour drive to and from Target, standing in line at the checkout with the screaming babies. Internet retailing is one of the greatest time-saving inventions ever, and Amazon perfected it. Maybe you should… send him a thank-you note? Do you remember all the negative press that Bezos got for launching into space, how this super-rich jackass was going up in a rocket that was shaped like a giant dildo? Do you remember (you probably don't) when people assembled a makeshift guillotine outside of his place in D.C.? How people compared him unfavorably to Dr. Evil, with his bald head and droopy eyelid? Most recently, he commissioned a giant fucking yacht to be built, and got a bunch of negative press around that. It's not as if he hasn't given to charity—he wrote a big, unconditional $10 billion check to fight climate change, which of course, appeased nobody.

Why do people hate Jeff Bezos?

Because he is good.

They don't hate him in spite of his virtues, they hate him because of his virtues. What are those virtues? The usual stuff: intelligence, hard work, foresight, and leadership ability. They hate that he accomplished what they never could. They don't hate his wealth—the wealth is simply a byproduct of the virtues that were used to create it. I don't know a lot about Bezos. I never read any of the biographies. Maybe he is a dick, maybe he isn't. I kind of get the impression that he was successful in motivating a bunch of already-successful people to work very hard in building his vision. When you're worth triple-digit billions, you probably don't suffer fools. Nonetheless, he created a company that is so good, we literally could not live without it. And if it vanished overnight, it is too complex and intricate for someone to build another one. Our lives are better because of Jeff Bezos.

And we hate him for it.

You might call this "human nature." Well, I don't particularly like human nature. I don't like this tendency to tear down people who are successful. I'm not sure I could even conceive of being as successful as Jeff Bezos, and that's why he's him, and I'm Jared Dillian. I am a fucking piker. But at least I have the ability to say the three magic words that all good people should be able to say:

Good for him.

Good for him! I genuinely hope he is happy. It sure seems like he is happy. Terrific. Let's put this plainly in terms you can all understand: Jeff Bezos is better than me. And I'm okay with that. He's had a much bigger positive impact on the world than I have. And he deserves everything he has. I'm not one of those people who is going to cop a resentment against you because you have a jingle in your pocket. And there are plenty of people like that—more than you can imagine.

Let's talk about a more relevant example. Let's say you live in a nice neighborhood, an area where the houses are big and the HOA is hyperactive. One of those types of places. There is a guy in the neighborhood who is very successful, and he lives in the biggest house in the neighborhood. How did he make his money? He has a dildo factory. He has a sprawling dildo manufacturing operation. Let's say, for the sake of argument, that the dildo business is growing, and he is making $7 million a year. He has a couple of supercars (that sit in his garage), and hired staff to manage the house, and the buzz in the neighborhood is that he is kind of a dick.

Wait, the buzz in the neighborhood? That's right—the rest of the people in the neighborhood, when they go to their parties and dinners, talk shit about this rich, successful guy living in their neighborhood. Did you hear that he did XYZ? Did you hear about ABC? And so people wage the subtlest of subtle forms of character assassination against the guy with the dildo factory. Maybe he is a dick—doesn't matter. You can't bring yourself to say *good for him*.

There are levels of this. I've been on the receiving end, believe it or not, and I am nobody special. There are people who hate my guts. They hate my books, they hate my newsletter, and they hate my small pile of money. There is an interesting psychological process here—when you hate someone for their virtues, you are effectively defining yourself as the opposite of those virtues. When you look at me or Jeff Bezos and hate our success, you're effectively saying "I'm a piece of shit." You actually define yourself as a piece of shit, and you feel even worse about yourself. There are two types of people in this world: people who hate Jeff Bezos, and people who aspire to be Jeff Bezos. There are some people who go around hating Elon Musk, Jeff Bezos, fill-in-the-blank billionaire, but also the person who got appointed as department chair, the person who was named realtor of the month, the person who got elected to city council, and that woman who picks up her kid from daycare in a Mercedes. They also hate big corporation Procter & Gamble for their toothpaste commercials, and practically any business that does not lose money. They go around hating everyone, hating the good for being good. And there is a word for that, too: a communist. And that is how evil killed 100 million people in the 20th century.

Hate, these days, has been dumbed down as some sort of racial animus. But that's not really what hate is. I would call that kind of bigotry *antipathy*. Real hate is when you spend your life wishing that bad things would happen to Jeff Bezos or your rich neighbor. I don't wish bad things would happen to anyone. And neither should you.

The definition of a good person is someone who can be happy at another man's achievement. The obverse of that is evil. That's the philosophy lesson for today—go forth and do good in the world.

BE CONSCIENTIOUS

As you know, I am a DJ, and I like to throw parties. About five years ago, my friend DJ Adam Silver and I got the idea to invite David Solomon to play at one of our shows. At the time, David Solomon was number two at Goldman Sachs, and while it wasn't necessarily a secret that he was a DJ, it wasn't out in the open either. There were a few posts about it online, but it didn't become big news until he was named CEO.

So I cold-emailed him. We guessed his email address, and I told him that I threw these Wall Street parties with other Wall Street DJs at Hotel Chantelle in the Lower East Side, and wouldn't it be fun if he headlined the show? To my surprise, he replied within a day or two, and he was down. Oh, he was down. I opened, DJ Adam Silver played the middle set, D-Sol closed, and to my surprise, nobody paid much attention to the old guy behind the decks. Like I said, this was before he became CEO.

But one thing struck me about my interactions with David Solomon that will always stick with me—if I texted him, he always replied within ten minutes. Ten minutes! From the president of Goldman Sachs. That's a big job, and he was a busy guy. Not only did he reply in ten minutes, he was unfailingly polite. I'll go further and say that all the bad press that he received in 2023 was completely unwarranted. He's a lovely man, and he treated this sketchy newsletter writer with dignity and respect.

I have a lot of friends who do not reply to me in ten minutes. I have a lot of friends who do not reply to me in an hour, three hours, six hours, a day, three days, a week, or ever. They are not as important as David Solomon. And you know what I think about that? They're dickheads. All my friends know that if you text me anytime during the day, I will reply within seconds, unless I am in the car. For me, it's a little easier because I'm typically in front of a Mac, and I have iMessage, so I can just respond on my keyboard. But I'm not making excuses for anyone else. If you get a text, you should respond. Be conscientious. It's the right thing to do.

This is where we talk about ghosting. Maybe I'm old, like an armadillo, but I think that ghosting someone is a really scummy thing to do. Apparently, it's very common nowadays among the kids. You don't feel like talking to someone, you just don't talk to them. Look, I get it. There are some people who have my phone number who I really wish didn't have my phone number. I get texts from people I don't particularly like that I don't particularly want to answer. But I answer them anyway, out of courtesy and respect. Life is about doing the hard things, you know, and not avoiding the painful things. It's called being an adult. Not that I get ghosted a lot. This frequently comes up in romantic relationships. You're dating for a while, things are going well, then—wham! Ghosted. Be an adult. If you want to end the relationship, call, don't text; be a grown-up and explain why you are cutting it off. I think I am the only person who thinks this way. It's the golden rule, right? Treat people like you would want to be treated.

I've found that there is a common phenotype of an un-conscientious person. First, they live in New York. Thirties, married, one or two kids, semi-important job like midlevel banker or something like that, important enough to induce self-absorption, but not important enough to really be doing anything of consequence. These are the people who never respond to texts. CEO of Goldman Sachs? Responds to texts. And to be clear: he's not a CEO who happens to be conscientious, he is CEO *because* he is conscientious. See what I am after, here? What I'm suggesting is that conscientiousness is a habit of highly effective people, and conscientious people tend to rise to the tops of organizations. Yes, we are all busy. I get hundreds of emails a day, and I try to respond to them all. Not everybody does, and those people will hit the ceiling at high six figures and their ID will stop working at age 47.

If you've heard of the Big Five personality test, you know that conscientiousness is one of the tested attributes. I score reasonably high on conscientiousness, but I have been known to space and forget a Zoom meeting from time to time. But I have a business that is entirely based on email, and you don't last very long if you don't reply to emails. I also generally don't let calls go to voicemail if I can help it. Though I will admit that I never listen to voicemails, because voicemail is the most inefficient form of communication in the world. I never leave voicemails. The phone tells you who called, you can call back.

For some people, a text going unreturned can be very anxiety-inducing. It used to be for me, but not anymore. If I text someone and they don't text back, my assumption is that they have some crisis or problem in their life, and I will find out about it later, or maybe I won't. Either way, it's not on me, it's on them. It's their volleyball. But many people are consumed by the idea of someone not returning a text. They'll stew on it for days, thinking that the other person doesn't like them. We've had text messages for about 20 years now, and I can tell you that in a career of sending text messages and having them go unreturned, only once it was because the other person didn't like me, and that wasn't the worst thing in the world, either. Remember: you are not in control of what other people think of you. In any case, one of the reasons I am so conscientious is because I know other people experience anxiety about this. Again, it's the right thing to do.

We are all busy. Well, maybe not all of us, but many of us are. It's hard to respond to every email and every text. But you know what? Some people manage to do it, and they do it because they make it a priority, which is pretty much the definition of being conscientious. Politeness is about putting people's needs above yours. Years ago, I read *How to Win Friends and Influence People*. There wasn't anything about responding to texts and emails, but I'm sure that if it was written today, there would be.

Let me appeal to your self-interest. If you do this, you will get pay and promotions. You will make more money. Do I have your attention now? I'm not sure if you've ever had this experience where you're dealing with someone in the service industry, like a doctor's office or something like that, and you call, and you ask them to do something, and they say, *I will do the thing*, and then, like clockwork, they call you and tell you they did the thing, and you're... surprised! You never expected it. You never expected a $40,000-a-year receptionist at a dentist to be so conscientious. In my newsletter, I don't always get the highest marks for my market calls, but I do get the highest marks for customer service, and that's why I have the highest renewal rate in the industry.

I am never surprised when someone rises to the top. And I am never surprised when someone gets spit out the bottom. These things all have a way of working themselves out.

WHAT IS YOUR CONTRIBUTION?

I HAVE ACCOMPLISHED A lot in my life. Degrees, awards, money, books, etc. I am pretty proud of my accomplishments—I have a very long and illustrious curriculum vitae.

Is that how I measure my contribution to this world? No, it is not.

I think back to my time at Lehman Brothers. I was an ETF trader, a block trader, providing liquidity in exchange-traded funds to hedge funds and other institutions. If I saved a client $10,000 on a trade, that was $10,000 that was passed along to investors, which were often rich people, but also pension funds for teachers and firemen and stuff. The job wasn't socially useless. Providing liquidity in the financial markets is an important function, but it's easy to lose sight of that. You are very disconnected from your positive impact on other people. I never got any thank-you notes from the teachers or firemen. Still, after a day of knife-fighting with hedge funds, it certainly did feel like a socially useless job, and after a while, you start to think about your purpose in life, and you start to believe the people in Zuccotti Park who think you are a drain on society.

On the other end of the scale are social workers, and also teachers. With those jobs, there is a very tangible connection between the work that you do and the effect you have on other people's lives, which is why people do those jobs. As a teacher, I can tell you that I do occasionally have an impact on a student's life, but most of the time, I am pissing into the wind. Not everybody wants help. And help is for the people who want it, not the people who need it. As a social worker or a teacher, you spend an entire career trying to fix problems that are essentially intractable, with only a handful of success stories. It's not that there aren't social workers in the Tenderloin; there are hundreds of them. And they make practically zero progress.

As I get older, I think less and less about padding my stats and more and more about helping other people (and animals), with the knowledge that a lot of help is iatrogenic and often counterproductive. And I really am powerless to change someone's life. I am powerless to get someone to stop using drugs. I am powerless to keep someone from killing themselves. I am powerless to turn a lazy slob into a productive member of society. The addict is being told by everyone to stop using drugs. So what you do is you spend some time with the addict, and maybe you say the same thing that everyone else is saying, but you say it in such a way that it finally clicks, and they decide to get sober. That is the best you can hope for. But this doesn't happen unless you give someone the gift of time. It's easy to throw money at a problem and hope it goes away—we do that all the time. If you really want to change the course of someone's life, it takes time. Lots and lots of time. And nobody has time, right? We don't even have time to answer text messages.

But there are a lot of ways to help people. Driving a tow truck is helping people. Painting a house is helping people. Doing someone's taxes is helping people. Being an entertainer is helping people. Pretty much everything is helping people except for sitting at home, playing video games. I'm hard-pressed to come up with a job that doesn't help people in some way. Former Goldman Sachs CEO Lloyd Blankfein said that he was doing God's work, and he got roasted for that—but it was

WHAT IS YOUR CONTRIBUTION?

true. It is true about every occupation. If you start a small business and hire people and pay salaries and service customers and pay taxes, you are doing a lot of good in the world. And I also think that doing good and making money are not two mutually exclusive things. Jeff Bezos has done a lot of good in the world—he has saved us all thousands of hours going to the store. Elon Musk is doing a lot of good in the world, cutting carbon emissions and sending stuff into space. He also has a thing for free speech. They both got fantastically rich in the process, but it doesn't diminish their contribution to mankind. Where would we all be without Steve Jobs?

We all contribute in different ways. Some of us swing a hammer. Some of us take out the trash. I write. Lots of people will read this essay, but my goals are very modest: if I can reach one person with my writing, and change their life for the better, then I am happy. Sometimes I write to gratify myself, sometimes my aim is to entertain, and sometimes I have altruistic motives. If my essays didn't enhance your life in some way, I guess you would have stopped reading by now. This is my small contribution. Would I like ten times as many readers so I could make ten times the contribution? Absolutely, but word of mouth is slow and very little of the content I create goes particularly viral. I was poking around on Amazon today, looking at some of the bestselling books. Morgan Housel's book has about 45,000 reviews, and it has sold four million copies. James Clear's book has 150,000 reviews, which means he has probably sold 15 million copies. That is helping a lot of people. I'd like to have that kind of reach someday, not just to stroke my ego, but because I think I have good ideas that could help people, so why not reach as many people as possible? There's no cap on the number of books you can print. There's no limit on how much an email can be forwarded. My contribution is small, but I would like it to be larger.

I learned recently that I have more money than Alyssa Milano. I don't like to think of myself as rich, but I probably am. My financial goals are as follows: have a place in Pawleys Island, have a place in Miami Beach, and maybe have enough for private air travel back and forth between the two. Everything else is gravy—I don't have material needs beyond that. It will all go to charity, mostly because I don't have any kids to leave it to. But that's not the point—to accumulate as many gold coins as possible, unless you plan on doing a lot of good with the gold coins. There are competing philosophies on how much money you should leave to your kids. You can make them rich and spoiled, or bitter and resentful. There are no good answers. Maybe you think that your kids should make their own way in the world, but then you think that you're making things unnecessarily hard. I have met useless heirs and useful heirs. But I have heard some stories. A friend of a friend inherited close to a billion, and is an actual large-C hammer and sickle Communist, though tellingly, he hasn't given any of the money away. Stuff like that. If your contribution to the world is going to be money, it takes a great deal of forethought and planning. Charity is a better use for the money than taxes, but even charity can be wasted. Giving money away is actually one of the hardest things you can do. I talk to people who say that if they won the Powerball they would give it all to charity. Number one, that's pure horseshit, but number two, good luck giving $400 million away without creating some powerful misaligned incentives.

But like I said, we can all contribute in our own way, through our work, or our wealth, or our efforts. My derision is reserved for the people who do not contribute at all, who consume more than they produce, and criticize others. I have my share of detractors. What I say to them is: How many people have you helped?

GRATITUDE

ONE OF MY favorite topics.

Sometimes things don't go so well, and you are feeling sorry for yourself. *Poor me. Life sucks.* What I suggest you do in these situations is to make a gratitude list. Make a list of everything you are thankful for. Spend an hour on this. There are the easy things—your job, your spouse, your house. Then there are the little intangibles. Rack your brain until you can't think of any more. My guess is, if you do it right, you will have a list of 50-100 things that you are thankful for.

And at the end of it, you probably won't be feeling sorry for yourself anymore.

I live life in pretty much a permanent state of gratitude. Why? Because I am afflicted with a mental illness so severe that, if left untreated, I would be out on the sidewalk, picking through trash cans, and barking at traffic. I am a miracle. I have a lot of good things going on in my life, which is a massive understatement, but if I ever pause to reflect on my life pre-diagnosis, I am just happy to be alive. Jails, institutions, or death—that is what awaited me had I not sought help.

Now, if I am being honest, I am not in a state of gratitude all the time. I have the *more* disease. I want more money, more power, more fame, and more sex. And I spend pretty much every day sitting at my computer thinking up ways to get more of everything. Now, there are competing philosophies on this. Some people say that you shouldn't want more—ever—you should be satisfied with what you have. You have three squares, a roof over your head, and Netflix—what else could you want? That's pretty much a king-size crock of shit. What is life without ambition? I know lots of people who don't want more, who are satisfied with what they have. And it works for them. But it wouldn't work for me. Twelve years ago, I said that when I got to x net worth I would retire and open my own nightclub. Well, I got to x net worth two years ago, and I haven't slowed down. There is nothing wrong with moving the goalposts. There is no vice in wanting to accumulate material possessions and encomiums. There is no vice in wanting more.

But more can be taken to an extreme, if it leads to an obsession. I saw that Elon Musk's $55 billion pay package was denied by some court in Delaware. Even for me, that is a bit much. Now, it's not a question of need—Elon doesn't need $55 billion more, not after he already has $250 billion. But I guess the hedonic treadmill never stops no matter what level you're on. I'm not going to fault him for it. I would like to think I would tap out at a certain level and retire and open my own nightclub—but probably not. Some people are just wired differently. On Wall Street, they say that the money is a way of keeping score. But I'm not in competition with anyone else—just myself. I don't need to make more money than other people—I just want to make a shitload of money in absolute terms. At Lehman, I never got upset about making less than other people—I just wanted what I thought I was worth.

There is not a lot of gratitude on Wall Street. If you've ever worked at a bank, you know what bonus season is like, with all the angling and politicking. It is gross behavior. Someone will make a stick and will be incensed that they didn't make one point two, but they never stop to think about the fact that, hey, they made a million bucks, which is more money than some people will see in a lifetime, so settle down, Beavis. It is all about ego. And ego and gratitude cannot coexist in the

GRATITUDE

same space. Wall Street rewards this behavior to a certain extent—the guys who have gratitude, like I did, and are happy with what they made, are generally never overpaid. The system rewards the angling and the politicking. I felt very lucky just to have a job on Wall Street, and the last thing I was going to do was to be a prima donna and risk everything I had worked for.

I have spent a lot of time talking about finance and rich people. What I've found is that people of lesser means often have more gratitude than the country club folks. For most of the country, a job is a precious thing. Half the country lives paycheck to paycheck, and the loss of a job is a huge disruption, to say the least. Yes, there is unemployment insurance, but the emotional impact of losing a job can be enormous. I feel differently about it. If tomorrow, the government made financial newsletters illegal, I would do something else, like manage money, and if that didn't work out, I would get into real estate, or maybe I would just retire and open the nightclub. I can do a lot of different things. I would just write books, but that does not pay the bills. The point is that, if you're capable, you're never too worried about losing a gig, because there are always options available to you. I have a friend who was a CEO and is enjoying a full year of a noncompete. He has no immediate plans to do anything. I'm sure he will get another great opportunity, which is what typically happens to talented people. But for 99% of the world, a steady paycheck is a lifeline, and people are often very grateful for it.

I am grateful for my fuzzballs. Last night, I got in bed, and Wendy snuggled up next to me for about an hour, and then she slept next to my head, purring. People think I am a little nuts for having seven cats, but I can tell you that it's the best thing in the world. And they're all amazing—no stinkers in the group. I am grateful for my new book, which everyone loves. I am grateful for my new house, which is truly going to transform my life for the better. I am grateful for my wife, my patient wife, who puts up with all my crap. I am grateful for my lifesaving medication. I am eternally grateful that I survived 9/11. And it goes on. I am not going to put my complete gratitude list in this essay, but you get the picture. Not many people out there have it better than me. Sure, there are people with more resources, but I doubt they are as happy. Having gratitude keeps you grounded, but it is perfectly acceptable to want more. Where people get twisted up is when they outwardly say they don't want more, but they secretly do. This describes a lot of people: *I'm not a greedy bastard like these billionaires, but I am still going to buy lottery tickets.* Most psychological problems come from internal conflicts like these, when people's insides don't match their outsides. I am transparent about my desires: I want more money and a condo in Miami Beach. I want my book to be a runaway bestseller. For sure, I'm grateful that I was given the opportunity to publish a book in the first place. But we can all dream.

It wasn't supposed to work out this way for me. There are a billion alternate histories, and in the vast majority of them, things didn't go as well. Ironically, the one thing I don't have is my health, and at the moment, I'm forced to choose between work and money and life expectancy. I feel like Mozart, my face a pale shade of green, composing the Requiem on my deathbed. I'll move a muscle in the new house. The point is, if you have your health, you should be grateful for it, which is a general principle about gratitude in general—if you have something, there is a good chance that someone else out there wants it.

THE THRILL SEEKERS

MY FAVORITE WORD of the moment is *sybaritic*, which I learned from my friend Chand Sooran, who wrote the foreword to my essay collection, *Those Bastards*. Sybaritic means fond of sensuous luxury or pleasure; self-indulgent. This started with the Boomers back in the 60s—but if you ask the average person today about their code of morality, they will probably tell you that you can do whatever the hell you want as long as you don't hurt anyone else. That's modern American ethics summed up in a single sentence.

I think there should be more to it than that. The older I get, the more I think it is a virtue to deny yourself sensuous pleasure. Sensuous pleasure can mean a lot of different things: it can mean drink or drugs, or sex, or video games, or TV-watching, or anything we do as an escape from reality. This isn't rocket science. You probably know someone who experiences a bit too much sensuous pleasure, whether in drink or drugs, or sex, or video games, or anything else. What do you notice about these people? They are very unhappy people, or at least, hollow and unfulfilled. I don't get the impression that whatever Hugh Hefner was chasing gave him a richer, more fulfilling life. Stories are starting to come out about the Hefner days, and it's ugly. How would you behave in the same situation, if you had the ability to have as much sex as you want with the hottest women in the world, 24/7/365? It was never enough. The same is true of alcoholism or drug addiction, where one is too many and a thousand is never enough. It leads you down a path of complete and utter spiritual bankruptcy. There was probably a point in my 20s when I thought Hugh Hefner was pretty cool. You may think he was cool, but he was not cool.

The libertarians say that you can and should treat your body like an amusement park. The Republicans say that you should not. The Republicans also try to legislate away your ability to treat your body like an amusement park. I am somewhere in between—I think that treating your body like the Lightning Loops should be discouraged, but allowed—the cost of enforcement is just too high. You might have seen recently that there was a bill making its way through the Oklahoma legislature to ban adult pornography and make the mere viewing of it a felony. There is a lot of evidence that pornography is harmful, but the idea of locking thousands of people up for lingering on a wet T-shirt on Instagram seems a bit authoritarian to me. If you legislate away the ability to be immoral, and don't offer people a choice of whether to be moral or immoral, then people aren't really moral, are they? They have no choice in the matter. We went through this a century ago with Prohibition, and trust me on this—there should be no debate about the harmful effects on society of alcohol—but the cure was worse than the disease. Of course, drug prohibition these days is in name only—except in certain parts of the country, it is practically not enforced at all.

There is a reason why predominantly older people go to church. Sensuous pleasure is the antithesis of spirituality. The more you drink, do drugs, have a dishonorable discharge, the further away you are getting from God. There is a reason people feel remorse when they do these things, why they feel pangs of guilt after the 15 seconds of bliss are over; they know, deep down, that it is wrong, but they can't quite articulate why. And a lot of morality and legislated morality is simply that the things that feel wrong, *are* wrong. All of these things allegedly fall into the category of things that hurt you, but nobody else. And that is a common fallacy, when people think that the consequences of their actions don't extend beyond themselves. Addiction, of any kind, can tear apart families, and often the consequences are worse for the people surrounding the addict than for the addict himself. For the past ten years, we have been experimenting with drug decriminalization. There have been experiments with decriminalization around the world, none of them successful, not even Portugal, which we are supposedly trying to emulate.

As someone who gave up drinking 18 years ago, I can tell you that I have very few good memories of drinking. I will tell you one: My wife and I took a trip to Atlantic City in the summer, spent the day on the beach broiling in the sun, then headed inside the Showboat casino to play penny slots and get slowly sozzled on free gin and tonics. We were giggling our asses off. But no, most of my memories around alcohol involve puking, getting beat up, doing embarrassing stuff, and waking up massively hung over the next day. My life is infinitely better without it. Let's put it this way—I wasn't writing any books when I was drinking. I couldn't spell cat if you spotted me the "c" and the "a." In fact, my life didn't even really begin until I stopped drinking. From age 18 to 32 was a complete donut. All I was capable of was dragging my ass out of bed in the morning, scratching my way to work, putting in a minimal amount of effort, and limping home so I could unwind with a drink. Fourteen years of my life—gone. There is something about alcohol, in particular, which makes it unique among all drugs, in that it destroys your character in subtle, insidious ways. You find yourself doing things you never said you'd do—the unacceptable becomes acceptable. There is a reason they banned this stuff in 1920. I get it. We will have correspondingly similar, but different problems with cannabis 10-20 years from now.

By this point you probably think I sound like some uptight Tipper Gore character, some church-lady morality scold, or maybe some straightedge skinhead in Sacramento. Many people think of religion and spirituality as being in conflict with the material world. Like, you can't be rich and go to heaven. There are competing philosophies on this, but there are sects of Christianity that believe that you glorify God if you are productive, and I tend to agree with that. I don't think that there is a conflict between the spiritual and material world. I think there is a conflict between real spirituality and fake spirituality, the kind you get at a Phish show. I'm not saying that you have to spend your mornings on the back porch listening to the birds. You're talking to a DJ here. You can be spiritual and have fun, and you can even be spiritual and have excitement. Really, it comes down to the concept of escape. And that is the funny thing about the sensuous pleasures, that people really are trying to find a spiritual solution—they are just looking in the wrong place. I mean, look at Hunter Biden, the perfect example of an immoral, pleasure-seeking person, the running butt of all jokes in politics. That guy is trying to find God; he is just taking a shortcut. And there are no shortcuts.

You will know when you have a spiritual experience. I have had a few, if you're speaking in terms of white-light moments. You know when you are having one of those experiences; you cry. But for me, every day is a spiritual experience, showing up and doing good work, being fully present for the death of my cat Uma, being fully present for my wife and her achievements, building, growing, helping people, and slowly becoming a better person after a period of decades. Spiritual experiences don't happen exogenously—they are earned, over a lifetime of work and effort. It is just like anything else.

FINISH WHAT YOU START

This may describe you—maybe you are the type of person that will take on a big project: a book, a song, something like that—and you get partway into and you're like, *gee whiz, this is harder than I thought it would be*, and you capitulate, putting it away, and never coming back to it.

I did this recently.

I took up guitar. How hard can it be? Well, not that hard, in principle—I've been a musician for years, and I know music theory and chords and stuff, so that part was easy. But I have tiny hands, and in the physical universe we occupy, barre chords are an impossibility. My index finger simply does not stretch across the fretboard to mute all the strings. I mean, sure: with infinity time and infinity resources, and maybe with the use of a Procrustean finger-stretcher, I could make it work. I was able to play songs without barre chords, like Coldplay's "Yellow," but if you can't play barre chords there is really no point to the guitar. So I put it aside and said that I would come back to it. And no, what they say about guys with small hands is absolutely not true.

Generally, though, I finish what I start. I started my MFA program, figuring that it would be a cakewalk, and after a few months, said, *shit, this is hard,* but I stuck with it, and finished it over three years. I finished two other degrees in such fashion. I stayed at Lehman longer than pretty much anyone else in my associate class—not many of us were left at the bankruptcy. There were 12 MBAs hired in Equities in 2001—in 2008, I was the only one left. *The Daily Dirtnap* didn't exactly come roaring out of the gates, but I stuck with that, too.

A behaviorist would say that I have a high tolerance for frustration, which is another way of saying that when the going gets tough, the tough gets going. And in any new endeavor, the going will get tough, particularly in startups. If you want to read a good story about that, read about Ben Horowitz at Loudcloud in *The Hard Thing About Hard Things*. I can tell you this for sure: I have never met someone who started a business and said that it was easy. I mean, after a while, it gets easy, when the business matures, and then you can sit back and collect fat dividends, but in the beginning, there are hard problems to solve. Some people have a low tolerance for frustration. They take up a new project, then two weeks into it, they're like, *shit, too hard,* and they go back to dicking the dog or whatever it is they do with their free time.

I would put a graph in here, but I don't believe in visual aids in essays. Just imagine a graph where you have some visual representation of things being easy in the beginning, then they get very hard in the middle, then they get very easy at the end. It is the middle part that you have to power through. I call this "the resistance." Actually, someone else called it that first—Steven Pressfield, in *The War of Art*. You have to power through the resistance. I have had variations of this in all my essays, about the relationship between pain and growth, and doing hard things, and how there is no growth without suffering. And maybe quitting something is perfectly rational behavior—you do a cost-benefit analysis of how long it will take you to learn a skill, and what the expected return is from learning that skill, and you decide in the end that it isn't worth it. And that's fine. But there are some people who demonstrate a repeated pattern of starting things they don't finish. They don't finish anything. They never see a project through to completion. These are the people who tell you at cocktail parties that they've been working on the same book for the last 15 years. They're not really working on the book, obviously, and that book is unlikely to ever get finished. Lots of bad books get published in the U.S. every year. You know what's worse than a bad book? No book! Also, there are a lot of bad books that sell millions of copies. The David Goggins book is terrible. Bestseller. There is no accounting for some people's taste.

So a lot of life is powering through the resistance.

When *Street Freak* came out in 2011, I got a Goodreads review from a publishing dude in Minnesota. As it turns out, he was in my Swab Summer platoon at the Coast Guard Academy in 1994. I will briefly explain: "Swab Summer" is the Coast Guard Academy's version of basic training, where the upper-class cadets train the incoming freshmen. It is what it sounds like: a lot like *Full Metal Jacket*, at least back then. Anyway, this guy takes a shot at me in the review, telling everyone that he hated my guts, that I was a "faux drill sergeant-type character," and then went on to write a nice review of the book and said that he'd like to grab a beer with me someday. Well, we still haven't had the beer, and I'll give you the reason why: He didn't demonstrate a lot of introspection about his two weeks at the Academy before he quit ignominiously. He didn't power through the resistance. And if I was responsible for running him out of that place, it is highly likely that I did him a favor, that he ended up long-term happier for not having a career in the Coast Guard. I was a tough sonofabitch back then. More kids processed out of the Academy in my platoon than any other platoon, by a lot—saving them a lifetime of misery, something I take pride in. Doing hard things is a good thing in general, even doing some things just because they are hard, because of the way you feel at the end. At week two of my Swab Summer, when I was a freshman, I was having panic attacks. Pushed through the resistance. Did something hard. Finished what I started. At graduation, I was doing the happy-happy dance.

Then you get these people who are resolute—they will simply not give up, no matter what. Music production is like that. If you hear a track on the radio or at a club, hundreds of hours went into that piece of music. And it's not simply musicianship—it's technical proficiency with the software. It's not something you just pick up. It's thousands of hours in front of the computer, making mistakes, and making more mistakes, and noodling around with stuff, tinkering, learning all the while. Buying your 14-year-old child Logic or Ableton might be one of the greatest investments you ever made. Those kids will sit in their bedrooms until four in the morning, hammering away at the computer, until they finally figure it out. They are resolute. I went through this three years ago, fancied myself a producer, starting messing around in Logic and discovered it was a lot harder than I thought it was going to be. Some time you should read about Matt Fax. As a 12-year-old, this kid had dozens of tracks up on Beatport under the alias Mike Duz. At age 14, he was producing tracks with BT. In terms of production ability, I'd rate him in the top five in the world. That guy put in his 10,000 hours a long time ago.

The thing I happen to be an expert on is books, having written seven of them, five of them published. You know how you write books? You write books. You can't write books not writing. A lot of people think that everything they write has to be perfect, but the perfect is the enemy of the good. Write something down, put it in the freezer for two weeks, and come back and revise it. Also, you get a lot of people who think they have to write like a writer, and they're writing like what they think a writer should write like, and their voice gets lost in the bullshit. Which brings me back to the Goggins book—the dude is barely literate, but he has a strong voice, and it comes through, which is why the book is so popular. He's not trying to be someone he's not. It's that authenticity that people are looking for. If you are writing with a desire to look good, then it's not going to work out.

If you start something, you should finish it. Unless the costs are high and the benefits are low. But there is something to be said for finishing what you start, even in those cases. There is shame associated with quitting. When the police train German Shepherds, they talk about the dogs that have *drive*, which is another way of saying motivation. Those dogs make the best police dogs, because they are the easiest to train. Humans can have drive, too—they'll run through a brick wall to accomplish a goal. You don't have to run a Tough Mudder to be resolute. Sometimes, it's as simple as answering an email.

CRITICAL OR COMMERCIAL SUCCESS

I WENT TO MIAMI two weeks ago, and stopped at the Books & Books store in the airport. It's a pretty substantial bookstore for an airport. My recent finance book *No Worries* wasn't there, but you know what was? *Rich Dad, Poor Dad*. Its author, Robert T. Kiyosaki, is one of the world's great ding-dongs, and the book is still selling 30 years after its initial release, even though everyone knows it's a ridiculous book and Kiyosaki himself almost went broke taking his own advice. But *No Worries* now has 561 reviews on Amazon, nearly all of them five-star.

Everyone loves *No Worries*.

But everyone buys *Rich Dad, Poor Dad*.

I have written four critically acclaimed books and one that was not, but the one that was not just went over everyone's head. It is my favorite of the four. None of them have sold particularly well. *No Worries* still might, if the mainstream media stops covering it with a pillow until it stops moving. I hold out hope. I write very good books, but they are not particularly good-selling books.

CRITICAL OR COMMERCIAL SUCCESS

Which begs the question: If you are an artist, would you rather be a critical success or a commercial success? If you are a writer, would you rather be James Patterson, who has sold more than 100 million books, or Barry Hannah, who never sold more than 7,000 copies of any book on its first print run? Can you have it both ways? Yes, you can be Jonathan Franzen. But the number of writers who enjoy both critical and commercial success is very small. Practically zero. The same is true of movies, too, unless, of course, you are Christopher Nolan. But everyone wants to be Christopher Nolan, and they can't be. On one end of the spectrum is *Moonlight* and on the other end is *Iron Man*. There is not much in between.

I have spent the last few years trying to break into the world of literary fiction. I have written a bunch of short stories and submitted them to over 100 literary journals. I have had one publication and a handful of close calls. Now, there are other forces at play here: I am the wrong demographic to be getting published these days, and there has been much written about that phenomenon. Plus, as a writer, I'm kind of a 90s throwback, with a real focus on characters and storytelling. I'll admit: my literary chops are not the best. I have a strong first-person nonfiction voice, and that doesn't translate automatically to fiction. But if this were 1995, I would be getting published like nobody's business.

Anyway, the point here is that I think any artist, myself included, would want to be recognized by the people that count. And in the literary world, that's what they do—they write for journals that nobody reads, they publish at presses that sell 300 copies, they all sit around smelling their own farts, and nobody makes any money off it. They do it for praise and recognition, and nothing else. I happen to like money. I would like to write a book that sells five million copies. But then, it would be—gasp—mainstream. It would be selling out. You can't have it both ways.

And then there is the idea that the taste of the masses is not exactly highbrow. I feel IQ points sublimating out of my ears whenever I read James Patterson. *The Fast and Furious* movies are not known for nuance and subtlety. Things that are popular tend to be pretty dumb—this is a fact. When was the last time you watched *Law & Order*? It is absolutely a bad show, with terrible writing and terrible acting. It's been on TV for decades. I'll give you another example. *Arrested Development* was a smart show about dumb people. *The Big Bang Theory* was a dumb show about smart people. Which one got canceled, and which one stayed on the air? I just gorilla-dunked my point on you. I don't read lowbrow books, I don't listen to lowbrow music, and I don't watch lowbrow TV. Shouldn't be a surprise that I write highbrow books. Maybe I will be the Barry Hannah of the finance world. All I ask is that Bloomberg sends out a push notification when I roll a seven.

If you get some time, I recommend you check out what's on the *New York Times* bestseller list. Not exactly Masterpiece Theatre. We made it this far in the essay and we haven't even talked about music. I'm not going to get into the aesthetics of Taylor Swift, but it's not exactly The The, which is what I was listening to circa 1989. And let's just say that "Wet Ass Pussy" is a long way from Simon and Garfunkel. There is no highbrow music left, and if there is, you have to know where to find it. Even in the dance music world which I inhabit, there is highbrow and lowbrow, with Steve Aoki (fuck that guy) on one end, and someone like Tim Green on the other. As a DJ, I have spent the last 17 years trying to raise the taste of the masses, actually with some success. I'll find some track from a 16-year-old in Belarus producing with a cracked version of Ableton on his laptop, play it out in a club, and everyone goes nuts. That's basically why I do what I do—to expose people to great art. Steve Aoki isn't art. He's a hype guy throwing cakes. The The, the winners of the Flesch-Kincaid lyrics contest, did reasonably well, all things considering, but that was before the winner-takes-all internet. A whole book could be written about how the internet has made all forms of art—visual art, music, literature—demonstrably worse.

There is something about the book business that is worth mentioning. In the old days, you'd go to a bookstore, and you'd browse. Maybe you'd stand in the aisle and read an entire book without paying for it. I remember the store clerks at Waldenbooks gave you the hairy eyeball if you tried doing that. But you could walk through the store, see thousands of different books, and flip through them. People generally only buy books on Amazon if they hear about them, and the only way they hear about them is through this thing called *buzz*. It gets mentioned on a podcast, or on a TV show, or on YouTube, or something like that. Or people post about it on Reddit. So today, if you're an author, you essentially have to be a hype guy like Steve Aoki, whereas before, you'd get some reviews and it would sit in a bookstore and people would pick it up. Amazon does suggest other titles to you, but who knows how that algorithm works. Or you have to get struck by lightning. I am standing out in a rainstorm with an umbrella and nothing is happening.

Which brings me back to the subject of Barry Hannah, who is my all-time favorite writer. If you asked 100 of the world's greatest writers who they thought the greatest writer ever was, half of them would probably say Barry Hannah. And yet: never sold more than 7,000 copies of a book. Not coincidentally, he was a man of the right. Got up at an AWP conference and told everyone to find Jesus, which nearly caused a riot. I have actually thought of taking a month and living in Oxford, Mississippi as a sort of writing retreat, thinking that something in the air or soil would bring out the best in me. So, to answer the question, would you rather be Barry Hannah or James Patterson—and let's just say for the sake of argument that you can't be both—I would rather be Barry Hannah. I really would. Patterson is a Play-Doh fun factory, a monarch of monosyllables, writing books to help people take a shit. I would rather write good books that nobody reads, than bad books that everyone does. You might say that Patterson is laughing all the way to the bank. Well, good for him. Who knows—maybe I'll get to be both.

COMPLIMENTS

Last week, I was in Kansas City for the AWP conference (Association of Writers & Writing Programs), and I sat down at my designated booth next to a 24-year-old representative from my MFA program. After I introduced myself to her, she said:

"Nice hair!"

I have been blessed in the hair department. When I was a teenager, I had Michael Hutchence hair down to my shoulders. There's a picture of it far down my Instagram. I was about 50 at the time of the AWP compliment, and I still had all my hair. It's more than 60% gray at this point, and it looks rather striking, or so I'm told. I'm very fortunate. Bald guys pretty much have to grow beards, or else they look like babies. I can't grow a beard, so if I didn't have any hair, I'd look like Charlie Brown. My hair started going gray very rapidly about three years ago, and the process should be complete in 2026. Combined with a young-looking, unblemished, tan face, it's about the best thing I have going for me right now.

The next day I went back to the booth, and she said:

COMPLIMENTS

"Nice jacket!"

I was wearing a rather dastardly peak lapel corduroy jacket, sort of a combination rockstar/college professor look. I like the jacket, too. It's comfortable, and you can wear it in about every situation. I don't often get compliments on my appearance from 24-year-old women, so getting two in a row was pretty special. It cushioned the blow of what was otherwise a brutal conference. And the nice thing about compliments is that if one person says it, you know that other people are thinking it.

I like giving and getting compliments. When I first applied to that school, I got a recommendation letter from my literary agent. In the letter, he said—among other things—that I was one of the funniest people he has ever known. I am funny, but not in the sense that I could do a set of stand-up comedy. I have these witty asides and running sarcastic commentaries on life and this sort-of deadpan sense of humor, and yes, people do find it funny. He wrote that recommendation letter five years ago, and I remember that compliment to this day. A good compliment sticks with you for a while. *Someone said something nice about me.*

I get compliments all the time. Usually about my newsletter, from my readers. People will say that I said something particularly smart or insightful, and those compliments are always appreciated. I have gotten a lot of compliments about my books, *No Worries* in particular. I welcome those, too. It's nice to get complimented for stuff—it keeps me going. But the ones I remember are the ones that are from out of left field, like the compliments about my appearance—because I think of myself as a six-foot, 245-pound, ugly troll. I will say this: women do not understand what men want. At all. Men seek *admiration*, whether they are deserving of it or not. It's a common misconception that men go to strip clubs because of the T&A—that's not why. It's because someone will pay attention to them, even for five minutes, and tell them that they are handsome, and otherwise worthy of affection, which is not something they're getting at home. Women are good at many things, but in America they are not so good at admiration. The short way of saying this is that married couples take each other for granted. They stop giving those compliments after a while, and they're absolutely crucial to a successful relationship. I was on the phone with my friend Buck the other day, and he asked me, *what do you think of your wife?* And I told him, I think she is absolutely the most beautiful woman in the world. I go out to dinner and I just stare at her. And then it occurred to me… that I have never told her that! We have our domestic duties at home, she cleans the house and I scoop the poop, and there's things that we do together, as a team, but we don't often give each other compliments. Life being what it is, we get busy with bullshit, and forget.

But there is something to be said for being worthy of compliments. If you are a pile of shit and wear cargo shorts and sit on the couch drinking beer on the weekends, that's not very attractive behavior. Life is a competition, you know, and even in a marriage you have to compete for the other person's affection. You're constantly in competition, otherwise the grass might look greener someplace else. Having to be asked 15 times to put the dishes in the dishwasher instead of the sink does not really put your significant other in the mood to compliment you about your hair. Peeing all over the toilet seat does not put someone in the mood to compliment you about your jacket. I think that once people get married, and stay married for a while, they get comfortable, and complacent, and they think that they don't have to do any more work on the relationship. You see, the thing about compliments is that they cost nothing. They're free! They're certainly a lot cheaper than that David Yurman necklace you were going to get your wife for her birthday.

The etiquette about compliments has changed in the last 10–15 years. These days, women don't like it if you compliment them about their appearance. At least, they profess not to like it. And there is an order of magnitude difference between "You've got the sweetest ass I've ever seen" and "You look nice today." You're not even supposed to say the latter. There is a lot going on here. Somehow, today, everything is construed as a sexual advance. It's not from me, because I have the sex drive of a fake plastic plant. I'm just being nice. But I conform to the new normal, and I don't give compliments to women anymore—at least not about their appearance. So this is where we are. I think that would be a pretty lonely existence—you spend all this time and effort trying to look good, doing your hair, doing your makeup, doing your nails, and nobody notices or cares. Apparently, the origin of this is that some women get hit on all the time and they find it exhausting, so maybe I would feel differently if I were a woman and I were fending off thirsty guys with a cattle prod. The word is that gymnast and influencer Olivia Dunne only takes classes online at LSU, so as to avoid the swarming schools of piranhas on the way to class. And young girls are often told that they are pretty, but not smart. Anyway, this is a delicate subject these days, and I can only speak for myself: I want people to say nice things about me. And I want to say nice things about other people.

You know where compliments go a long way? On Twitter. On financial Twitter, you have a bunch of personalities and egos who spend a lot of time trying to look good. They're so focused on making themselves look good, they don't often compliment other people—publicly. Because business is a zero-sum game, and someone else might get a subscriber that I don't. It's not a zero-sum game. We can all win. If you are generous with compliments online, people notice, and it reflects well on you.

The world is full of people who work hard and never get recognized for it. I will say that the military is very good at recognizing people—they give out medals and awards quite frequently. The private sector, not so much. Your reward is your pay. But people need psychic rewards, too. I enjoyed my time at Lehman Brothers, but the maddest I ever got was when I was passed over for promotion to senior vice president. Which is weird, right? The bonus pool is finite, but promotions cost nothing. In retrospect, I should have cared more about the money. In the academic world, awards and recognition are a big deal, because nobody gets paid. There was a management article written decades ago called, "It's the Reward System, Stupid!" which talked about which behaviors you were trying to incentivize in your organization. Really, complimenting people on their performance is simply one of the best things you can do.

I didn't win Most Likely to Succeed in high school. I won Class Musician instead. In the joke awards, I also won Nicest Legs. The idea of all the senior girls lusting after my heavily muscled legs kept me going for a while. This guy didn't need calf implants. It was from all those hours running up and down stairs in wrestling practice. Thirty-two years later, I still tell people about the time I won Nicest Legs. Thanks, girls.

LETTER TO MY 22-YEAR-OLD SELF

In 1996, I was a walking sack of spermatozoa, a physical specimen who picked up heavy things and ran marathons—and wholly undereducated, from four years of sleeping through college. I had raw intelligence, but nothing in the way of accumulated wisdom. What I lacked in sagacity I made up for with pure, limitless ambition: whatever I tried, I was going to succeed at. If I was going to be a Coast Guard officer, I was going to be an admiral. If I was going to be a writer, I would make Granta's list of best young writers. If I was going to be a trader, I would end up in one of those Jack Schwager books.

None of those things happened. But in a couple of instances, I came pretty close.

Things might have turned out even better, if I knew then what I know now.

Here are a few things I'd like to tell my dumb 22-year-old self:

1. *Politics matter.* One of the things that turned me off about the Coast Guard is that politics was a big determining factor in

one's success, and I didn't see myself as someone who was in possession of adequate political skills. All it took was one bad tour where you didn't see eye-to-eye with your commanding officer and you found yourself having a passover party. Of course, the more politically adept officers were able to make it work in any scenario, and they invariably rose to the top. That wasn't for me. So I decided to work in what I thought was the most meritocratic industry in the world: capital markets. But while I was at Lehman, I was getting paid approximately 1% of what I made for the firm, while some people were getting paid 15%. All a function of politics. When you're young, you have this naïve belief that all that matters is performance—if you're the best at your job, you should get paid the most. Nothing could be further from the truth. So in any organization, you have to manage up as well as down. If your boss doesn't like you, you're not getting paid. And even if he does like you, if he thinks you won't leave, and you'll work for nothing, then you're not getting paid. I could write a book on this, but some have already been written.

2. *Get some sleep.* Boy, was I stupid about this. I used to think that the less time I spent sleeping, the more time I had to work. This is true, but you work a lot more efficiently if you've gotten a good night's sleep. I started getting a full night's sleep around age 32, and it changed my life. That is not an understatement—it changed my life. I couldn't write a book when I was sleeping two hours a night. I could barely think. It took me a while to finally stop the tough-guy act and go to bed at 10 p.m. To this day, I get eight, sometimes nine hours of sleep. Last night, I actually got 11. The next day, I'm Superman. My performance in school would have been a lot better if I wasn't constantly pulling all-nighters on stuff, and managing my time a bit better.

3. *Sex is not that important.* It's just not. It's one of the least important things you can do. Stop thinking about it all the time. You'll have more space in your head to think about more important stuff.

4. *Generosity matters.* Not in the sense that you should donate 10% of what you make, because when you're young, that's hard, and you need to be accumulating wealth and letting it compound. But don't be a lousy tipper. And if you can't donate money, donate time. A mentor of mine was trying to get me to volunteer in animal shelters about 12 years ago. I demurred. Why did I say no? Well, I thought that my time was valuable, and that I was so important, etc. Not the case. Give the gift of time, if you can't give the gift of money. Visit with sick people, old people, and animals. I can tell you that charitable organizations would be very surprised—and happy—to see a 22-year-old show up and help out.

5. *Pursue your dreams, sort of.* When I was 22, my dream was to become a writer. A family member told me that was a terrible idea, because I would be poor. Most young people, when they get that advice, plow ahead anyway, and end up poor, and poverty is no fun, no fun at all. I went to business school instead, made some money, and now I am pursuing my dreams. I think I did it in the right order. Now, if your dream is to be a musician or a poet or something like that, and it's really what you love, then who am I to say no? Just know what you're getting into—a lifetime of deprivation. Money matters. Creature comforts matter. The economics of the artistic world are terrible, so you might as well be a working stiff and do music or art or writing in your spare time. If I had obtained my MFA right out of college and gotten a job at a university somewhere, I'd be content, but under constant financial pressure. Pursue

your dreams, but make some darn money, and don't blame someone else for your choices.

6. *Do it without the rope.* Remember that scene from *The Dark Knight Rises*, where Bruce Wayne is trying to climb his way out of the underground prison, and the old blind man tells him to do it as the child did—without the rope? When I left the Coast Guard for Wall Street, there was no plan B. If I didn't get a job, I was totally stuck. No rope. When I left Lehman Brothers for the newsletter, there was no plan B. If it failed, I was completely stuck. This is part of a larger discussion about taking risk and risk appetite in general, and also betting on yourself. Betting on yourself is like trading on inside information—you have an edge, because you are in control of the outcome. I hear that Zoomers are not big risk-takers. That is too bad, because we need young risk-takers. We need people to bet it all on themselves, and win. And the nice thing about taking risks when you are young is that there are very few consequences if you fail. When you get older, there are huge consequences if you fail. No spouse, no kids, no house—take the risk. There is no point playing it safe in your 20s.

7. *Be hungry like the wolf.* I have had about 12 interns over the years, all very bright, very capable people, but none of them were as hungry as I was. When I was getting started in my career, I read every single book on finance, over 200 of them. I subscribed to *Barron's* and *The Wall Street Journal*, and read them religiously. I learned absolutely everything there was to know about finance. Other people were not so hungry—they went home at night and watched their shows. I was going to outwork you, and I was going to outsmart you. I've never met anyone like me, who has that level of passion and intensity. I bring that level of intensity to writing, too, going to get my

MFA and publishing books and submitting to hundreds of journals. And here is the thing about being hungry—it can't be taught. It absolutely cannot be taught. So if you are 22 and reading this, and think you might be slacking off, it is because you probably are. There will be time to relax—later.

8. *Don't drink or do drugs.* I never made any career-ending mistakes while drunk, but I had some close calls, and I was drunk a lot. There was a lot of drinking on Wall Street. Half the trading floor would show up hung over on any given morning. Which is crazy—we were like highly-paid professional athletes, supposedly performing at our peak, and we'd be out at strip clubs until four in the morning and roll in with a bacon, egg, and cheese, barely able to function. I regret every drink I took. Plus, it messes with your sleep. Ninety percent of people who get fired for cause are dismissed as a result of some alcohol-related incident. Sounds like Zoomers drink a lot less than Xers, so you are well on your way. But stay off the weed, too—it's an ambition-killer, which is worse.

9. *Think big.* Let's say your goal is to become CEO. Well, there are a lot of steps in between where you are now and becoming CEO, so it is going to take a lot of time, and it is going to take a lot of patience. But have a goal. Maybe the goal is to make seven figures. Maybe the goal is to become head of the desk. Maybe the goal is to retire at 50. What's always shocked me is the number of goal-less people who kind of plug along, punch the clock, earn a paycheck, and don't think too hard about the next steps. I still have goals, and I'm still reaching them. My goal was to publish a short story collection, but that's secondary to my real goal: to revolutionize literary fiction. I'm a one-man wrecking crew. You'd much rather think too big than think too small. There are no consequences to thinking

too big, but the consequences to thinking too small are severe. Don't just think big—think huge. Your ambition is your most precious commodity.

10. *Communication skills are the most important thing.* If you are the best public speaker in the world, you know what you get to be? President. If you are the best writer in the world, you know what you get to be? Maureen Dowd. Kevin Williamson. The people who rise to the top of any organization or industry are always the best communicators. I got a Commendation Medal in my second tour in the Coast Guard because of my writing skills—no joke. I was a legendary trader on Wall Street because of my writing skills—also no joke. If you're good at a thing, like manipulating spreadsheets, you will be a worker. If you're good at a thing, and you're also good at communicating, you will be a leader. All the job interviews in investment banking test the wrong things, unless your goal is to simply hire indentured servants. But if you want to hire someone who will eventually lead your investment banking division, you can't just look at their spreadsheets. And now, because of AI, nobody will learn how to write ever again. It's terrible.

This is only a partial list—I could go on. College graduates have the foresight of a ferret, and the attention span of a goldfish. You should sit down and write out a plan for the next 20 years—all your goals, and how you are going to achieve them. Print it out and save it. Read it again in 20 years, and have a good laugh. God laughs at our plans. But God has a much bigger imagination than you do, and He has a bigger imagination for you, too.

TRAUMA

THIS IS A fact: All the bad stuff that happens to us before the age of seven, all the trauma we experience as a child, becomes a part of who we are. It is in every cell in our bodies. It is true of all ages, but it is especially true before the age of seven.

I'm past it, so I have no need to relitigate it, but I grew up in a violent house until the age of seven—at which point my parents divorced. Let's just say that I experienced physical discipline far above and beyond spanking. And I was a 9/11 survivor, so there is that. And I had some trauma while in the Coast Guard, too. Throw in the financial crisis while you're at it. If you were to draw charts of various addictions, criminality, and other social ills, you would find that they have a one-to-one correlation with trauma in childhood. Which means: If you are getting married, and you are having children, your first and most important responsibility is to shield the child from potential trauma. That is the difference between a future Nobel Prize-winner and a convict. It is very, very hard for people to succeed in spite of their trauma. Some people do, but it is exceedingly rare.

I watch some TV. You want to know what I notice about TV? Everyone is smiling all the time, like on *American Idol*. Lionel Richie, Katy

Perry, and Luke Bryan are always joking around. They seem to be really enjoying themselves. None of them have that haunted look like me, or people I know who have experienced trauma. People tell me to smile all the time. What the hell is there to smile about? If you had been through what I have been through, you wouldn't smile either. I know some people who have been through what I have been through, and much worse, and they're not big smilers. They are serious as a heart attack.

Right now, there are some people pushing a narrative that talk therapy is next to useless. I can see why some people might think that. I think talk therapy is like a lot of things in life—you get out of it what you put into it. In other words, it is work, and you have to do the work, in and out of sessions. Most people just sit there, passively receiving information, a spectator to their own recovery. After 9/11, in the beginning I would have panic attacks if I heard the sound of jet engines. I finally came to terms with it around 2009, through years of therapy. I came to terms with a lot of things through therapy. I will add that a lot of therapists are patently unskilled, so in order for it to work, you need someone who knows what the hell they are doing, and you need to be willing to put in the work. You have to want it, which is true of just about everything. You have to want to get better, and deep down, a lot of people don't really want to get better. They like to sit in the pain, because it is familiar and comfortable. You have to get honest. When therapy doesn't succeed, the vast majority of times it is because of the insouciance of the patient, not the acumen of the therapist.

Most people, when they experience trauma, spend the rest of their lives seeking out things that are soothing. This is where the addictions come in. Some people might be soothed by drugs or alcohol, resulting in addiction or alcoholism. Some people might be soothed by prostitutes. Some people might be soothed by obsessive-compulsive disorder or other ritualized behavior. All of these things allow the person to perpetuate the illusion of *control*—if I can change the way I feel, the thinking goes, then I have control over my situation. Of course, all of these behaviors are self-destructive, and lead to bigger consequences down the road. The solution to this is to not pursue behaviors that are soothing, the solution is to do things that bring joy. For me, most of the time, it is music. I play music in my house and time disappears. The cats also bring me joy. For some people, it might be swimming in a pool, going for a walk in nature, or going to a concert. Joy is the antithesis of trauma, and seeking it out is the best alternative to self-destructive behavior.

The number of people who experience a quiet, drama-free childhood is actually pretty small. All of us are carrying around one trauma or another. We are all a bunch of screwed-up people, trying to find our way in the world, bumbling into shit and making mistakes, and trying to clean up the mess. I'm big on forgiveness, for just that reason. I have only not forgiven someone once. Usually, if you're dealing with someone and you find their behavior disturbing or incomprehensible, just know that 90% of the time, you're dealing with trauma, addiction, mental illness, or some combination of the three. Mentally stable, healthy people generally don't go around leaving a path of destruction in their wake. There are some assholes out there, but not many. The number of truly evil people in the world is breathtakingly small. I always, always bet on the goodness of people.

And then you think about the people in positions of leadership who have experienced trauma. John McCain, for example—one of the greatest war heroes in history, but when you learn what he went through in Vietnam, the torture he endured, and he came within 4% of becoming leader of the free world? Look, I'm not saying he wouldn't have made a fine president, because he was a man of character, and that is what is important. But remember what I said about trauma—it is in every cell in your body, and affects your decision-making in ways that you can't even comprehend. I keep bringing up the Goggins book, as much as I disliked it—the one thing I kept thinking about when I was reading that book was that he also grew up in a violent household from age zero to seven, even more violent than mine. All these triathlons he's running—that's not perseverance, that's not willpower, that's soothing, and it doesn't take a psychology PhD to figure that out. But we live in a society that values superhuman endurance and physical prowess and tolerance of pain, so a few million books later, he's a hero. I wonder what you'd find if you did a psychological study of Navy SEALs and what trauma they endured in childhood. It would be pretty interesting.

I can tell you how I deal with trauma—I write about it. You know how I finally, finally put 9/11 to rest? I wrote about it. I wrote a 2,000-word piece for *The Daily Dirtnap* for the 20th anniversary in 2021, and then I turned that piece into an essay for my book *Those Bastards*. That was how I finally came to terms with it. I am not the only one who does this. Graham Greene wrote, "Writing is a form of therapy; sometimes I wonder how all those who do not write, compose, or paint can manage to escape the madness, melancholia, the panic and fear which is inherent in a human situation." If I didn't write every day, I would… never mind. I would be pretty unhappy, to say the least. People thank me for writing stuff all the time. Hey, don't thank me. I don't do it for you, I do it for me. The alternative is to bottle it up and turn into a miserable bastard. No thanks.

DEPRESSION

Depression is the most common form of mental illness. Millions upon millions of people suffer from it.

First, we must distinguish between bipolar depression and unipolar depression, which is what most people have. Bipolar depression is far less frequent, but exponentially more severe. People with unipolar depression are more or less depressed all the time—but the risk of suicide is much lower. I have no personal experience with unipolar depression, but I have many friends who do, so I think I can speak with authority on it.

Depression is characterized by feeling like shit, weight loss, sleeping much more than is necessary, losing interest in things you like to do, and having low self-esteem. You feel unworthy. Often, this is accompanied by substance abuse, which—guess what—only makes it worse. Self-medicating your depression with alcohol or anything else is never a good idea. Short-term gain, long-term pain.

I don't have the cure for depression, but I can tell you what helps, if only momentarily:

1. *Move a muscle, change a thought.* Go out for a walk. Go out for a drive. Go work in the garden. Go to the batting cages. Go for a run. Go play tennis. Do something with your hands. Don't: sit on the couch and watch TV or doomscroll social media. I like to say that the inside of my head is a bad neighborhood, and I don't want to go in there without a shotgun and a flashlight. So I don't go in there. I do stuff. But when you are depressed, the last thing you want to do is to do stuff. You have to force yourself to do it. Working with your hands is especially helpful. If you are the type of person who likes to work on cars, or likes to make things out of wood, this is the best way to get out of your head for a few hours. I hate getting my hands dirty, so gardening is not for me, but many people extol the virtues of gardening. The best thing you can do for your mind is do something.

2. *Avoid isolation.* When you are depressed, you don't want to talk to anyone. This is the exact moment that you should be lighting up your phone, talking to as many people as possible. Talk to them about how you are depressed. If you talk to ten people, you are bound to get two or three good ideas. But again—it will get you out of your head. Here's one for you—call someone else and ask how *they* are doing. Call someone you know who is going through some shit and try to be of assistance. Nothing will get you out of your head faster than helping someone else. Also, you might realize that your problems are not as bad as you thought, compared with those of some of your friends. You might call up a guy who is going through a really hellish divorce. You can help him out, and you can help yourself out in the process. I make a lot of phone calls on any given day. I am really not that social—I am doing it for my mental health.

3. *Take medication, if necessary.* I don't have a lot of experience with antidepressants—took Prozac for a while and found it to be a bit stimulative, which wasn't what I was looking for. Also, antidepressants take a while to build up in your system, so it's not a break-glass-in-case-of-emergency kind of drug. Some people resort to short-term fixes, like Valium and Xanax, and while those provide some temporary relief, they are not a long-term solution, and they can cause chemical dependency. Anyway, the goal of any psychiatric medications is to get off them eventually—you shouldn't be a lifetime user of Prozac or Wellbutrin. But they do help. Note: if you are suffering from bipolar depression, the SSRIs are to be avoided, as they can trigger a manic episode.

4. *Don't stop, don't give up.* Don't call in sick to work because you are depressed. Put on your pants and get in your car and go. Depression is a real disability, but you have to fight through it, which is the message that I want to get across here: keep fighting, keep pushing. Don't let the monsters win. If you spend a day laying on the couch, it is not going to help, and it is going to make things worse. The worst depression I ever had lasted about four months when I was at Lehman Brothers. I lost 42 pounds. I never, not once, called in sick to work.

5. *This, too, shall pass.* The way you are feeling right now is not the way you are going to be feeling forever, though it sure feels like it. You think that you are going to feel like shit for the rest of your life. You won't. It will pass. It might take a while, but it will pass. It probably won't pass if you don't take care of yourself, if you don't do the things in this list. It probably won't pass if you don't want it to pass. That's the thing about depression—people get used to living with it. They get used to feeling like shit, it becomes familiar, it becomes comfortable,

and they don't do anything about it. Do you want to get better? Then take action to get better. There might be someone reading this who thinks that I don't know what real depression is, the kind of depression where you're curled up in the fetal position on the floor, crying. Yes, I do. I've been there. And there is a good chance I'll be back there again. I survived it, so can you.

Sunlight helps a lot. Myrtle Beach gets 230 days of sunlight a year. New York gets 115. I totally underestimated the impact that sunlight has on my mental health until I moved to South Carolina. Seattle gets 88 days of sunlight a year, and to compound it, in the winter, the sun doesn't come up until 8 and sets at 3. Remember, Washington is at about 48 degrees north latitude, so the days are very short in the winter. Nothing but darkness and rain. I lived in Washington my first two years out of college, and it was brutal. When I was in the Coast Guard, I took a trip to Kodiak, Alaska in late November. Twenty-two hours of darkness. The Coast Guard had a big suicide problem in Kodiak for a number of years. They call it seasonal affective disorder, and it's a real thing. Though you can be depressed even in Arizona or Southern California.

Remember: Nobody is at fault for being depressed. It is a matter of brain chemistry. Some people have it, some people don't. There shouldn't be any social stigma whatsoever, but there still is, a little. Having said all that, we all have a role to play in our own recovery. I don't know about you, but I don't want to spend 30% of my life depressed. I want to be happy, joyous, and free. I am happy, joyous, and free about 2% of the time. How do I know when I am happy, joyous, and free? When I am having singalongs in my car and I just don't care. Most of the time I am worried about one thing or another. I am actually suffering from very, very mild depression at the moment, which is common for me after I have a book come out and there is a letdown after the initial flurry of sales. Another book that doesn't make the bestseller list—I am still a failure, or so I think. But I'll snap out of it eventually, and go back to feverishly working on some new project. I've been through this a bunch of times before.

Depression is not a choice. But it is also not *not* a choice. Pop psychology will tell you that it just hits you—*whammo*—and you have no role to play in your recovery. But there are things you can do.

THE FUTILITY OF PLANNING

Probably the best speech in movie history (aside from John Goodman's rant about fuck-you money in *The Gambler*) is The Joker's peroration to Harvey Dent in *The Dark Knight*.

It goes like this:

> Do I really look like a guy with a plan, Harvey? I don't have a plan...
>
> The mob has plans, the cops have plans. You know what I am, Harvey?
>
> I'm a dog chasing cars... I wouldn't know what to do with one if I caught it. I just *do* things. I'm just the wrench in the gears. I hate plans. Yours, theirs, everyone's. Maroni has plans. Gordon has plans. Schemers trying to control their worlds. I am not a schemer, I show the schemers how pathetic their attempts to control things really are. So when I say that you and your girlfriend was nothing personal, you know I am telling the truth...
>
> ...

THE FUTILITY OF PLANNING

> I just did what I do best—I took your plan, and I turned it on itself. Look what I've done to this city with a few drums of gas and a couple of bullets. Nobody panics when the expected people get killed. Nobody panics when things go according to plan, even if the plan is horrifying. If I tell the press that tomorrow a gangbanger will get shot or a truckload of soldiers will be blown up, nobody panics. Because it's all part of the plan. But when I say that one little old mayor will die, everybody loses their minds!
>
> Introduce a little anarchy, you upset the established order and everything becomes chaos. I'm agent of chaos. And you know the thing about chaos Harvey?
>
> It's fair.

That was one of those moments in the cinema when you're sitting there and you're like, *you know, the bad guy is making a lot of sense*. Now, I'm not going to blow up any hospitals, but I do want to talk about the futility of plans. As I mentioned earlier, God laughs at our plans. You want to know what I do to prepare for interviews? Nothing! Because the unplanned is better than the planned. The spontaneous is better than the rehearsed.

If you make your living in the financial markets, you are familiar with the ways of chaos. We all have plans for trades. *I'm going to buy it at X and sell it at Y and make Z.* How often does that work out? It has worked out precisely one time in my entire career. Shit goes sideways. You adapt, and improvise. I'm sure you know people who plan out every aspect of their lives, and correspondingly, they are not so good at adapting and improvising.

I make plans. But the plans are basically just a rough outline. A good example of this is air travel. If you are not able to adapt and improvise with air travel, you are going to be miserable. I was on a flight from Hartford to DCA a few days ago, and a toddler got some allergic reaction while we were sitting on the tarmac, waiting to take off. Back to the gate. I was going to miss my connection. Did I freak out? No, I adapted and improvised. I texted a college buddy who lived in D.C. and asked if I could crash at his place. As it turned out, it wasn't necessary, because I made my connection anyway, because my connecting flight was late too. Either way, my heart rate did not go up one bpm. I had extra clothes. I had a toothbrush. I was going to be fine. Sometimes, shit happens.

The communists in communist countries make 100-year plans. Everyone talks about this with the Chinese. *Oooh, they're so smart, they're thinking out 100 years.* Then, a year later, the plans are totally useless. The U.S. government lurches from one crisis to another, without any clear plans. Actually, this is the correct way to do things. And besides, in a democracy, there is no continuity from administration to administration, so long-term plans are pointless. I get the impression that this is how Elon Musk manages, constantly putting out fires and dropping bombs on Twitter. It seems to work for him! Boeing, on the other hand, has plans, thinking out 30 years. Yet they cannot see the trees for the forest.

I have some plans to do things in the coming years. Like I said, they are rough outlines. I know I will encounter some challenges along the way, and then I will adapt and improvise. Things are never as easy as they seem. But you solve one problem, then another problem, then another problem. Teachers can plan, more or less. You can write up a syllabus and stick to the syllabus. In the business world, you can't plan—it's too dynamic an environment. Fossil probably thought things were pretty good until the Apple Watch came along. Stock down 90%. Nobody saw that one coming. Blackberry probably thought things were pretty good until the iPhone came along. Nobody saw that one coming. All it takes is about 12 months for you to be disrupted out of existence.

In my writing, I don't plan. I didn't plan this piece. I figured I'd start with The Joker speech and go from there, and see where it took me. When I write short stories, I never know how they are going to end. Whenever I plan my writing, it ends up immeasurably worse. *All the Evil of This World* is a maddeningly complex book. There is a lot of engineering between the different overlapping storylines. You might think I would have mapped it out in a diagram ahead of time. Nope, started on page one, went to page two, and at the end, I had a book. The most I will ever do for a book is have a chapter outline, which I had for *No Worries*. I will admit to doing chapter outlines for books. But that is all the planning I will ever do. Because the unplanned is better than the planned. The spontaneous is better than the rehearsed.

This is the point in the piece where I point out that capitalism is entirely unplanned. You have a phone. Someone had to design the phone, which required chip experts and software experts and hardware experts. Manufacturing takes place somewhere around the world, with different contractors and subcontractors providing various parts for the phone. The materials for those parts were obtained from around the globe. And you know what? There is no phone czar sitting in Washington, D.C. orchestrating all these activities. Each person working for their own benefit, for the mutual benefit of others. Nobody had to be told what to do. That's magic. That is the kaleidoscopic energy of capitalism. Planning an economy has been tried, and it results in chronic shortages and hardship. No one person can anticipate and organize the activities of millions of people, and the result is crushing deprivation. Because the unplanned is better than the planned. The spontaneous is better than the rehearsed.

Bloomberg was a good mayor in many respects, but he was a planner. And I suppose, at Bloomberg L.P., where you have all that recurring terminal revenue coming in, you have that luxury. In particular, I am thinking of the effort to reroute traffic around Times Square by cutting off Broadway and turning the entire place into a giant pedestrian walkabout. Not long after that happened, you had costumed characters and the *desnudas*, along with the return of crime and drug dealing. I watched a midnight showing of *The Crow* in Times Square in 1994 and felt safer then than walking through there today in broad daylight. That's by far the least egregious intervention in New York City that I can think of, but probably the most visible. Things are the way they are for a reason. Leave it the fuck alone.

I do not remember the details of this story, but here is a story: There was a college with a quad where students were walking back and forth to classes. The planners at the college wanted to put in an array of sidewalks to keep the kids from mucking up the grass. *Wait,* the college president said. After a few months, there were paths across the quad where the grass had given way to dirt. That is where they built the sidewalks. This is also known as spontaneous order.

I do not have a high opinion of TV news shows or the people who go on TV news shows, but I recognize that it is a demanding discipline that requires a great deal of flexibility. You have a one-hour program planned out, and then some drunk sets off a car bomb in Omaha. Within seconds, you are talking about Omaha. It is a dynamic environment, and the hosts have to be ready for anything. This is true of media in general: newspapers, radio, and the like. 9/11 happened on a Tuesday. Not sure if you knew this, but all book launches are on Tuesday. Some poor sap had his life's work released the day of 9/11. The thing about chaos is that it's fair; sometimes you just have bad luck.

I planned on doing an entire career in the Coast Guard. God laughed at my plans. I planned on doing an entire career on Wall Street. God laughed at my plans. These days, I have no idea what the hell I am going to do. I am going to do something if it works, and when it stops working, I will do something else. I think this is the right way to live.

CLASS

THE GENERAL FEELING is that people with money are high class and people with no money are low class. This is broadly true, but there are exceptions. I met some rich primates on Wall Street, and I have some family members of very modest means who are the classiest people I know.

So class is not necessarily about money. But I just got off a flight from Nashville to Charlotte where a couple of old hayseeds behind me were playing *Candy Crush* with the sound on, on their iPads. Like a teacher in the summertime: no class. This is why people buy tickets in first class—not for the comfy seats, but to get away from the riffraff picking their toes in coach. I get upgraded to first class fairly often, and I've only sat next to a complete rube there one time. There is something about having and acquiring money—you get a bigger house in a nicer neighborhood, you drive a nicer car, you start hanging out with people with nice houses and nice cars, and you generally don't have to put up with people setting off fireworks in their driveway or leaving Bud Light cans everywhere. The Bud Light can phenomenon is real: If I go on vacation, I tell my travel agent that I don't want to go somewhere where there are going to be Bud Light cans around the pool. That kind of place. I want somewhere where there is deep house thumping softly on the pool speakers, not "Sugar Pie Honey Bunch" playing on a loop at the swim-up bar.

I'm sure you've had this experience where you've walked into an apparel retailer and the offerings are sparse—a few garments on hangers, a couple of pairs of shoes, that's it. Like a YSL store. The lowbrow stores, like Johnston & Murphy, are filled with shit everywhere. You walk into one of these high-class stores, and there is virtually no inventory out on the floor, and everything is neatly folded, and you're like: *I can't afford this.* So you walk out. It's a screening process—those empty stores are intimidating to the riffraff. The type of place where there are no price tags. If you have to ask, you can't afford it. For what it's worth, my favorite clothes in the world (for men and women) are Tom Ford. I'm not at the point in my life where I can afford $1,200 for a pair of sneakers, but I hope to be someday.

And there is a difference between real luxury and aspirational luxury. The luxury goods business is fascinating to me, with its huge gross margins. Aspirational luxury is Coach. There is a Coach store in Myrtle Beach, or more accurately, a Coach outlet, and that is populated by the $120,000-a-year crowd. You buy aspirational luxury, then you make more money, then you do the real luxury. I'd throw Kate Spade in that category, too, and Michael Kors, though that is a step down. A Louis Vuitton bag is a whole different animal. I know next to nothing about this stuff. True story: One of my favorite reads used to be *Departures* magazine by American Express. I'd read it just for the ads. I'd get it in the mail, and take it with me on a flight, and drool over watches and clothes and stuff. Years ago, *The Robb Report* was a big thing too. I find this stuff to be highly motivational—I don't know how you feel about it. Anyway, *Departures* magazine went online and nobody reads it anymore. The articles weren't bad, either. They used to get some legit writers—travel writing is a genre unto itself.

But class is a state of mind. I am building a fancy house in a fancy neighborhood and my table manners are still pretty bad. And I kind of don't care. Not terrible, mind you—I'm not eating with my hands. But I have resisted all attempts to civilize me. But that's not really what class is all about. Class is something very, very intangible, very ephemeral—it's about how you carry yourself, how you act, how you speak. Some kids are born into it—others are not. There was a whole Wall Street firm that catered to this demographic, the *poor, smart, and determined*, that cratered on March 17th, 2008. That was an aggregate loss for the poor, smart, and determined.

Since we're talking about Wall Street, it is pretty much fucking impossible to break into Wall Street as a poor kid these days—unless you get a math degree from Caltech and go to one of the quant firms. But if you are going to be working in debt capital markets at JPMorgan, there is a 98% chance you will grow up in the tri-state area, play lacrosse, and go to an Ivy League school. The open-outcry trading floors were the great democratizers, and that's where I got my start in the industry. If the P. Coast hadn't existed, I'd probably be selling insurance, and that's not an exaggeration. Lots of Wall Street guys in my cohort got their start on the CME, the CBOT, the CBOE, the AMEX, the PHLX, the PCX. Nassim freaking Taleb was a bond options trader on the CBOT. If you want to know where the class hierarchy is, it's in private equity. There is no poor, smart, and determined in private equity. They hire from the best colleges, the best high schools, and the best neighborhoods. I have never met a poor kid in private equity.

I like to dump on Myrtle Beach, and Myrtle Beach definitely has an underworld, but it also has an underground city. There is wealth in Myrtle Beach. Much of it is inherited, in the form of land passed down from generation to generation. But there are some strivers, mostly in real estate and insurance. When I moved there, in 2010, it was moribund, but now it has a real economy made up of people trying really hard. Some of this is the Northern influence, but some of it has to do with the proliferation of opportunities. People are throwing money at each other. It used to be a very economically cyclical place, dependent on tourism, but now it is virtually recession-proof. People work pretty hard. Don't get me wrong, the parking lot at my building is fairly empty on a Friday afternoon, but I remember a day in 2010 when the power went out for 15 minutes and everyone went home. This is part of a larger phenomenon of the North becoming the South and the South becoming the North. The South is rising again. Nashville is a food fight, and it didn't get to be a food fight by people screwing off. There is a Ferrari dealership in Nashville. Ten years ago, you could get a house for $200,000. Now it's a milldog. You can thank the SALT taxes for all this.

Class is really about treating people decently, regardless of any socioeconomic differences. One thing I've noticed when visiting New York is the complete indifference that people will treat wait staff with when going out to dinner. They're not being rude, but they're not being personable either. A high-class person will make the one ounce of effort that it takes to make someone's day a little bit better, and that doesn't necessarily mean a bigger tip. That means making a small personal connection with everyone you meet. Trust me, I'm not always in the mood to be making conversation in the elevator, not at 7:45 in the morning when I have a million things to do queued up in my brain. Basically, don't be self-absorbed. This does not come naturally to me. I spend most of my waking hours thinking about myself, thinking about how to get what I want, and thinking of ways to make more money. I suspect many people are the same.

The best low-class movie I have ever seen was *Boys Don't Cry*, about a transgender woman living in Kansas. They were all poor as shit, and the movie does not disguise or gloss over that fact. If you really want to read about class, read Anton Chekhov's story "The Peasants," about the most anti-communist thing I have ever read. Now, I just told you to read it, and nobody is going to read it, but I highly recommend you read it. In fact, I think we should send a copy to every member of Congress.

I'll add one more thing: I'm not much in favor of taking steps to conceal one's wealth. We all have a moral responsibility to live at our means. *At* our means. If you can afford a palace, buy the palace. I have a friend who never posts vacation pictures on Facebook for fear of offending people. Screw that. For some people, it will cause envy and resentment, but for others it will be aspirational. You care about the latter's opinions, and not the former's opinions. Surround yourself with people who will celebrate your achievements, and everyone else can jump in a lake.

THE 80% SOLUTION

I WRITE A FINANCIAL newsletter, as you may have heard, and I publish it every day. If I wanted to, I could make it perfect—I could wordsmith the shit out of it, I could make it literary as hell, and I could spend three hours copy-editing it, or paying someone to do the same. I could send out the perfect newsletter every day. And you know what? I would probably not make any more money off it.

What I send out is an 80% solution. It typically takes me two hours to write the thing, but if I wanted to be a perfectionist about it, it would take six hours, and it would only be incrementally better. This is called the 80% solution—D for done, and move onto the next thing. If I spent six hours writing each issue of *The Daily Dirtnap*, I wouldn't have time for other things, like this essay, or perhaps another book. There is the occasional typo in the newsletter, and sometimes, someone will give me shit about it, but that is a small price to pay for all the time the 80% solution frees up.

I have worked with some perfectionists, and I can tell you that perfectionism is a disease. I used to be a perfectionist myself. The military mints perfectionists. The rack has to be perfectly made. The shirt has to be perfectly ironed. The shoes have to be perfectly shined. I used to shine my shoes so much that I could read my nametag in them. And you know what it got me? A bunch of Bs in college. I was focused on little shit that didn't matter, instead of the big shit that did matter. That cost me later in life. Let me say that again—perfectionism cost me dearly.

I started to become an 80% solution guy on Wall Street. By necessity. Let's say a customer wanted to sell 676,204 shares of SPY. Now, I could calculate the correct hedge in S&P futures to the contract, which would take me a minute, but I have to hedge this in a matter of seconds. So I hedge with 1,300 S&P e-mini futures, which is off by a little bit, but I will clean it up later. I might lose a couple thousand bucks on my hedge being off, or a might make a couple of thousand bucks on my hedge being off, but the important thing is that I am mostly hedged. The 80% solution. If I sat there with an HP-12C trying to figure out the correct hedge to the contract, I could lose $50,000 or more, as the market moves while I am tapping away on the fucking calculator. So in trading, you quickly become an 80% solution guy.

The hilarious thing is that they teach you the exact opposite in school. In a finance class, you will get a question on the test about hedging with S&P futures, and if you don't get it right to within ten degrees of precision, you get the answer wrong. I teach finance, and I try to keep this in mind when I grade exams. If someone gets the concept right, but flubs the math a little bit, I usually give most of the credit. Now, if you're supposed to sell and you buy, or vice versa, then you get no credit. I want my students to be 80% solution people, too.

Writing is an area where perfectionism runs rampant. I mean, if you're going to publish a book, it *has* to be a perfect book, right? Well, there are typos in all of my books (except *All the Evil of This World*). There are typos in every book. Our friend Nassim used to go thermonuclear on editors for messing with his work. He once said there were 200 typos in *Fooled By Randomness*. Anyway, the typos are not really my job. I'm the 80% solution guy, I write a book which is mostly perfect, and then I give it to a copy editor, who is a perfectionist, who cleans it up. The right people are in the right jobs. The 80% solution guy makes all the money, and the copy editor makes God knows what, maybe $500 for editing a manuscript. Perfectionists always, always make less money.

Now, there are some fields where you must be a perfectionist, like when you are working at NASA. You remember about ten years ago when they crash-landed a spacecraft into Mars because they mixed up the English/metric system? Oops. One line of code can ruin your whole day. I wouldn't be able to function in a job like that—I really couldn't. I think big, in terms of concepts and values and ideas, and someone else's job is to think small. You can probably tell that I don't have a great deal of respect for people who think small. They do have a role in society, but they're not going to be the CEO. There is probably something about personality typology in here, too, but I don't know what I am talking about.

I keep going over this. You have a project, like a writing project. You can have an 80% (or even a 98%) solution in two months, or a 100% solution in a year. Time is life. Get it done and move onto the next project, because every day you're working on the original project is one day closer to death. You are dying while you work. You die a little bit each day. People ask me all the time: *How do you get so much shit done?* It's because I'm an 80% solution guy. Get it done, shit it out there, onto the next thing. I get so much done because I'm dying, and I'm the only one that seems to realize it. This is another way of saying that I am impatient. I am the most impatient person in the world, and I haven't gotten any better. But I think all successful people are impatient. Elon Musk is impatient. Jeff Bezos was impatient. Don't dick around—life is passing you by.

That doesn't mean you put out crap. And my 80% solution is really a 98% solution. This essay, for example. I will give it one pass for editing and typos, and then I hit send. I spend no more than 15 minutes editing these things. So my first pass is usually very high quality, which isn't true for everyone. When I went to AWP in Kansas City and I was talking with indie publishers, and I realized I was looking at two-plus-year publication lead times, I was like, *fuck you, I will do it myself*. I can do quality control and put out an even better product in less time. And it's not like you, the publisher, is going to help with marketing or distribution, outside of maybe getting one or two reviews. The publishing world is full of perfectionists—there are people who will literally agonize over a semicolon. Blow me. That is the semicolon of death. I mean, the publishing industry does serve an important function as a gatekeeper—a book that is traditionally published is usually good, as in, free of errors and published well, as opposed to the janky self-published POS that your neighbor just put on Amazon that 20 people will buy to be nice and no one will read. It is true that most self-published books are crap. It is true that most traditionally published books are good, as in, professionally done. You don't see self-published books in the chain bookstores. But occasionally there is one that breaks through. Were you aware that *The Martian*, by Andy Weir, was a self-published book? He had it up for 98 cents on Amazon. It was in no stores, got no reviews, and no media coverage. It was a good book, and people find good books.

I am not a perfectionist about anything, not even cleaning the litter box. I'll get most of the pee and poo, but I'm not going to spend an extra 60 seconds chasing around the one tiny turd left over. It can sit there another day. I am not a perfectionist about washing my car, even the Corvette. I could be out there all day with a toothbrush making it perfect. Nope, I'll hire another perfectionist to do that. Strangely, the one thing I am a perfectionist about is music. If I make one small beatmatching error while I am playing out at a party, it burns me. It will ruin my whole night. I will spend hours recording a mix to make it amazing. Everything else in my life—"fuck it."

Procrastination will destroy your dreams one day at a time. You know what else will? Perfectionism. My two favorite words in the English language are *good enough*. Think big. Move fast. Create. Don't dick the dog.

OBSESSIVE-
COMPULSIVE

Just over 2% of the population has obsessive-compulsive disorder, known colloquially as OCD. I had pretty severe OCD for a while from about 2003-2013. I was a door-locker. When I left the house in the morning, I would lock the door, walk about 20 steps, turn around to make sure the door was locked, go back and get in the car, drive about 500 yards, turn around and make sure the door was locked, confirm that it was indeed locked, get back in the car, drive about a mile or two, have feelings of crippling anxiety that the door wasn't locked, go back and check the door, and so forth. On an average day, it would take me a full 45 minutes to go through this process before I could go to work. I got smart and started locking the door in a specific pattern: 2-4, 3-6-3, 7-10, and that worked for a while, but then I didn't even trust myself to do it correctly. It was a real handicap.

OCD is part of a class of what is known as anxiety disorders. Hoarding, by the way, is also an anxiety disorder. And the problem with anxiety disorders is that they're basically untreatable with medication. There is medication, and it works—a little. In the best-case scenario, there is a

40% reduction in harmful activity. The best way to get rid of an anxiety disorder is to get rid of the source of anxiety. But that is a lot harder than it sounds. I will say that my OCD got significantly better when I left Lehman in 2008. I would not allow myself to believe that my job was causing me anxiety on that scale. In retrospect, it was obvious. As an ETF trader, I was getting bombs dropped on me on a daily basis, and living in constant fear of compliance and regulation. But it wasn't just the job—I had anxiety about everything. I have written before about ways to combat anxiety.

I had a psychiatrist appointment recently, and the doc asked me about my OCD. I told him that it was about 98% better, and he said, *without medication?* And I said, yes, without medication. He said that was exceedingly rare. Basically, I had to come up with some Jedi mind tricks to fight it. After I left the house, I would focus on a problem at work, and I would start thinking about it, which would crowd out any thoughts about whether or not I had locked the door. By the time I remembered the door, I was a half hour away, and it was too late to go back. I would feel anxiety about it, but there was nothing I could do. And I would get home at night, and inevitably, the door would be locked. I have never, not once, forgotten to lock the door.

Most people don't really know what OCD is, and are glib about it. People think it is OCD when you're at the gas pump and you have to get the dollar amount to a round number. That is not OCD. That is perfectionism, or something else. People confuse the two all the time. Real OCD is not funny, not a joke at all, and people suffer badly from it. There was a guy at Lehman who was a compulsive handwasher. Every time I was in the men's room, he was in there, washing his hands, in the same repetitive motion. He must have spent two hours a day washing his hands.

Let me tell you how this works, and why obsessions and compulsive behavior exists. You have something that is causing you anxiety, say a lawsuit or something like that. As a defense mechanism, your mind decides to focus on some small thing as a distraction from the bigger thing that you have anxiety about. It is all about control. If you can control how clean your hands are, or whether the door is locked, then you cannot think about the lawsuit for a while. It is a distraction technique. So the real way to fight OCD is through talk therapy, and to work through the big things that you actually have anxiety about. I talked about the door-locking with my therapist, and he told me that working at Lehman was the cause, the big anxiety that I was avoiding. I didn't listen to him. I said, *no way, I love my job, that can't possibly be it*. But that was it. Like I said, I am 98% better, and that 2% still gets me. I still check the door—once—when I leave the house. If the compulsion flares up again, I will know that there is something bigger that I am worried about, and that I had better do something about it.

There are examples of pediatric OCD. And I had it. When I was five, I had an obsession with how the seam in my sock lined up with my toes. During the school day, in kindergarten, if I felt the seam out of place, I would take my shoes off to fix it, and then I would get in trouble for taking my shoes off in class, which would get me a beating at home, which was obviously the source of the OCD. Pediatric OCD is about 60% less common than adult OCD, but it is usually a harbinger of worse things down the road.

Hoarding, as you know, can be debilitating—and dangerous. People who hoard objects are more than just nostalgic—they have memories associated with objects, and they feel that if they discard the object, they will lose the memory forever. Of course, over time, this morphs into shopping at yard sales, and acquiring other people's objects, and co-opting their memories as your own. It's an anxiety disorder—the purpose is to distract from some larger issue. They made TV shows about this 20 years ago, which were unhelpful, sort of a window into the depths of this mental illness and a contest to see whose house was the grossest. Not much different than a freakshow at a carnival. These people deserve our sympathy, but out of all the manifestations of OCD, hoarding is the most difficult to break. The afflicted individuals generally do not want help, and the worst thing to do to a hoarder is to throw their shit out. Pandemonium.

How do you know if you have OCD? If you're engaging in compulsive behavior and you want to stop. You know that it's harmful, you know that it's impacting your life, and you really wish you could stop checking the door. If you're engaging in repetitive behaviors and you don't want to stop, then you have something else. It is possible that you have autism spectrum disorder, for one. People on the autism spectrum arrange objects sequentially, engage in ritualized, repetitive behavior, but crucially, either they aren't aware that they are doing it, or they believe that the behavior is functional. If they don't want to stop, it's not OCD. By the way, the whole field of psychology is dedicated to helping people with certain behaviors stop doing those behaviors. That's why it's called *behavioral* health. If you're a PhD or an LCSW and you can't reliably help people from harming themselves, then you're just bad at your job. Good therapists can help people with these sorts of things. I will add that addiction and OCD have a lot in common, and these two things naturally co-occur in lots of people.

I will probably never stop checking the doors. There exists that kernel of anxiety that someone my break into my house and steal shit, or my cats might get out. That would be the worst thing in the world, so I take out insurance on the worst thing in the world by checking the door every day. Behind all of these compulsions is a kernel of truth. And also lots and lots of trauma, as I mentioned earlier. If you have OCD, I'd advise against the medications—they don't do much anyway—but get a good therapist who specializes in OCD, or addictions, or both. And then you actually have to put in the work. The good news: you can beat it if you try! I did. And there is a lot of letting go involved, which is hard to do.

WHY SOME PEOPLE GET RICH AND OTHERS DON'T

I'M SURE YOU'VE had this experience where you see someone who is a dummy who has lots of money. Or you know someone who is a genius who is scratching by on $60,000 a year.

I have thousands of stories. Maybe more. I'll give you one—there was a derivatives sales trader at Lehman, a rotund fellow with a greasy lunch-counter mustache, who allegedly took the Series 7 exam seven times, failing each time, and eventually applied for a waiver because of a real or imagined learning disability. He was also addicted to painkillers. But when it came to trading options, the guy could really swing the lumber. Especially on the day that the new LEAPs got listed—his genius clients would come in with a few thousand contracts and pick us off on a mispriced vol surface. He made millions of dollars of commissions in the process. I have no idea where he is today—possibly dead—but at the time, he was very, very rich.

Richer than me. I got a 96 on the Series 7, had a business degree, and a fancy math education in university. Lunch-counter guy probably wouldn't know vega convexity if it punched him in the nose. But he was getting paid, and I wasn't. And it's not that I wasn't doing well at my job.

So like I said, I spend a lot of time thinking about this. I know rich dumb people and smart poor people, and the one thing that most rich people have in common is that they *care about money*. As in, they want to make a lot of it. The first step in making money is to want to make money. I wrote about this in *No Worries*, and it actually is true. If you don't want to make money, you probably aren't going to get any money. Right? I mean, on rare occasions, you might fall ass-backwards into money, winning $200,000 on a scratch-off, but that is the exception rather than the rule. If you want money, you have to go out and get it. And some people are better at that than others.

There is a Hebrew word that means "to have a nose for money," and I think I know what it is, but there is no chance I can spell it, so I won't include it here. Some people have it. And some people care very deeply about making money, like me. I am always looking for ways to sell more subscriptions, to take on new business ventures, to invest in hedge funds or startups, to trade futures. It doesn't always work, but I am never complacent. There are not too many rich people who are complacent. Sure, they might get complacent eventually, but that is usually the point at which they stop making money. They have enough. And there is nothing wrong with that—I know many people who made their $40 million and retired to play golf. Maybe if I got to $40 million, I would do the same thing, except for the golf. "Enough" is a different amount for different people. For Jack Bogle, $20 million was enough. The guy was responsible for maybe the number-one financial innovation of the 20th century, outside of perhaps the 30-year fixed rate residential mortgage, and he could have been a billionaire many times over. But he had enough, and he wrote a book called *Enough*, and he said that everyone else should have enough, too. He had a real aversion to accumulating wealth, like it was immoral or something. Well, screw that guy. I don't feel that way at all. And no, Jack Bogle didn't like me, either.

There is an element of rapacity to shareholder capitalism, I'll admit. Elon Musk wants bigger and bigger pay packages, at the expense of current shareholders. He needs the money! He wants to go to Mars! You might wonder why a billionaire needs all that money; well, in some cases, they do. I have a hard time coming up with ways to spend a billion dollars, but maybe I do not have a big enough imagination. I don't like yachts—I get seasick. I suspect I would also get sick in space, and there are only so many houses you can buy. But there are things I still want, even after building my dream house—I still want the pied-à-terre in Miami, and maybe I will get there someday. I have a friend who once said to me that the most powerful thing in the world is liquid net worth. Not houses, not hard assets, but cash and marketable securities that you can turn into cash, because cash is a big pile of options. Houses are great, but better than houses is a bunch of cash and stocks and bonds. That is a mistake that a lot of people make—they get rich, and then they put it into a bunch of illiquid stuff, and they lose optionality.

All of this is a roundabout way of saying that you should be greedy. That word. But the word "greed" implies a zero-sum view of the world—I have more and you have less. If you create something or produce something, and you make money incidental to that, then you've done something admirable. People usually draw the line at money managers, saying that they are socially useless. *They don't produce anything*, they say—*they simply move money from one pile to the next*. Well, that is actually an important social function these days, especially since fewer and fewer people are evaluating securities, owing to all the indexing. The indexers are the ones who are immoral, free-riding off the efforts of others to keep the market efficient. Also, as you know, the asset management business is not easy—people fail all the time. Try it for yourself and find out.

Every once in a while, you run into these people who go into business and fail because they simply don't charge enough. Why don't they charge enough? Well, the reasons are complex, but at the core of it, they just don't feel as if they're worth it. It's a self-esteem issue more than anything. Philosophy has a lot to say about this, too—you should charge as much as you possibly can, as much as the market will bear, and not a penny less. There is a field of study devoted to this, and it's called microeconomics. If you charge too much, you won't have any business. If you charge too little, you are leaving money on the table. If you charge too little out of some hangup you have about making too much money, then I don't know what to tell you. I was friends with a home design guy (someone who is a step down from an architect) who was charging $50 an hour. He was complaining that his phone was ringing off the hook, that he had so much business that he could not keep up. I told him that he should charge $100 an hour. He actually sorta took my advice and raised his price to $75/an hour—problem solved. He had more money, and he didn't have his hair on fire. What was keeping him from charging more? It was purely an issue of self-esteem. And that's the thing about capitalism—doing business is a positive statement that you are worth it.

I'll say that some people are not really cut out for business, and those people should stay in academia or government. Go into work at nine, navigate the bureaucracy, take a long lunch, head home at 2:30, life is good. It's a nice life, but what you have done is traded away your upside for safety and security. And the people I hang around with—the people who care about money—would not trade away their upside for anything. I heard a story about a lottery winner in New Jersey who won $20 million. He started a business and turned it into $200 million. A lot of people were sour grapes about that, and said that he was simply lucky, and yes, he was lucky, but he had an idea, and he previously didn't have the capital to deploy, and suddenly he did, and as it turns out, he was pretty good at business. And the amazing thing was that $20 million wasn't enough—he had the same amount that Jack Bogle had, and freerolled it into an enormous fortune.

I think it's been long enough since Bogle passed to dump on him, but it's hard to come up with someone who has done more damage to the world with their poisonous ideology, and the damage has been done in such a way that it can never be unwound. The good news is that they will never make another Jack Bogle. You see these memes on Facebook about Edison and Tesla, and how Edison was such a bastard because he tried to monetize all of his inventions, while Nikola Tesla was just a starry-eyed idealist who gave his ideas away from free. You know where I fall on that debate.

So do you want to make money, or not? If you do, just understand that it's a lifetime of struggle. But it's worth it, and even if you don't have much in the way of material needs, you can always give it away if you want. And that's the really fun part.

SPIRITUALITY

THERE IS A saying: *Religion is for people who are afraid of going to hell. Spirituality is for people who have already been there.*

I went to church regularly until age 15. I enjoyed it. After age 15, I started playing organ in church. So I have always been around church.

I also went to the Academy chapel in college, and went to church on-and-off until about age 24, at which point I got really fucking busy, and I didn't go back for 12 years. When I went back, in South Carolina, I saw things that I didn't see before. I saw people who wanted to be *seen* as being devout, rather than actually being devout. Politicking. And after sitting in Sunday morning services about six or seven times, the priest took me back to his office and told me that I had to give him 10%. Top line! Pre-tax! At the time, I was making about $350,000 a year, and there was no freaking way I was going to give this dude $35,000. So that about did it for church for me, and I haven't been back.

Maybe I just haven't gone to the right church. Maybe there is a church out there for me. Could be, but keep in mind that I am an Episcopalian, and the Episcopalian church today is not the white-shoe Episcopalian church of George H. W. Bush. It is very far left, politically. At my mom's behest, I accompanied her to an Episcopalian service about five or six years ago. It was all about how rich people are going to hell. Haven't been back.

So I think it is good to separate religion from spirituality. You don't need to sit in a building with a bunch of other people on Sunday morning to have a relationship with God. And before we go any further, I use the word "God" to refer to a higher power—you can substitute any word you like. I call him God for convenience. People go to church for all sorts of reasons. Some go for a sense of community. Some go to meet people. Some go for their kids. Some go because they're afraid of some supernatural consequences down the line. It's been my experience that only a small percentage of people who go to church do so to have a deeper relationship with God.

I don't have the statistics at my command, but I suspect that smarter people tend to be disbelievers. They are skeptics. They spend their entire lives trying to prove the nonexistence of God, which, from a philosophical standpoint, is very difficult to do. I was one of those skeptics, and then I discovered that life is full of miracles, if your eyes are open. I have experienced many such miracles—the first was in 2006. My ass has been saved so many times in succession that it can't possibly be a coincidence. For example: I was in New York City last week for meetings and media appearances. I was walking down Madison Avenue, and I tripped over a whammy stick, one of those construction barrier-things, that had been folded sideways across the road. I flew through the air and faceplanted—right in front of a car. I looked up and saw a tire two feet from my head. That is grace. I suggest you read some books about the study of near-death experiences if you are still skeptical. I'm not proselytizing—I'm just telling you that, for a period of time, I considered myself to be an agnostic, and then I saw the proof.

When I was an agnostic, I believed in the power of my rational, scientific mind. So, a few things happened. First, I started to realize that even the most rational people are truly irrational—we are emotional beings, first and foremost. Then, I began to realize that the human mind, even at the upper reaches of IQ, is just not all that powerful. I

SPIRITUALITY

believe there are phenomena which are unexplainable and beyond the comprehension of any human brain. I believe that there is a vast spiritual world within and beyond our material world, and I believe that what we do in our spiritual realm is far more important than that we will do materially. That's not to say that you shouldn't fight for the extra $50,000 in your bonus—that's important, too—but it's trivial compared to our preparation for all of eternity. All things in their place.

Some people see God in the intricacy of a spiderweb, or in the dusky hues of an evening sky, or in the rolling waves crashing on a beach. I see God in the spirit of my cats—I have Xenia cuddling up next to me as I write. I hear God in music—many people can attest to having a religious experience at a concert or in a nightclub. I see God in the achievements of man—skyscrapers, factories, or Amazon.com. I see God in the kaleidoscopic energy of capitalism. You don't need to know how it works, only that it works, which applies to spirituality as well. Capitalism is an unexplainable phenomenon—you can't prove *why* capitalism works. A superior system would be one constructed by man's mind, right? As it turns out, that particular system unleashes the horrors of the worst of humanity.

What I'm talking about here is faith. Faith is belief without evidence. Well, some people need to see the evidence. Do you need the evidence that a microwave will cook your food when you push the start button? And if it doesn't work, do you need evidence that someone qualified to fix it will show up to your house and fix it? We are dependent on our cars and microwaves and espresso makers, in much the same way that we are dependent on God. Most people don't like to have a dependency on anything. They are independent, or so they think. When I am driving, I depend on other drivers not to swerve into my lane. I depend on the airline to ensure that the pilots are trained and the crew is present and the bags are loaded and the plane is cleaned and checked and inspected so it can take off on time, so I don't miss my connection. We are all interconnected, and interdependent. It's funny—one of my heroes during that 12-year period away from spirituality was Penn Jillette, who wrote an article on cnn.com about being a libertarian atheist. I don't know what the hell I am these days, but I am not a libertarian, or a Republican, or a Democrat. Uncategorizable. My basic philosophy of life is that the hard way is usually the easy way, and the easy way is usually the hard way.

Which brings me to the subject of prayer. Some people say that you should leave your shoes under the bed so that you can hit your knees in the morning and pray. I don't do this. I did this for a while, but it felt inauthentic, so I stopped. If prayer is a way of communicating with God, I do it on an ad-hoc basis, like the other morning when I was in my home office and the deluge of all deluges poured down from the sky. That was a spiritual moment. I grab time with God in fits and starts, and it works for me. I do occasionally have those foxhole prayers: *Please, God, let me get out of this jam this one time, and I'll never do it again.* I think everyone has those. As long as those aren't your only prayers, I think you're fine.

Up until this essay, I have been quiet, even taciturn about my spirituality. People get touchy about this stuff, and they don't talk about it. Well, I am talking about it. I mentioned God in passing in my commencement speech at Coastal Carolina University in 2022, realizing fully that some people might be offended by it, but I didn't care. What I said was that God has a bigger imagination than I do. When I got out of the psych ward in 2006, the only thing I asked from God is that I wouldn't kill myself and would maybe keep my job. Think of all the things that have happened since then. Successful businesses, teaching, speaking, DJing, five books, writing op-eds, and much more to come. The best I could have asked for in 2006 was that I would continue to eke out a living at Lehman Brothers and pay my mortgage. God had a bigger imagination than I did, and he has a bigger imagination for you too. God laughs at our plans, the utter futility of them, which is why I turn my will and my life over to his care without reservation.

These are words that I couldn't have imagined myself writing in 2001. How could 9/11 happen in God's world, I thought? What I didn't see was that grace was present on that day, too—even my own life was spared. I don't have good memories of those 12 years. And it is one thing to believe in God, but another thing altogether to trust God. That is the next level in the game. God hasn't given me anything I can't handle, and he won't with you, either.

NEVER ENOUGH

How do you stay hungry when you have everything you need?

This is a phenomenon: People will continue to grow and learn and get paid and promoted up until the point at which they are *comfortable*, at which point they will stop growing and rest on their laurels, sit on the couch and eat Harvest Cheddar SunChips. For some people, that happens when they make $100 million, for others, $1 million, and for still others, $100,000. *Life is good. Instead of hustling, I'm going to watch football this weekend and zone out.*

Not that there is anything wrong with that, in its place. It is always good to take a moment and enjoy your success. But if you don't grow, you die. I've seen a lot of people do well and then get complacent, and it doesn't have a happy ending.

Little-known fact about me: When I was at Lehman Brothers in 2007, I tried to switch from trading ETFs to treasury bonds. Under a cloak of secrecy, I went upstairs and talked to the co-heads of rates trading and pitched them on the idea of me trading part of the yield curve. They entertained the idea seriously, but said that pretty much every seat was occupied at that point. They offered to make me a desk strategist instead, but that wasn't what I wanted—I wanted to trade bonds. So I went back downstairs and continued to sling ETFs in the salt mines. But even at that point in my career, I was willing to try something new.

One of the reasons I did this was because I saw the increasing automation happening in the equity world, and one day that automation would claim my job. It wasn't happening in the bond market at that point, so I figured I could stay a few years ahead of technological advancement if I traded something else. Also, I would learn something new, which would be fantastic, and make me much more marketable. I'm really sorry it didn't work out. I also liked the guys on the treasury desk personally, and thought it would be a good fit. I was 33 years old at the time.

But you see some people who are in a buggy-whip runoff business, and their plan is just to try to stick around as long as possible and ride it to zero, hopefully somewhere close to retirement age. That usually isn't how it works out. You get to age 47, you get riffed, and you have no marketable skills. This is how most people become real estate agents, actually. A lot of people who become real estate agents are people who got spit out the bottom of something else. It wasn't their lifelong ambition to become a real estate agent. And the world needs real estate agents, but even that business is going to be disintermediated eventually. So the conclusion here is that you have to be adaptable, and constantly changing, and always learning to survive in a capitalist economy. Some people do this better than others.

But beyond trying to stay ahead of obsolescence, you should learn and grow... because it is good to learn and grow. And you should try to make more and more money... because it is good to make more and more money. You know what sounds like the worst thing in the world? Getting lucky at age 25, making $50 million, and having nothing to do for the rest of your life. I wouldn't wish that fresh hell upon anyone. Of course, to a lot of people, that sounds pretty good. Make enough money so you don't have to work, and then don't work. Everyone has their number, I suppose.

This is the point at which I bring up John Bogle again, the inventor of the index fund and the founder of Vanguard. At his death, as said, Bogle was only worth $20 million—incomprehensible. His counterparts, like Ned and Abby Johnson at Fidelity, are worth tens of billions. Bogle simply didn't want the money. In fact, as I mentioned, he wrote a book about it in 2002, called *Enough*, which said that we should all be satisfied with what we have and not work for any more. It would be one thing if these were simply the oddball rantings of a fuzzchin philosopher, but this was a real book published by a real publisher which told people not to make any money, and that we should be satisfied with enough.

I cannot even begin to describe the profound philosophical differences I had with Bogle. In fact, if I were to write a rebuttal to that book, it would be called *Never Enough*. It's not simply about the money—for God's sake, if you don't want the money, give it away. Really, what it's about is growth and progress. With every action you take, you're either moving towards death or further away from death—but never standing still. To simply exist is to be moving towards death. What are you contributing to the world? Your contributions do not necessarily have to be financial. If you want to make a pile of money and do philanthropy for the rest of your life, then great! If you want to make a pile of money and then go down to the country club to drink at 11 a.m., not great. I feel the Gordon Gekko speech coming on: *Greed, in all of its forms—greed for life, for money, for love, for knowledge—has marked the upward surge of mankind...* That index fund you own in your IRA was created by a guy who didn't want any of it. And, of course, the core philosophy behind indexing is that the average is better than the great. And maybe for a lot of people it is. Not for me. Just because it's hard to beat the market, doesn't mean you shouldn't try. Hard things are worth doing, you know.

Does anyone *need* a billion dollars? Well, in the case of Elon Musk, he actually does—he needs it to go to Mars. He will spend it all to get there. That's pretty ambitious. Maybe there are billionaires who are not too ambitious. Maybe they will donate it to children's hospitals. Maybe they will bequeath it to their shiftless offspring. It's not up to us to tell them how to dispose of it. It is, after all, private property.

Greed for knowledge. I went back to grad school at age 46 to pursue a degree in writing from the Savannah College of Art and Design. This, while I was running two businesses and doing a radio show at the same time. I finished my MFA three years later, and let me just say that there was really no reason for it, other than greed for knowledge. I'm not getting paid more because I got an MFA. It's not really getting me published anywhere. All I got out of it was knowledge, which is good enough. And it was life changing—it turned me from an amateur writer into a professional writer, and my goal, now, for the rest of my life, is to publish a book a year. Writers write, you know—that is the one thing I learned from that program. And I would absolutely do it all over again.

There is never enough life, enough love, enough knowledge, enough money, and don't let anyone tell you otherwise. That's the leper's bell of a second-rate intellect approaching. Don't ever let anyone tell you should be satisfied with what you have, at any age or stage of your life. If you're not going forward, if you're not constantly challenging yourself, you're going backwards. Never get comfortable. Never get complacent. The most important decision you will ever make in your life is what to do with the next 24 hours.

CREATIVITY IS WORK

I AM A PRETTY creative guy. Ten million words written, hundreds of hours of music recorded, radio, podcasts—you get the picture. A word that people like to use nowadays is *content*. I dislike this word. Like, would you say that Jeff Koons produces content? No, you would say that he is an artist and that he produces art. I don't think my books are content—I think they are literature. And even these essays are not content. There is an artistry and a craft that goes into them. I have been called a "content machine." I would rather be called an art machine.

Now that we've got the semantics out of the way, some people create a lot and most people create nothing at all. There's nothing wrong with that. Most people are not creative people. But even creatives are not continuously creative.

There are days when I have nothing to say. I find that I have nothing to say about politics or political thought anymore—I have given up trying to proselytize people. Some people make a very good living preaching to the converted. That seems very boring. Yes, they have influence, but it is the wrong sort of influence. People cannot be persuaded until they are ready to hear the message, and often they aren't ready to hear the message when enjoying great prosperity. So it is all noise. I could play that game if I wanted to. And in a way, I do. My writings are full of ideas, but I soft-sell them to the point where they are unrecognizable, persuasive brainworms that, bit by bit, chip away at people's intransigence. You can't argue with people about politics. You can't argue with people about ethics. But upstream from politics and ethics is philosophy, and when you're talking philosophy, you're talking about reason and logic. In another life, I would have been a philosophy professor, but I like big houses.

There is a saying: *I only write when inspiration strikes, but fortunately it strikes at 8 a.m. every morning.* Writers write. Painters paint. If you've ever run into a writer who's always "working" on a book, and has been for ten years, and can't seem to finish it, that is not a real writer. That is a writer who waits for inspiration to strike. I never got the Stephen King book on writing, but I gather from the book that he basically treats it as a job. If you write 1,000 words a day, you'll be done with a book in two-and-a-half months, which is not a lot. Spend a couple of hours writing, go to lunch, go swim in the pool, go walk the dog, and recharge your brain for tomorrow when you can write another 1,000 words. I am actually not that disciplined—I write in spurts. I will go for a week or two when I'm writing 3,000 words a day, and then take a month or two off. But I get to the same place in the end. I have an artist friend who is very prolific, creating 100–200 works of art a year. He has his routine—he works at night until the wee hours. I write in the morning and the evening, but not in the afternoon. In college, I fancied myself one of those tortured soul writer-types, tapping away at stories at 2 a.m. I do know a woman who took ten years to write a book, but it was a big project, and it turned out to be one hell of a book, reviewed in the *New York Times* and all that. No freaking way I could stay focused on something for ten years—I need instant gratification.

A thousand words a day. One painting a week. One song a month. I think a lot of reasons creatives don't create is because they are unable to break down a big project into smaller, bite-sized pieces. A book is made up of 12 chapters. So write a chapter. Too hard? A chapter is 150 paragraphs. Write a paragraph. Write a sentence. Write a word. Staring at the blank document in Microsoft Word is pointless. I don't often get stuck, but when I do, sometimes I'll just write nonsense, like, *the quick brown fox jumps over the lazy dog*, and then it will remind me of a story about a dog, and then I am off and running. You don't think, then write—you write, then think. That is true of all creative endeavors. I bet if you ask most artists, they don't really have an idea of how a painting is going to turn out when they start. I know for a fact that music producers have no idea what a song is going to sound like when they open the project file. When I write a story, I have no idea how it is going to end. I make it up as I go along. You write, then think. When you stop writing, you stop thinking. No, it's not going to be perfect. You go back and edit and clean it up later. But I don't write with my brain—I write with my hands. I've told people that if my hands ever got chopped off in some horrific farm equipment accident, I'd be finished as a writer. I should take out an insurance policy on my hands.

Part of being a creative is throwing shit out. Not everything I write (or play) is good. In fact, prior to writing this piece, I got halfway through two others and deleted them. Maybe I should delete this one. I've spent an entire afternoon recording a DJ mix, and then shitcanned it. I can't go back and read my old books, because I will find fault with them. I just have to accept that that was the best job that I could do at the time, with the information I had available to me. And part of being a creative is knowing that not everything you do is going to be perfect, and accepting that. This is no business for perfectionists. I've known music producers who can't stop fucking with a track, twiddling this or that, trying to get it perfect, and the next thing you know, six months have gone by, and it's still not done. You know what's better than perfect? Done. There are very few pieces I've written that would have benefitted greatly from a complete teardown. I am not a perfectionist. Even the *New York Times* makes errors. They make so many errors, there is a Twitter account dedicated to them.

CREATIVITY IS WORK

The thing I enjoy writing the most is short stories. They are also the hardest. Imagination is like an air conditioner in the summertime that is struggling to keep up, and then you end up with a $500 electric bill. It consumes as much energy as an AI data center. So even though I love writing short stories, I dread them—they just take so much out of me, mentally and emotionally. Eighty percent of people who write fiction cheat—they're actually writing about their own experiences, just changing the names. I have done that once, and only once. When I write fiction, I write *fiction*—it is pure imagination. By the way, the vast majority of movies you watch these days are based on books. It was not the movie studio or the director with imagination, it was the writer—like Annie Proulx out in Wyoming writing about gay cowboys, with *Brokeback Mountain*—that was the basis for the acclaimed motion picture. The creatives are doing all the heavy lifting. Ludlum with *Bourne*, Herbert with *Dune*, even *Requiem for a Dream* by Hubert Selby Jr.—all books. Someone had an idea, a vision, wrote 1,000 words a day, and it became part of the cultural lexicon.

Creativity is not genius. It is work. You have as many good ideas as I do, but you're spending your weekends at little kid birthday parties.

LIVING IN THE PRESENT

IN MY OFFICE, I have a clock. The clock says "NOW" on it. The purpose of the NOW clock is to remind me that the only thing that matters is what I do in this moment—not the future, and not the past. I actually toyed with the idea of taking the minute and hour hands off the clock, leaving only the second hand, to drive the point home even further.

Living in the present is a good thing to do. Most people spend half their time projecting into the future, and half their time dwelling on the past, and absolutely zero time in the present moment. That's not to say you shouldn't plan for the future—it's good to make plans—but when people think about the future, they're typically projecting, and 99% of all projections are negative. When people think about the future, they have anxiety, and they engage in catastrophic thinking. This terrible thing will happen, or that terrible thing will happen, *I'm going to lose my job, my kid is going to get abducted, my house is going to get robbed*—very few people look at the future with anticipation. It's always dread.

Before we go any further, let me tell you that I do a terrible job of

LIVING IN THE PRESENT

living in the present. I am either living in the wreckage of the past or the wreckage of the future. This, in spite of the NOW clock. I find myself thinking of some awkward date I had in high school, spilling wine on someone's shoe at a holiday party, or lamenting big losses I've had trading in my personal account. I have made a million mistakes in my life, and I've probably rehashed each of them a thousand times. Most of this involves broken relationships, things I could or should not have said, or things I could or should not have done. But you can't unfuck them whores. What's in the past, is past. *The past is history, the future's a mystery, and today is a gift, which is why they call it the present.* Super corny—but true.

You know who is the best in the world at living in the present? Yankees shortstop Derek Jeter. Those who played with Jeter said that the guy had absolutely *no memory*—if he struck out, he would forget it immediately, and move on to the next plate appearance. If he made an error on the field, he didn't dwell on it, and would concentrate on the next play. Derek Jeter had over 3,400 hits in his career, but notably he never really had extended slumps. The vast majority of hitters, after having a few golden sombreros, begin pressing at the plate, making the slump even worse. The failure of the last plate appearance led to the failure of the next plate appearance—they were serially correlated. Jeter had a fresh approach every time, which is why he is considered one of the greatest baseball players in history. But it's not just baseball—talk to any professional athlete: basketball players, football players, and they will talk about the importance of moving on after a bad play and concentrating on the task at hand. Living in the present isn't just about your mental health—it's about operating at peak performance.

I've done some things in my life that make me cringe in horror. What is the purpose of your past? The purpose of your past is to help you learn from it, and not make the same mistakes again. Well, duh. If you keep screwing up the same stuff over and over again, you are a dunce—or it means you have an addiction. Me, I don't make the same mistakes twice, but I keep finding ways to make new ones. But no, I don't look at my past in horror anymore, and I don't let my past define me. It's part of who I am, but not the person I will be going forward. My conduct has not always been unimpeachable, which is a fancy way of saying that up until about 2006, I was a scumbag. Do I wish I could do things differently? Absolutely. But you can't put the toothpaste back in the tube.

Meanwhile, the future can be a dark place, and I don't want to go in there without a 4×4 on my shoulder like The Rock in *Walking Tall*. In my mind, I have been broke, bankrupt, arrested, and humiliated—but none of it has ever actually happened. Life continues to get better day after day. I put myself through all this torture *in my head*. For no reason! We all do it. I know you do it. It is completely unproductive. I could power a ten-terawatt power plant with the amount of mental energy I spend living in the future. Long ago, I used to calculate probabilities of bad things happening. I'd say, *there is a 1 in 100 chance of this bad thing happening, and a 1 in 100 chance of this bad thing happening, so there is a 1 in 10,000 chance that I will end up in jail*. This was not really a good use of brain space. I don't do that anymore, though I still worry, which is also unproductive. By the way, the bad things that we are always catastrophizing about never happen. That's not to say that bad things don't happen, but it's never the things that we are worrying about.

So the goal is to not live in the future, and to not live in the past, but to live in the present. I'm sure you've had these moments in your life where you're on vacation in Riviera Maya and you walk out on your hotel room balcony in the morning, sit in a chair, and watch the sunrise. And for one fleeting moment—you are living in the present. You are enjoying this moment for what it is. Imagine if you could live your entire life like that? Not sitting in a chair in Mexico, but with that peace and serenity that comes from living in the present. I'm making it sound like it's easy, but it's not. There are monks and religious people who spend their entire lives trying to live in the moment. I suppose this is where meditation comes in, but I have never been any good at

LIVING IN THE PRESENT

meditation—I have a very busy brain, and ten seconds into it, my mind is off and running. Whatever works for you.

At the present moment, I am sitting on the couch in the living room in my new house, with my cats Tars, Yellow, and Zeus. I also have the Yankees game on. Am I living in the present? Not really—I owe a lot of money on this house and some ding-dong just canceled their subscription, so in my mind, there was a tiny increase in the probability that I will go bankrupt someday. I also have some other things on my mind at present. But I have had moments. Last night, I was in bed, listening to the rain on the roof of the house—that was cool. I will tell you the story of the first time I ever spent any time in the present—it was in 2009, and I was visiting a bank customer down in the World Financial Center, and when I walked out of the building, the sun was shining, and I was listening to my iPod. I even remember the track: "Landmine Hopscotch" by Shiloh. And there was something about that day, the temperature, the wind, the sun, the music, and for a few seconds—I was present in the moment. I never had many moments like that in my 30s. In my 40s, they became more common. I'd say that today I spend about 20% of my time living in the present, up from 0% 18 years ago. I am not the Dalai Lama—I will never get to 100%. My mind is often troubled. But I am much better than I used to be.

I will give you one piece of advice for living in the present: practice gratitude. If you are spending time thinking about things you don't have, or things you want, you will be living in the future. If you are grateful for the things you have—your house, your marriage, your kids, your job, your health—you will be centered in the moment. So make a gratitude list—write down all the things that you are grateful for. Spend an hour on it, and don't leave anything out. See how you feel afterwards. That's all I got.

RISK

"PEOPLE WHO DON'T take risks work for people who do." That quote is attributed to Linda from Substack. Someone forwarded it to me, and it hit me over the head like a flying can of corned beef hash.

I hate to break it to you sell-side traders, but you don't really take risk. Yes, it is bad if you lose money, but the bank will frequently tolerate losses for a long period of time before your ID doesn't work. If one desk is losing money over here, another desk is making money over there. Your bonus is sometimes dependent on how much money you make, but frequently not. If you were in business for yourself, you would have tapped out a long time ago. The hedge fund guys are risk-takers, though the hedge fund world has become much more institutionalized in the last 15 years. When I think of a risk-taker, I think of an independent trader sitting at his desk in his underwear, whose ability to buy food depends on his ability to produce profits. *Eat what you kill.*

But this is all capital markets stuff. The reason America is so special is because of the efforts of *crazy gamblers*, Elon Musk being the foremost example, the craziest gambler of all. Investing alongside Elon Musk is a high-volatility proposition. We take risk in America. Big risk. I am

RISK

kind of wondering if some behavioral finance person somewhere could run an experiment to determine risk appetite in America versus other countries. In the mid-2000s, we had internet poker. Now we have sports gambling on our phones, where people do crazy six-leg parlays to try to win a million bucks. There is a certain species of individual that always needs to have action on something. I knew a guy who was betting on the now-defunct World Sports Exchange 20 years ago, the online offshore sports book, when FBI agents showed up at his door. That did not deter him from gambling. People will bet on anything. I was the *American Idol* bookie on the trading floor at Lehman. For a time, people were trading Michael Jackson suicide futures. Again, this doesn't really exist anywhere else in the world.

Most of this is nonproductive. A more productive use of taking risk is starting a business. You invest some money, you rent some office space, you hire some people, and if it doesn't work out, you lose what you put into it, and if it works out, you get to keep it all. This is known as a *call option*—every single business started in America has call-option-like returns. And I think something else that is unusual about America is that there is absolutely no stigma, none, zero, if your venture fails. In some quarters, it is considered a badge of honor. So if there are really no consequences to losing—you get nicked up, you get leaves in your hair and arrows in your ass, and you lose a little bit of money—you can keep on taking risk over and over again. Or, if you take a risk and it works out, you can freeroll it into something else and pyramid it, kind of like what Elon Musk has done. Exponential returns.

But I want to get back to that quote that I led off the piece with—if you're not taking risk, you're working for someone who is. There are a lot of people who don't want to take risk—I'd guess 95-97% of people have absolutely zero interest in starting a business. Which means that the actions of a few crazy gamblers are what propels the economy forward. And if you're sitting in a policymaking position, you'd probably want to ensure that you don't create impediments or roadblocks for the crazy gamblers. That is often not the case. I know a guy here in town who made a living doing repairs and mods to RVs. He recently quit his job and went into business on his own, competing directly with his old firm. I talked to him about it. He said, *why should they get all the money?* Correct. An economist would look at this and say that there is a business out there that is earning excess returns, and sooner or later, competitors will appear on the scene, driving returns lower, in the economic state known as *perfect competition*. But if you work in the private sector, you have probably had similar thoughts about your own employer. The guy that is running the place is driving a Porsche. *Why him? I can do that.* Well, then go do it. Form an LLC and get a business license and invest some money and buy some shit and hang up a shingle. Many people get rich doing this. I can tell you that this is exactly what happened in the newsletter business. I was an early entrant, and people looked at me and said *why him? I can do that.* And they did, and now it's tougher than ever, and the industry is much more mature. That's capitalism.

The longer I do this, the more I think that being a W-2 employee is a really unattractive proposition, unless you're getting a lot of stock and you can participate in the upside. Okay, so you get insurance, and health insurance is expensive. The insurance thing is interesting—there is a whole class of people out there who don't want to strike out on their own simply because of the health insurance. They get it at their current job, and they don't want to lose it. If I were in a policymaking position, that is something I would want to look at. I mean, single-payer healthcare is bad, bad, bad, but there is one silver lining—it would release people from the insurance plans that are tied to their employer, and maybe some of them would go out and take risks. A lot of entrepreneurs, like myself, have a spouse who is a W-2 employee with health insurance. If you're single, and you're paying $30,000 for Obamacare, it makes it a lot tougher. My health insurance is hardly gold-plated. It is basically a high-deductible insurance plan, and I am paying for most doctor's visits more or less out of pocket. But I don't have to worry about ending up on an iron lung and spending $2 million.

There is another reason to take the risk and start your own business:

you will be happier, even if it fails. I set an alarm in the morning, but if I want to roll around in bed for another half hour, I can. If I want to get some exercise at two in the afternoon, I can. If I want to kill 20 minutes doomscrolling on Twitter, I can. I don't have to manage politics up, and I don't have to manage politics down. I don't have to think about what I wear. I don't have to think about how I carry myself. I can hang up my pants on the door when I enter my office like Mister Rogers. Beyond all the creature comforts, it is just good to be your own boss. You own all the successes, and you own all the failures. A couple of months ago, I saw a Twitter interaction involving the economist Claudia Sahm. She went after someone unprovoked, and that person responded (and I am paraphrasing the hell out of this) that she had never taken risk in her life, and she replied that she was proud of that fact. What? That's not really something to be proud of. Kamala Harris was going around in the 2020 primary telling anyone who would listen that she had never worked in the private sector. It takes all kinds to be president, but I prefer someone who is a decisive risk-taker, and someone who at least has had some contact with risk-takers or who has some idea how the private sector works. And no, I don't think a trader should be president; traders are not good with nuance.

Not to say that I didn't take risk when I was in the public sector. I carried a gun, for crying out loud. I got in small boats and boarded vessels in dangerous seas. A captain of a Coast Guard cutter or a navy ship must have a very sophisticated understanding of risk: the right risks to take, and which ones will get you in trouble. So people in the military are risk-takers. People in the intelligence agencies can be risk-takers. A lot of people in government are risk-takers. But it is a different sort of risk—no upside, versus all downside. Kahneman would have something to say about that. I read something recently that controlling for all other factors, golfers will make a birdie putt more often than they make a par putt. They are betting on upside, rather than avoiding downside. That should tell you something about taking risk.

Begin with the end in mind. Think about you, on your deathbed.

You will regret the risks you never took, rather than the ones you did. If you've been thinking about starting a business for a while, and you haven't done it, what are you waiting for?

THE 60/30/10 ASSHOLE RULE

Let's say you have a job and you are dealing with a co-worker who is an asshole extraordinaire. Just a miserable piece of shit.

I have a theory about this.

- 60% of the time, that person has a substance abuse problem
- 30% of the time, that person has a mental illness
- 10% of the time, they are actually an asshole.

So the thing about this is that 90% of the time, you have no reason to be angry at that person. They can't help it—they're sick. You may not like their symptoms, but that doesn't change the fact that they are dealing with some issues and deserve your sympathy, not scorn. This isn't a joke—I'm deadly serious about this. If you are at work and you are working with a lying, backstabbing jerkface, that person is probably an alcoholic. Or bipolar. Or both. I worked with a lot of assholes at Lehman Brothers—all alcoholics or addicts. I personally have a mental illness, and I was pretty much an asshole back then. I got treatment, and I am no longer an asshole. Funny how that works.

Sometimes I am fooling around on Twitter late at night, and some troll flames me. My first assumption is that the person is drunk. One guy once said my wife was ugly as a dog. Probably drunk. Alcohol and social media do not mix. If you look closely, it is pretty easy to pick out the drunk posts, especially on Facebook.

Alcoholics and addicts can be pretty hard to get along with, even if they're not currently drunk or high. For starters, they lie all the time. They lie about things big and small. Another way of saying this is that they are incredibly full of shit—all the time. Substance abuse gives rise to behavior that evinces a certain kind of psychopathy. And all those studies that say that x% of Wall Street people are psychopaths? They're just drunks. And that's not exclusive to the finance industry—there are drunks everywhere, and they leave a trail of destruction in their wake.

Many decades ago, we started to view substance abuse disorders as a disease. It is an allergy of the body—some people simply react differently to substances than others. And it is an obsession of the mind. And a disturbance of the spirit. The upshot is that if you have someone who is an alcoholic or addict, you don't view them as a bad person, you view them as a sick person. And sick people deserve your sympathy—even if they're fucking you over. I worked for a guy at Lehman who took all the money for himself and left scraps for everyone else. Let's put it this way—he was not in the 10% of true assholes.

If you're dealing with someone who you believe to be an asshole, and they're not actually an asshole, and they fall into the 60% or the 30%, you must be aware of the fact that this is a profoundly unhappy person. You may be wishing for karma to take over—karma has already taken over. But instead of wishing ill on them, you should be wishing for them to get better, to undergo a profound psychological change. You would not wish for a sick person to get sicker. Unfortunately, if this person is your boss, then you are kind of stuck. Patience and tolerance are our code. It is hard to exercise patience and tolerance with an addict or a mentally ill person, and it is important to note that they will not seek help until things get really bad, which means that things will probably get really bad for you in the meantime. This might be the point at which you polish up your resume, which is part of a broader theory of mine—it is often better to go around than to go through. You're not going to be able to work with this person.

The world is full of assholes. The world is also full of alcoholics and drug addicts, and people with mental illnesses, and people who have unresolved trauma. There are a lot of sick people out there, and the thing about social media is that they are pouring out their sickness onto the internet for everyone to read. This is one of the reasons I don't spend much time on Twitter anymore—drunk people can make you drunk. Crazy people can make you crazy. It is not a psychologically healthy place to be. There is someone I know who retweets every single nice thing that someone says about him on Twitter. Doesn't take a psychology PhD to get to the bottom of that one. But again, I can choose to be annoyed by this behavior, assuming that this person is an asshole, or I can have sympathy, and operate under the assumption that he falls into the other 90%.

It is worth pointing out that there are some people out there who really are true assholes, either through nature or nurture. There are people out there who take pleasure in hurting people. I think I have only met two in my life, and one of them is a family member. The only possible course of action in these situations is to disengage, get as far away as you possibly can. I can deal with sick people—they're pretty easy to figure out. I can't deal with bad people. Some of these people are in prison, but a lot of the people in prison belong in the 60/30 category as well. I have heard stories of people committing all sorts of crimes while drunk or high. In fact, the number of crimes that are committed by people who are stone cold sober is probably pretty low. And as you know, the mentally ill population has shifted from psychiatric institutions to jails. Which brings us back to the idea that there really aren't that many true assholes out there—even in the criminal justice system.

This all ties in with another general philosophy of mine which is that you should be gentle with people. We've all dealt with a lot of shit in our lives—crappy parents, abusive parents, trauma, bullying, random exogenous events—the number of people who had a drama-free, happy childhood is actually pretty small. We are all sick in some way, shape or form. We all have our things. We all have our baggage. And whenever you are observing someone's behavior, and it confuses you, remember: it makes sense to them. Even the most rational among us have our blind spots.

When dealing with what you presume to be an asshole, the best you can hope for is to be a power of example. If you are a stable, happy person, the asshole might reach out to you one day and ask for help, and then you can be in a position to do good in the world. But remember, alcoholics (and mentally ill people) generally don't want help. Sick people want to stay sick. I wouldn't start dropping any hints that someone should go to rehab. All you can do is to be there when the wheels come off, and then you can lend a helping hand. Other people did this for me, in 2006, when my life was completely unmanageable, and I have never forgotten it.

It's one of those things that once you see it, you can't unsee it. The world isn't full of bad people, it's full of sick people. I call this the 60/30/10 Asshole Rule. If more people understood this rule, the world would be a kinder place.

JOY

THE WRONG QUESTION to ask is:

"What makes you happy?"

The right question to ask is:

"What brings you joy?"

Joy is the antidote to anxiety, depression, addiction, and compulsive behavior. Boredom is the antithesis of joy. Boredom leads to incomprehensible demoralization.

I would suggest that you make a list of things that bring you joy. I will include a short list of my own here:

- Writing
- Trading
- Playing music
- The cats
- My house

- Helping people
- Traveling (when the flights don't get screwed up).

If I am doing things that bring me joy, then I'm not sitting around feeling sorry for myself. You know what's strange? Sometimes I don't want to do things that bring me joy, even if I know they will bring me joy. There is this inertia, this resistance, that prevents me from doing them. I would rather be bored or feeling sorry for myself.

You probably have a different list of things that bring you joy. Like your kids. Can't relate, but you probably can't relate to my cats. I see pictures of my friends with their kids on Facebook, and I'm like, does not compute, but they probably say the same thing about my cat pictures. Anyway, the point is, it doesn't matter what brings you joy. Walks in the woods or walks on the beach bring people joy. Neither make my list. But if a walk on the beach brings you joy, then—why not go for a walk on the beach? Maybe every weekend? Maybe as much as you can?

I try to spend as much time in a state of joy as I can. Here's the thing: If your work doesn't bring you joy, you are going to have a tough time of it. Because we spend a lot of time working, and if you hate it, that's not a recipe for happiness. So, step number one in seeking joy is doing something that you love. Here we run into problems, because there are a lot of people who get paid very good money to do a thing, and they would rather be doing some other thing, and would have to give up the money. I am not going to sit here and tell you that you should quit your high-paying job so you can ride ponies. That is something your fifth-grade teacher would tell you, and she probably hates her job. I mean, you can do that if you've worked that job for a number of years and you have a few million saved up, which brings me to the very obvious personal finance advice that saving is very good. When you've saved enough money, you can say blow me and ride ponies. If you're living in deprivation in pursuit of joy, you won't be experiencing much in the way of joy. So do it when you're financially ready to do it, and not before.

You may be led to believe that drinking or doing drugs or surfing porn brings you joy. I assure you that they do not. I'm going to dive into conservative philosophy for a bit, and say that when you use a thing to change the way you feel, it is a shortcut to true joy, and joy is a matter of the spirit, not the body. We have all treated our bodies like an amusement park at some point in our lives, and achieved a high that we thought could never be replicated by a real-life experience. But it can. The real-life experiences are fuller and more meaningful, and bring you closer to God, while cocaine and hookers are a fake experience that take you away from God. You become spiritually bankrupt. But where I part ways from the conservatives is that they think you shouldn't be allowed to do the cocaine and hookers—it should be prohibited by law, and enforced by the coercive state. Fuck, let people try it, and come to their own conclusions. Some of the best spiritual experiences around are when people give up the cocaine and hookers, and instead pursue real, honest-to-goodness joy. The liberals (and the libertarians) think that joy comes from treating your body like an amusement park. I have been there, and it is a spiritual dead end, with nothing but shame and regret.

I used to derive a lot of joy from working out and staying in shape, or so I thought. It was all driven by vanity. I was a gym rat, a real lunkhead, and spent many years picking things up and putting them down. Then I'd stare at myself in the mirror, and go around strutting like a peacock. In 2013, I had a horrific knee injury, with surgery and seven months of physical therapy, and that was pretty much the end of the working out. These days, I don't care much what I look like. I spend good money on clothes, but that is about the extent of it. I eat whatever I want, I weigh 240 pounds, I'm not so fat that I can't fit in an airplane seat, and it's not like I need to run a six-minute mile to do my job. I'm happy with who I am and what I look like.

With the benefit of hindsight, all the working out and watching my diet was an obsession, driven by pride. I'm okay with the dad bod. Some women like dad bod. I found that my trying to maintain my physical appearance was taking a huge amount of mental exertion. Going to the gym, working out in the gym, coming home from the gym, taking supplements, drinking gallons of water, weighing chicken—I can say this for sure, when I stopped obsessing over my body, I started making a lot more fucking money. There was almost a perfect correlation. So if you're one of these workout fanatics, ask yourself why you're doing it. Are you doing it to feel healthy, or for some other reason? About the only thing I do these days is walk on the treadmill for 30 minutes a day with a sauna shirt on. Get a sweat going, get the endorphins going, and burn a modicum of calories. I do it for my mental health more than anything. But it does not bring me joy—it is simply maintenance.

I mentioned that the antithesis of joy is boredom. Being unproductive. I have difficulty explaining the first-world human desire to check out, zone out, grab a beer and sit on the couch and passively watch *America's Got Talent*. I mean, TV and entertainment has been around for 75 years, and at various times in those 75 years, people have said that TV is responsible for all sorts of ills. It's a *passe-temps*. Something to pass the time. I would be remiss if I did not mention social media. If I have free time, which I rarely do, I don't want to spend it passively watching TV or social media. I want to spend that time on something that brings me joy, which is usually writing. The good news is that I can write and watch TV at the same time. I can work on my laptop, and look up when Gleyber Torres makes another boneheaded baserunning error, and yell at the TV. Then I go back to writing. I have a lot of writing projects backed up, months' worth of work—and joy. When work is fun, you tend to be pretty happy. I was this way at Lehman Brothers, too—I'd head up to my office in my house, fire up Bloomberg, and pull charts all night. I was happy being a military officer, I was happy being a trader, and I'm happy being a writer.

Maybe I'm just… happy? Maybe happiness is a choice?

It is. And if there is one thing that you could possibly learn from this collection of essays, it's that happiness is an inside job. We choose to be happy or not be happy. It is not a matter of exogenous events, random good or bad things that fall on your head. I want to be happy, so I do things that make me happy, I spend time with people who make me happy, and I end up happy. That's not to say that everything is perfect. Life is always a struggle. But if it wasn't hard, it wouldn't be worth doing.

There is an old saying in trading—*do more of what works and less of what doesn't*. Frequently, people do the opposite! They do less of the things that bring them joy and more of the things that don't. And they're stumped—totally baffled—as to why they're unhappy. So make that list, that list of things that bring you joy. And make an effort to do a little of it each day. Life is short, man. I'm sure I'll regret some things at the end, but I sure don't want to regret not having done the things that made me happy. I want to leave it all out on the field.

CONTEMPT PRIOR TO INVESTIGATION

There is a principle which is a bar against all information, which is proof against all arguments and which cannot fail to keep a man in everlasting ignorance—that principle is contempt prior to investigation.
—Herbert Spencer, "An Artist's Concept"

HERBERT SPENCER (WHO is my kind of philosopher, by the way) was referring to the principle of *openness* in this quote—our willingness to try new things. Most of the time, we don't want to try new things—we want to stay in our comfortable little bubble and do what we have always done.

I run into this most often:

Me: "Hey, I just recorded this mix, you should check it out."

Villain: "What is it?"

CONTEMPT PRIOR TO INVESTIGATION

Me: "It's house music."

Villain: "I don't like house music."

Me: "Are you sure? What house music have you listened to?"

Villain: "I don't know. I just don't like house music."

Me: "Well, mine is different. It's very downtempo and melodic. I think you'll like it."

Villain: "I don't like house music."

Six months later…

Villain: "Hey, I finally tried that music you gave me, it was pretty good!"

Me: *Roll my eyes so hard I break them. Now I am blind.*

Music is a very small thing. People have different tastes in music, and that's fine. Some people like the Allman Brothers. I don't like the Allman Brothers. But crucially, I have listened to the Allman Brothers! I have tried it! I have tried it enough to understand its essence. Not for me. And that's fine.

But some people will have contempt prior to investigation about something that could save their lives.

Me: "I think you have a drinking problem."

Villain: "Eh. I'm fine."

Me: "Have you thought about going to Alcoholics Anonymous?"

Villain: "It's a cult."

Me: "Are you sure? How many AA meetings have you been to?"

Villain: "Well, none."

Me: "So how do you know it's a cult?"

Villain: "That's just what I've heard."

We tend to have *preconceived notions* about things. Indian food is too spicy. *American Idol* is stupid. New York is dangerous. We miss out on a lot of life because of these preconceived notions. With regard to the New York Is Too Dangerous thing, there are people here in South Carolina who have never been to New York and never will go because they think it is too dangerous. Yes, it is a bit more dangerous than it was in the 2000s, but it is orders of magnitude less dangerous than it was in the 70s and 80s. If you stay in the tourist areas, you're going to be fine, and even if you don't stay in the tourist areas, you're also probably going to be fine. It's certainly no more dangerous than the south side of Myrtle Beach after dark. So people miss out on a lot of life, because of their preconceived notions, and because they have contempt prior to investigation.

It also applies to romance. We have preconceived notions about people because of their appearance. That person is too tall, that person is too short, or too fat, or dresses weird—you dismiss a lot of people out of hand because of these superficial characteristics. In the electronic dating world, people set filters. How many women do you know who refuse to date someone who isn't at least six feet tall? The best husband in the world might be five-eleven and you would never know. People exclude, rather than include. Mr. or Miss Right might be out there somewhere, waiting for you, and you would never know because you filtered out Trump supporters. I have no experience in modern dating,

CONTEMPT PRIOR TO INVESTIGATION

because I have been married for 27 years, but if I were on the dating scene I would set no filters at all. Age, height, weight, education, nothing. Because you never know.

About ten years ago, a broker invited me to deep-sea fishing in Miami. I hadn't fished much since dropping a hook with a worm on it into a pond in Connecticut. Well, I got on the boat and we went offshore and I puked my guts out. I puked, and puked, and puked until I felt something hairy in my mouth—and then I swallowed that back down, because that was my asshole. It was rough, and we were pretty much all down for the count—my wife was the only one who wasn't seasick, and the only one catching fish. It was a complete bust. But… I'm glad I did it! Now I know what deep-sea fishing is all about.

I have a friend who is always trying to get me to do yoga. Now, I have nothing against yoga, and I would actually like to try it, especially hot yoga—I love heat and I love to sweat. I live pretty far away from a yoga studio, and to be honest, I don't think there is hot yoga anywhere in Myrtle Beach, but I would like to try it. I mean, I do have preconceived notions about yoga. Yoga people have a reputation for being hippy-dippy. And there seems to be a belief that there is a spiritual element to yoga, and it's supposed to mellow you out or something like that, but I know plenty of assholes who do yoga. Bill Gross, for starters. I have a friend who lives in the Gulch in Nashville (the same guy who wants me to do yoga) and there are all these young girls walking around in yoga pants with yoga mats. White girl culture, you know. Still, Ichiro stretches for about four hours a day, and he's in the Hall, so maybe yoga would do me some good.

Had a bout of contempt prior to investigation recently with the new house. My wife wanted to order automatic blinds off of Amazon. She said that we could save thousands of dollars on blinds than if we hired someone locally for a custom job. I was skeptical. My wife tends to buy cheap crap, and I don't want to spend a ton of money on a house and then fill it up with cheap crap. We did the second guest room as a test case. And you know what—it turned out great! Easily as good as the professional blinds. So I had to concede she was right, which is something that happens not infrequently at our house.

Try not to say things like:

- "I will not"
- "I will never"
- "I don't like"

I'll give you yet another example. I had preconceived notions about NASCAR. A bunch of hillbillies! I said *I will never go to a NASCAR race*. Then my mom got interested in NASCAR, and she was going to races all over the country. After a great deal of encouragement, I accompanied her to a race in New Hampshire. I was hooked. It's not so much that I care about the sport or who wins, but the experience of being down on the track while the cars are roaring past is… well, something that you cannot describe. You feel it in every cell in your body. So then I went to a bunch of NASCAR races, and even dragged my Wall Street buddies. And yes, there are hillbillies—but the hillbillies are great! I don't go anymore, but I have great memories of it.

There is so much contained in this concept of contempt prior to investigation. Say yes to things. Go to the party. Go to the conference. Try new things. Meet new people. It's the difference between having a big world and a small world. Sometime in the future, someone is going to come to you with an opportunity that might change your life. If you have contempt prior to investigation, and you say no, you will be cutting yourself off from the world. Well, the couch is comfy and the beer is cold.

MOMENTS THAT CHANGE YOUR LIFE

I SUFFERED FROM BIPOLAR disorder while I was a trader at Lehman Brothers and spent about three weeks in a psych ward. When most people think of a psych ward, they might think of *One Flew Over the Cuckoo's Nest*, or something like that. That is not too far from the truth. Plastic spoons, no shoelaces, Velcro shower curtains. I checked myself into the hospital because I thought that the federal agents wouldn't be able to get me there. It was beyond a delusion—I was experiencing psychosis and literally seeing people and things that weren't there. It was the scariest period of my life.

A psych ward is… boring. There is not much to do. There was a TV in the common area, but I was never much in the mood to watch the idiot box. There was a ping-pong table, too, but I never took advantage of that either. I just wanted to be left alone. There was a bookshelf, and I read a book about a woman who was stranded in Antarctica, as well as some John Updike books that my wife had brought me. There were some activities—there was yoga in the morning, but the yoga was sad, because inevitably someone would start crying in the middle of it. There were meetings for people with a dual diagnosis, but those meetings were sad, because people would cry in those too. When people asked me what I was in for, I told them that I was in to get away from the federal agents. I was that far gone.

One of the activities I did was painting—they gave us these plant pots to paint, and let me tell you, I am a terrible painter, and I painted the terrible-est plant pot in the group. I thought it was good. I saved it, and I have it on a shelf on the third floor of my house, the one artifact from that period of my life. It gives me gratitude.

One night, I was hanging out in my room, and one of the nurses came by and asked if I wanted to go to a writing seminar.

"No thanks."

"You should really go."

"No, I'm fine."

"Please, let's go to the writing seminar."

I relented.

So I go in this room with a rectangular table and about eight other patients. There was a complicated woman sitting at the other end. She looked as if she was wearing about five scarves. She *looked* like a writer. What I didn't realize was that I was sitting in the presence of a literary giant. The woman was Siri Hustvedt, who has written a whole bunch of fiction and non-fiction books and was even published in the *Best American Short Stories* series at least once. She was in her fancy clothes and I was in my socks.

She had us do a writing exercise called "I Remember," to write about a period of your life, perhaps from your childhood, and the feelings associated with it, including as many details as possible. We had about 20 minutes. I had a pen and paper. I wrote about my childhood on Governors Island, which used to be a Coast Guard base. I wrote about my best friend, I wrote about playing tee-ball, I wrote about my abusive father—oddly, it was one of the best things I had ever written. Then Siri asked us to read what we wrote.

Afterwards, she motioned for me to come out into the hall. From what I remember, she was taller than me. She looked me directly in the eyes, and said: "Have you ever thought about being a writer?"

That is the moment that changed my life.

So we chatted for a bit, and she told me her background, and I suddenly realized I was talking to a real writer, and here was this real writer telling me that I could be a writer.

There were no more invisible people after that.

So I think about that moment a lot.

We have talked about contempt prior to investigation. Back then, I had contempt prior to investigation. *Do you want to go to a writing seminar?* No. I want to sit in this room and feel sorry for myself. Imagine if I hadn't gone. What would my life look like today? Well, I'd probably still be trading, spit out the bottom of the bulge-bracket world by now, trading odd-lots of ETFs for some bucket shop with a bunch of other Wall Street castoffs. I'd be divorced, and an alcoholic. And perhaps I wouldn't have been med-compliant, and maybe I would have killed myself by now. That is what was in my future if I said "No." So today, I say yes to things.

I can't be clearer about this. Siri Hustvedt saved my life. Now, I am not the writer that Siri is—my froggish leavings just pale in comparison to what she does. She's smarter than me, and a better writer by a factor of 11. But I'm good at what I do. I don't have an expansive vocabulary of ten-dollar words, but I have insane flow, and a strong first-person nonfiction voice. And my career as a writer has been a bit uneven—two traditionally published books that were big hits, and three self-published books that did pretty well too. But I'm no Morgan Housel, no million-book bestseller. I hope I will have one, but that is not why I write—I write to live. If I don't write, I will go insane. I write for my own mental health. Even if I had an audience of my wife and my cats, I would still write—for myself. Yes, I take my medication, and yes, I get plenty of sleep, and yes, I get some exercise, but writing is a big part of staying mentally healthy. And it all started in that room in the psych ward in 2006.

Sometimes I think about those moments, because I have had a few of them, like the time I was on the options floor in San Francisco and almost got hit with a flying water bottle, which resulted in a job offer, and the beginning of my trading career. Or in 1989, when I laid down on a couch and put my head in a strange girl's lap and asked for a kiss. We are still together, 36 years later. Chance encounters. Pure randomness. And you never know in the moment that you are having one of those moments—you can only see it in retrospect.

Artists and athletes want to be discovered—they want to get that big break. A high school pitcher gets a visit from an agent. A DJ playing at a small club gets spotted by a promoter and is invited to play at a festival. You're writing a book, toiling in anonymity, you put it on Amazon for $0.98 and it sells a million copies. I am interested in those lightning strikes, those moments of serendipity that change the course of your life—for the better.

I haven't talked to Siri in a while. We corresponded briefly in 2011— I sent her a copy of *Street Freak* for a blurb, and she was really, really happy to hear from me. She also blurbed *All the Evil of This World*, but that was a tough book. I'd like to meet with her again someday. It's been 18 years, after all, so I can tell her in person that she saved my life. She knows it, but I want to tell her in person. It also speaks to the power of affirmation—you never want to piss all over someone's dream. If you tell someone that they can do something, they will probably do it.

I've said this before—I am the luckiest person in the world. I cry when I think about it.

I'M OFFENDED

IF I WRITE something, and you're offended by it, that's your fault.
What?
You heard me. If you are offended by an article, a TV show, a movie, a professor, a co-worker, a boss, or a relative—*that is your fault*.

Here is the reason. We are humans, not animals. And because we are human, we get to choose how we respond to any situation. If someone makes you angry, it is because you chose to get angry. You could also choose not to get angry. You could choose to ignore it. You could choose to keep on scrolling. I actually kind of like not being angry, therefore I never choose to be angry. Animals don't get to choose how they respond to situations—they simply react. So if you react to a tweet or a Facebook post, you are an animal.

I can't be any clearer.

Seems like a lot of people get offended by things these days, though that may be changing. A teacher says something politically incorrect, the students are *offended*, and they ride him out of town on a rail. That was happening a lot, for a while. What this means is that we are very psychologically unhealthy as a society. And there is nothing better than being offended to give someone a sense of moral superiority. Ego is tied up in this, too. If someone posts a Trump meme and you find yourself going to battle in the comments, you are a very psychologically unhealthy person.

Every two weeks I go on the local radio show, and last time I was there, the host asked me if I was offended by such-and-such thing, and I said of course not, I am offended by nothing. Nothing offends me—ever. There is no single word that could trigger me. This wasn't always the case. I almost got thrown out of law enforcement school in the Coast Guard because one of the instructors called me a "pussy" and I punched him in the head. I got a perfect score on every exam and was not the honor graduate, and that pretty much says it all. I used to be an animal. I used to react to things without thinking, which means I probably didn't have the temperament to be a law enforcement officer. These days, you can call me any name in the book, and my heart rate is not going to go up a single beat.

Being offended means you have *righteous indignation*. We feel superior to the other person. Elon Musk says something dumb on Twitter, we are offended, we have righteous indignation, and we feel superior to… the richest man in the world. Which is ludicrous! How many people out there feel superior to the guy who just had an astronaut walk in space? Lots of them. You are in dangerous territory whenever you start feeling superior to other people, whether it's billionaires or Haitians. Over a hundred years after Bolshevism came on the scene, and we are still carrying around this idea of the noble savage, that poor people are virtuous and rich people are vicious. If you are a poor person, and you feel superior to a rich person, then there is a 0% chance that you will ever be rich. Zero. And if you are a rich person feeling superior to poor people, then you are an asshole.

If you are the type of person to get offended by things, what you are really saying is that other people should have their speech and actions conform to your view of the world. You are the director of the play, and everyone else is the actors. The amount of ego it takes to sustain this worldview is staggering. *I know what's best for you and everyone else.*

In politics, the thinking is often that people cannot be trusted to think for themselves—they behave irrationally and in ways that are deleterious to their own health and well-being—and government is here to protect you from your own worst instincts. I admire Mike Bloomberg and what he's built, but the Big Gulps were a bridge too far. The idea that a politician should leave people alone, free to make their own mistakes—or succeed, perhaps—is so out of fashion that we can hardly imagine a time without it. I'd say that the last (and possibly only) president to get it right was Calvin Coolidge, literally 100 years ago. I read the Amity Shlaes biography, and I don't think it does him justice. Get out of the way, and let people work and produce and worship and thrive, and what results is a decade of breathtaking technological innovation and the biggest stock market boom in history. And inherent in Coolidge's worldview was the very psychologically healthy belief that he didn't know what's best for you. I can't possibly know what's best for you. These essays are about my experience and my journey to being psychologically healthy. I've been working on it for decades. I can't write about being physically healthy, because I am a fat fuck. You can go to David Goggins for that.

Social media is an outrage-producing machine, and when I say outrage, I mean being offended. Just keep scrolling. I am friends with a whole bunch of people, from all parts of the ideological spectrum, and I'm not in a position to tell people what they should or shouldn't believe. If they had my experience and my knowledge, they might believe differently, but they don't. I'm on my path, and they're on their path. I say that a lot. *I'm on my path, and you're on your path.* There are things I see on social media, and I say to myself, *well, that was inadvisable,* but it has been years since I was triggered by a social media post. And I don't curate my feed—I'm not "hiding" the people I disagree with. If you can't handle someone with an opinion different from your own, what does this say about you? That is the thing about social media—people just pour out their mental illnesses onto it on a daily basis, for all the world to see. Their insecurities, their foibles, their fears, their resentments—

let me put it this way, if I were actually trained in psychology, I would have a lot to write about. I can tell you one thing for sure—the people who constantly post pictures of flowers are very, very sad people, and possibly suicidal.

Instead of getting offended by other people's shitty opinions, I often find them to be funny. I find humor in it. If you laughed every time you were offended, instead of being offended, imaging how much happier you would be? Laura Loomer is in the news these days. Laura Loomer is very, very funny. And Marjorie Taylor Greene is funny. But people like this tweet their shitty opinions, and it's like feeding a gremlin after midnight—everyone gets triggered, and they get ratioed to the moon. Why do people fall for this again and again? Why can't you just let someone be wrong on the internet? Here's the way I look at it—if I say something on social media that triggers a bunch of people, I win. That's right, I am the winner, because I got 1,000 people to take five minutes of their day to come up with the perfect dunk, and I just wasted 5,000 minutes of the time of psychologically unhealthy people. I'm doing the world a service.

What I don't understand is these people who make a career out of political media, the people who are always in the middle of a fight. Glenn Beck, Dan Bongino, Rachel Maddow—why would you want to live like this? Financial media is bad enough. You're constantly in a state of outrage, whipping up outrage in other people, and your contribution to the world is... what? That has never been my ambition.

I have to reiterate this point, because it is extremely important: If you get offended, it is your fault. Not the other person's. Yours. You can choose how you respond to any situation, which you would know if you'd ever read Victor Frankl. Imagine if you could just choose to be happy all the time, no matter what the circumstances? You absolutely can. I am proof that it is possible.

MENTAL OBSESSIONS AND LETTING GO

I HATE TEXTING, BUT let's talk about texting.

Let's say you have a friend who is going through hard times. Wife crap, kid crap, job crap, other crap. You decide to send him a text:

> "Hey man, just letting you know that I'm here for you. You can call anytime."

And he doesn't respond. What is your response to him not responding? Do you get mad? Do you get mad at the guy who is going through hell because he didn't respond to your offer to help?

Some people would. Which would be dumb. Maybe he is too wound up in his own crap to respond to your text. Maybe he read it and appreciated it, but didn't think it merited a response. Maybe a lot of things. The point is that you discharged your responsibility as a friend when you sent the text, and you should let go of the results, because we are not in the results business. You send the text and you *let go*. The rest is up to him.

Ninety-nine percent of people can't do this. They can't send a text and let go of the results. They can't make a phone call and let go of the results. They can't let go of any results. They get personally and emotionally involved in other people's problems. They become codependent. They let other people's actions determine their feelings.

It is all about letting go.

This is probably the one thing I have worked on the most in the last 20 years. Let's say I have a business relationship with someone. There is something I want them to do, and they're not doing it. You have two choices. You can let it consume you, where it is the last thing you think about before you fall asleep, and the first thing you think about when you wake up, and your daily thoughts are eaten up with trying to figure out how to get this dick to do what you want them to do, and you can make yourself miserable in the process—or—after a certain amount of time passes, you can just say *fuck you* and go around and find someone else.

The latter option requires a lot less mental energy. I don't get emotional about this stuff anymore. I have a philosophy about situations like these—it is easier to go around than to go through. I spend much of my professional life going around people who aren't doing what they're supposed to be doing. I mean, if the incentives are there, everything works, but sometimes things don't work even when the incentives are in place. But let me be clear: I don't get upset. I don't get anxious. I just find another solution. It's not personal. This is an act of letting go.

I'm sure the Wall Street people will appreciate this. You think your bonus should be a million dollars. Your bonus turns out to be $600,000. Luxury problems, I know. What do you do? Do you get mad and resentful at your firm and management for screwing you out of $400,000? Does it consume you? Are you miserable at work? I assure you that it is not personal. So if it's not personal for them, it's not personal for you. Go find another job that pays more, and if they really want to keep you, they will meet or exceed the offer you got. And

MENTAL OBSESSIONS AND LETTING GO

they shouldn't get resentful at you, either. It's not personal. There were a few people who were upset when I walked away from Barclays when they bought the Lehman broker-dealer out of bankruptcy. I always tell them the same thing: *you should have paid me more!* It would have made the decision a lot harder. Nothing personal: I had other things I wanted to do with my life. Walking away from Wall Street was the ultimate act of letting go.

You have a child who is addicted to drugs. Severely addicted. You believe their life is in danger. It is the last thing you think about before you fall asleep, and the first thing you think about when you wake up. It is a mental obsession. You find yourself getting personally involved in his or her problems. Their success or failure dictates your success or failure. You are codependent. This is where it is time to let go. You make some options available: A.A., rehab, etc., you encourage them to go, but that is all you have control of. You can't make someone get sober if they don't want to get sober. If they want to get sober, they will get sober. It is that simple. So level 98 of the letting-go videogame is doing the footwork and stepping back and being willing to accept the possibility that your own offspring will fail, *even if that means they lose their life*. It's not on you.

This is the toughest thing to do in the world.

I find that the level of codependency is off the charts with parents these days. If the child doesn't start on the traveling team, they internalize it. If they don't get straight As, they internalize it. If they don't get into an Ivy League school, they internalize it. I see a lot of miserable parents because their kids are not following the script that the parents laid out for them. As anyone who has kids knows, how your kids turn out is 95% nature and only 5% nurture. You really have no control over the results. So *let go*.

All of this falls into a category of what I would call *mental obsessions*. Mental obsessions are things that you think about all the time. I am a very obsessive person, and I have become very disciplined about mental obsessions over time. If I find myself obsessing about this or that thing,

I quickly quiet the disturbance by redirecting my mind to something more productive. True story: I had a book signing for my short story collection, *Night Moves*, at my house for the folks in my neighborhood. I sold very few books. For about five to ten minutes, I found myself descending into despondency, obsessing about the idea that I was a loser and the book was a failure. Then, I realized what I was doing, and I quieted the disturbance, and redirected my mind to something positive. I let go.

I then drove to Savannah and spoke to a few writing classes at the Savannah College of Art and Design, trying to inspire them to become great writers. I can tell you what the antidote is to obsessive fears or resentments: helping someone else. When you help another person, it's like hitting the "clear" button on a calculator of all your obsessive thinking. If you didn't get paid enough on Wall Street, pick up the phone and help someone else going through the same thing. If you're worried about your child with a drug addiction, call the guy up the street who's going through a horrible divorce. Try it—it works every time, and you will get a sense of gratitude to go with it.

Everyone gets mental obsessions. Letting go is the answer. I'm not going to tell you it's easy. It's not. Mental obsessions can be crippling. *So-and-so didn't return my phone call. He hates me!* Ninety-nine percent of the time, this is a story that you made up and told yourself, and there is nothing wrong at all. One percent of the time, the person really hates you, and maybe you will get to the bottom of it, and maybe you won't, but either way, everything is going to be fine. I had a guy ghosting me one time who really did end up hating my guts. I no longer have a relationship with that person, but I'm fine, and he's fine, and everything's fine. It was a little stressful for a few days, but you get through it. I have never heard the story of a person dying because a relationship ended. I haven't heard that story yet. I have heard the stories of people who have killed themselves over mental obsessions. They didn't have the ability to let go. Your body is not a weapon—your mind is a weapon, and you can use it and its wildly destructive powers against yourself.

MENTAL OBSESSIONS AND LETTING GO

I would say that the number one determinant of psychological well-being is the frequency and severity with which you get mental obsessions. And I would say that the frequency and severity of mental obsessions is the number one determinant of happiness. Another thing I've learned over the years: nobody gives a shit about me or what I'm doing. I don't mean that in the pejorative sense—what I mean is that while I'm sitting here obsessing about whether someone's going to text me back, they're in Riviera Maya drinking out of a pineapple, *not thinking about me*. We tend to think that other people think about us all the time. Absolutely not the case. You're self-absorbed, and so is everyone else. You're thinking about your problems, and they're thinking about their problems—not about you. You are the center of your universe. They are the center of their universe. *I may not be much, but I'm all I think about*, the saying goes.

If you are a person who is plagued with mental obsessions, if you are a person who is going through a mental obsession *right now*, know that there is an answer. Know that there is another way. I can't teach you how to run an Ironman. I can't teach you to deadlift 800 pounds. I can only tell you how I went from being one of the most psychologically sick people in the world to one of the healthiest, and to let you know that it is possible. Imagine a life free from mental obsessions. Imagine having the ability to let go. It is within reach—you just have to try.

A FULL LIFE

I SLEPT IN UNTIL 8:45 this morning, which is pretty unusual for me. During the week, I get up at about 6:30 a.m., and on the weekends, about 7:30 a.m. I was tired. It was a full week, including a couple of nights I stayed up late to grade exams from my class.

Being busy is a good thing. When I say "busy," I don't mean drudgery, like the "busy work" of fatfingering stuff into a spreadsheet or putting addresses on envelopes. You can have a lot of mindless tasks and be busy, but that is not the good kind of busy. The good kind of busy is when you're fully engaged, working a long day at your job, you have social engagements, you have phone calls catching up with friends, you have exercise, you have concerts or sporting events to go to, you have trips for work or pleasure—basically, you have so much shit to do that you cannot possibly get it all done. I don't know about you, but when I am in that state—the state of having too much shit to do—I am at my happiest. The moments of unbusy, when I have time to park my ass on the couch and watch baseball, my brain tends to run wild with all kinds of conspiracy theories I made up about how everyone hates me. That's why being busy is good, because you don't have time to run around in your own head, and when you are working on big problems, the small problems seem smaller. But if you aren't working on any big problems, the small problems seem big. That's why I like to stay task-saturated.

But "busy" doesn't quite capture it, right? I prefer to call it *living a full life*. Here are some of the things that will help you life a full life:

- Meaningful work (and lots of it)
- Friends
- Family
- Challenges, physical or intellectual
- A spiritual connection
- Philanthropy
- Hobbies
- Travel

I want to talk about this *challenges* bullet point for a second. I know people with demanding jobs and great families and all the things on this list, except for challenges, and they are a bit unmoored. Challenges refers to the act of setting a goal and achieving it. A physical challenge might be entering in a jiu-jitsu tournament, and an intellectual challenge might be writing a book. One of the things I've found about challenges is that people who do physical challenges don't hold intellectual challenges in high regard, and vice versa. I can say that is definitely true for me—my books will live forever but my body will turn to dust. And the weightlifters probably look at me and say, *what the fuck is the point of writing a short story collection? You spend all that time on it and you make $10,000*. Then you have the guys like Hugh Laurie who do both and are just good at everything.

The point is, if you're not being challenged, physically or intellectually (or even emotionally), you are not leading a full life. You can have a house and money and kids and friends and cars and church and everything else, but if you're not putting yourself through the wringer for no good reason, you are not living up to your potential. You have to constantly try to be better. I am not gonna work out in the gym for three hours a day, but I respect those who do, because it is a hard thing and they are trying to be better, and I am a big fan of doing hard things for their own sake. I run into a lot of people who have good jobs and make good money, perhaps even a shitload of money, and life is good, but they are not pushing themselves. And it doesn't have to exclusively be writing books or working out. You can have spiritual goals, you can have social goals, or you can just go back to school and take a class in something random. Or you can (sigh) take the CFA. I think Stephen Covey called this "sharpening the saw."

The goal is to have a full life. The goal is to do things, not talk about doing things. The goal is to go out in the world and mix it up. The goal is to have a lot of friends. The goal is to meet new people. The goal is to travel around the country and see new things. As you do these things, your impact on the world grows.

Here's a question for you: *When you die, will you be missed?*

Oof. That's a tough one. The reality is that none of us will be missed—I am always amazed when someone dies and people get together for the service and a few weeks later they are forgotten, and people just get on with life. I can think of two people in particular who had an enormous impact on me, and I still think about them pretty much every day. They are missed. And of course, there are people who have an enormous impact on the world, and their influence is felt for decades afterwards. I've written about this before—I am a bit obsessed with legacy. I'm not strictly talking about being rich and famous. Will you be remembered as generous in spirit, or will you be remembered as a miserable fuck? Do you give people the gift of time, or are you jammed up in your own bullshit all the time? My experience shows that 98% of people fall into the latter category.

I have a great deal of respect for my brother. The guy spends two to three hours a day in the gym, he has a job which requires him to drive all over creation and spend hours a day on the phone, and he still makes time for family and friends, and oh—I can't name another person who is more generous with time or resources. I can't remember the last time I called him and he was sitting at home just dicking the dog. He's always doing something. He's not sitting around feeling sorry for himself. Is he rich and famous? I would not characterize him as rich and famous. But if he were to pass, there would be a giant hole in the world that would be impossible to fill. He has all of the things on that list. And, as a result, he is insanely happy. Funny how that works.

Look, I spent my early 20s reading a lot of Ayn Rand, who did not have good things to say about altruism. But in my 20s and 30s, I was not generous with time or money. I was pretty jammed up on my own bullshit. Every so often, someone one will call in the middle of the workday, and I don't feel like picking up, but I pick up, because if I needed something from someone, I would want them to pick up. And I am always glad I did, even if I'm in a personal fast market. And even if the person just wants to shoot the shit, it is a good thing to be spending 15 minutes shooting the shit, because relationships are important. It's called giving the gift of time. Time is more important than money. It is one thing to be generous with money, especially if you have a lot of it—you are not going to miss $1,000—but it is another thing to be generous with time.

The opposite of having a full life is having an empty life. An empty life means you don't have the following:

- Meaningful work (and lots of it)
- Friends
- Family
- Challenges, physical or intellectual
- A spiritual connection
- Philanthropy
- Hobbies
- Travel

These people are struggling. Because these are the things that give life meaning. If you are doing these things, you won't have time to think. You won't have time to breathe. You won't have time to make up stories and believe them. You won't have time for fear or resentment. You won't have time to feel sorry for yourself. You take action—because faith without works is dead.

ACCEPTANCE

God, grant me the serenity to accept the things I cannot change, the courage to change the things I can, and the wisdom to know the difference.

THE SERENITY PRAYER—so simple, and yet: it's taken me 20 years to fully comprehend what it means. And I'm still not there.

When people are spiritually disturbed, it's usually because they are trying to change something they can't. I will generalize here about politics, because politics is the act of trying to change the world, the idea that one person can make a difference, or that thousands or millions of people doing a small part can make a difference, when the reality is that none of that is true—*nobody* can make a difference. For example: I am a mishmash of many things—I am a Reason libertarian, an objectivist, and conservative about some things as well, but mostly I am a man of the right—and nothing is going to change that, really. There isn't going to be one thing you can say that is going to change my mind about taxes, about capitalism, about Israel—I am not persuadable. I am not going to "see the light" by reading your riposte on Twitter. I am not responsive to logos, ethos, or pathos. Not to say that I'll never change, but it's not going to be because of you—through a process of falsification, I'll arrive at a different conclusion over the course of many years. But no, you are not going to *change* me. And if you try, you are going to end up spiritually disturbed. Better to just accept me for who I am, to accept other people for who they are, because they ain't gonna change, and you are going to tie yourself up in knots if you try to change them.

No, you're not going to *change the world*. Isn't that what graduation speakers always say? Change the world? I take that back, a little—there are some people who actually manage to change the world, in a small way, but at great cost, and you have to ask yourself, are they happy? No, they are not happy. Because there is always more to do. Which gets back to my favorite question of all time: do you want to be right, or do you want to be happy? Hollywood likes these biopics of these heroes who sacrificed everything in order to change the world, one man against the system, and they beat the system, but that is not how it usually works out. If you are going to be one man against the system, the most likely outcome is that the system is going to squash you like a bug, and no one will remember your name. And if you do want to change the world, it will take more than Facebook and Twitter posts—you have to have skin in the game. I don't give a fuck about changing the world—I'm only interested in changing myself. I actually gave the graduation speech at Coastal Carolina University in 2022, and that was the focus of the speech—changing the world is a big waste of time, and will leave you unhappy and unfulfilled. Look at all the people in politics—they don't look like very happy people to me. Instead: get a job, make some money, buy a house, raise a family, be happy. *You can't change anything*. If people had any idea of the extent their impotence, their inability to change anything, they would give up immediately. But no, people think they are gods, and I don't know a lot about God, but I am getting there over time.

So when you read in the serenity prayer that you should change the things that you can, you have to realize that the universe of things that you can actually change is pretty close to zero. Some people take the serenity prayer too far: *I don't have a job, and I just have to accept that.* No, dumb fuck, you have to go get a job. That is within your control—to an extent. If you have a pair of pants with a stain on it, you can take them to the drycleaners. That is within your control. If you have a leak in your roof, you can get it fixed—that is within your control. If you are hungry, you can make yourself a sandwich. That is within your control. Who is president? Not within your control. Making managing director at your firm? Sort of within your control, but mostly not. Having a podcast with 100,000 subscribers? Sort of within your control, but mostly not. If God wanted you to be managing director, he would make you managing director. If God wanted you to have a viral podcast, he would give you a viral podcast. The results are not up to us—all we can do is do the footwork. Show up and do a good job every day, with consistency. That is all we can do. If you don't get any of these things, then God didn't want you to have them, and maybe you are better off. Maybe you will get other, better opportunities. Maybe you won't. And that's okay.

What are you in control of? Your own happiness. And that's pretty much it. No matter what the circumstances, we can choose our response and our attitude, which is basically the lesson of Mark Manson's *The Subtle Art of Not Giving a Fuck*, except Mark stole a bunch of other people's ideas without attribution and dropped a lot of F-bombs, and put an orange cover on it and sold six million copies. I wish I had thought of it myself.

Acceptance is the answer. And I am stealing an idea here: If there is a person or thing that is bothering you, the answer isn't to change that person or thing, but to accept it as it is exactly as it is supposed to be at this moment in time. Your efforts to change things are often counterproductive. If you have a family member who is an addict, have you had any success in trying to change the family member, and get them to stop being an addict? Of course not. They will change when they will change, and not a moment sooner. Are your tweets going to get Trump out of office? Or course not. So you can either accept Trump, or you can be miserable for four years, and maybe in a cruel twist of fate, JD

Vance will get elected two more times and you'll be miserable for 12 years, 15% of your life. Sounds like fun! And remember, if you complain about something, or if you attack something, you make it stronger, if you haven't figured that out by now. The answer is to accept things exactly as they are at this moment in time. If you can't do that, you are in for a lifetime of misery. Elon Musk seems to be pretty good at changing things right now. Well, you're not Elon Musk, and again—is Elon happy? Probably not. Would I trade places with Elon Musk? No, I would not.

Change is *puny*. So I am kind of a hypocrite, because here I am telling you that you can't change the world, but I have been and currently am an opinion journalist, and the point of that is to basically try to change the world. But change is puny. One thing I learned from my editor at Bloomberg Opinion is that you want to write about small things. If you write about big things— Trump is good/bad, capitalism is good/bad, health insurance is good/bad—people tune you out. If you write about small things, like raising the cap on SALT deductions from $10,000 to $20,000, people will be more receptive to your ideas. Innovations are puny as well. People don't like big change, but they can handle small change. The only time people like big change is when they are absolutely miserable and have reached the point of maximum pain, like FDR in 1932, or Javier Milei in Argentina in 2023. And big change isn't always good. Au contraire, it's usually bad.

Try to practice acceptance in every area of your life. Someone always makes smart-ass comments on your Facebook posts? Accept that person exactly as he is supposed to be. Kid not living up to your expectations? Accept him. Not getting the recognition you think you deserve at work? Accept it, or find another job—this is partially within your control. That last part of the serenity prayer—*the wisdom to know the difference*—you can live ten lifetimes and still never fully acquire that wisdom. Back at Lehman, we were judged on having a *bias to action*. These days, I have a bias to *inaction*. I don't do things. I don't try to change people or situations. Believe it or not, usually that problem will work itself out if you ignore it long enough.

FORWARD MOTION

I JUST GOT THROUGH *Lessons for Living* by Phil Stutz, probably the world's most famous living psychiatrist, where he writes about something he calls "forward motion." I am paraphrasing: when we stop moving forward, we die. He is more specific: when we stop creating, we die.

As you can imagine, I am in agreement. In my 50s, I am constantly taking on new challenges. I just built a big honking house with a big honking mortgage because...why? Because I was getting too comfortable. I am a big believer in blowing up your life and starting over. I started an investment firm this year, because... why? Because doing a newsletter was getting a little bit stale. I teach every semester at CCU. I don't have to do this. I am working on my sixth, seventh, and eighth books. I don't have to do this. I got an MFA in 2023, at age 49. I didn't have to do that. I probably spend 100 days a year on the road. Etc. And this year, I think I am going to try something new: screenwriting.

I have written about the dangers of retirement. I'm sure you know someone who worked their whole life in finance or law or some demanding profession, they retired, and were dead within a year? Cancer got 'em. That's not a coincidence. They stopped moving forward, and they rolled a seven. That's not to say that you should be doing finance or law or publishing or whatever high-powered profession you are doing until you die, but you have to *keep creating*. My grandfather-in-law is 102. He works in his wood shop every day. During the holidays, he is especially busy—he will make a few hundred toys for local children in need. A hundred and two years old, and the dude is still creating. He has a purpose. This is what it's all about.

No need to think about retirement at the moment. What are the ways in which you could be constantly pushing yourself? Well, if you are a small business owner, if you did $1 million top line this year, maybe you think about doing $1.5 million? Or $2 million? Maybe, if you made 9% this year at your hedge fund, you think about making 12% or 15% next year? Maybe, if you are a writer like me, your goal is to finish a book and start another one? Fill in the blank. When I use the word "creating," you might think of artistic endeavors such as painting or writing or filmmaking, but really, anything can be "creative," including being a corporate bond salesman. You're a creator, you're a builder, you're a maker of things, you're a doer, and you keep doing these things until your body or mind can no longer sustain it, and then you quit and create or do something else. John Updike is one of my favorite writers. He never stopped writing—he was writing well into his 70s, and published his last novel the year before he passed. He was worth $20 million at his death, could easily have stopped a long time ago, but he kept creating. I should add that he had some longevity.

I sort of implied that there is a connection between forward motion and physical health. There is. This has no scientific basis in fact, just a matter of observation, but people engaged in work or play or creating or living, tend to live a long time. People who sit on the couch with the TV turned up to 11 will die. There are a lot of people who watch their diet and exercise and don't eat seed oils and all that crap, and they think that physical fitness is what will keep them alive until age 90. Nothing could be further from the truth. Longevity is mental, not physical. I can't explain it. Let me put it this way: I never met someone in their 100s who didn't want to keep living. When they make a decision that they want to die, they will die. There are people in their 80s, 70s, or even 60s who decide that they want to die. This isn't a decision made on a conscious level, but on a subconscious level—why is it that physical afflictions always hit the people who have the least to do? The people who have checked out? Let me put it this way: I am going on 51 years old, and I am not in great health. I am about 40 pounds overweight, I have high blood pressure, high cholesterol, a bum knee, and spinal stenosis. I am going to outlive a lot of people, because I get out of bed every morning like the *Raiders of the Lost Ark* theme is playing, and run around like a crazy person trying to get all this stuff done. It would suck if I died, because there is so much left that I want to do. Maybe I get to a point where I run out of things to do, and I give up. You may disagree with me, but I would say that we all get to choose the time and place of our own death, whether it is a conscious choice or not. And forward motion doesn't have to be up and to the right in my chosen career. Maybe I get to be age 70, and I decide I want to do something completely different, and I become a bartender, and I put on a white shirt and black bow tie and become a purveyor and lifter of spirits, and that is my new calling.

TV is the enemy. Remember in the 80s when we all thought that TV would rot your brain? Newsflash: it actually does rot your brain. Now, I have a TV (one, for a giant house) and I do turn it on (mostly sports), but I am usually working on my laptop with the TV on. I'm not "watching" TV, per se. Maybe one time in the last five years I have sat down on the couch and zoned out watching *Judge Judy* or something like that. Theoretically speaking, the only time one would watch TV is when one has nothing to do. And I always have something to do. In our house, the TV time is for the family to hang out together on the couch—me, my wife, and the cats. Everyone gets cozy, there's some noise on the TV from the baseball game, I'm tapping away at my computer, and my wife is reading a book. It's a ritual, and ritual is important. But I basically wrote all of *No Worries* in front of the TV, and a good part of *Night Moves*, too. The foregoing also applies to social media, doomscrolling on Twitter or going deep into Facebook where all the ads for boner pills and hair growth live. I try to take social media in small doses. These days, my mom will ask me if I have seen something on Facebook, and I haven't, which I think is a good thing.

There was one year in my life when I was going backwards, not forwards: 2010. I had just moved to South Carolina, I had been running *The Daily Dirtnap* for about 18 months, and I inexplicably became *satisfied* with what I had, which wasn't much. I got practically no business that year. I'd write my newsletter in the morning, and then I'd walk about a mile to Starbucks and get a coffee and sit and stare out the window for the rest of the afternoon. I should add that by this point, *Street Freak* was already written, and was going through the editing process, so there wasn't much to do with that except to wait for it to come out. I wasn't depressed. In fact, I was quite happy to be living someplace new, I liked the weather, I liked the people, but instead of working on the newsletter, or another book, or something else, I was just killing time. By the way, killing time is one of the worst things that you can do. Time is our most precious resource. You wouldn't kill time any more than you would light a $100 bill on fire.

I'll give you one more example: Richard Russell, the famous financial newsletter writer with his *Dow Theory Letter*, who passed away at the age of 91. He wrote that damn thing up until the day that he died, and never missed a day. At one point, he had over 12,000 subscribers. He did not have that many at the end. But he kept doing it. I can tell you that writing a financial newsletter can be a grind, and it's tough to sustain that kind of enthusiasm over decades. I am on year 17. I have a long way to go before I catch up to Richard Russell. But you want to talk about forward motion—egad. That dude kept going and going and going.

We could talk about Buffett and Munger here, for sure.

Keep going. Never stop. Am I clear?

POWER

I READ A BOOK a few years back called *Power* by a guy named Jeffrey Pfeffer. The thesis is as follows: Many people naively believe that if they do the best job they possibly can, they will be paid and promoted, but then are disappointed to find out that less-competent employees are getting paid and promoted ahead of them. The solution? Your job—that thing you do every day—is not your job. Your job is actually to be friends with your boss. If it makes you feel better, you can be friends with your boss and do a good job, but mostly all that matters is that you're friends with your boss.

But then you say, *I refuse to play political games!* Earth to asshole: life is about political games. If you want, you can go on being the hardest-working, most underpaid person at your firm.

I'm not sure how much of this checks out, but I identified with it. At Lehman, I was the hardest-working, most underpaid person at my firm. I didn't realize it at the time, though. I never politicked for pay, and I got paid what I got paid, which was about 20 times what I had made in the Coast Guard in any case. I was vaguely aware that my ETF trader pals at other firms were making almost twice as much as me, but at age 32 or whatever, I felt fabulously wealthy, so I didn't complain. Editor's note: I should have complained. If I got paid an additional 30% in my last three years at the firm, that money, compounded, would be worth a lot today. Enough to pay off my mortgage.

I like money as much as the next person, but—and I am being honest when I say this—the money was incidental to being able to participate in the most amazing intellectual challenge of all time: the financial markets. I did it for the love of the game. And like I said, I was just happy to be there, and I think management knew that I was just happy to be there, so I traded at a discount. Now, usually what people do in these situations is get an offer away and hold up the bank, but I was loyal to a fault, and they knew that, too. I did get one offer, and I turned it down, and it was a good thing I turned it down, because it was from Bear Stearns, and I would have been on the beach six months earlier.

Anyway, I don't dwell on being underpaid, and now it doesn't matter, because I eat what I kill, and when you eat what you kill, well, let's just say that it's a good place to be, psychologically speaking, not having to depend on the benevolence of some guy making $5 million to give you another $50,000. But the part that I do think about is: how do you use people skills to get what you want? Because there are people out there who have copious people skills who are adept at getting what they want. Then you have the politicians, who basically do this for a living. We hate the politicians who are unprincipled, which describes about 95% of them. The Thomas Massies of the world, the principled ones, have no political future. Once he's ignominiously voted out of office, he'll start a libertarian gold mining newsletter or something, flying coach to MoneyShow Orlando, stay at the Omni hotel where the ice machine on his floor doesn't work. If you're a principled politician, that's what's in your future. When I think back to all the presidents we've had in the last 50 years, none of them are political slouches, with the possible exception of Biden. Bill Clinton had god-level political skills. My only experience with elected office was when I was elected class vice president my freshman year in college. After one year, I was voted out of office.

As I have written before, principles will get you in trouble. If you don't want to overtly be a political animal, think of it this way: You would want to be friends with your boss just like you would want to be friends with anyone else. It's just a nice thing to do. If you want a raise, have you tried asking for a raise? The cool thing about asking for a raise is that there is absolutely, positively no downside. Your boss can say *no—end of discussion*. But it's kind of hard to cold-ask for a raise if you haven't developed a friendship first. Life is salesmanship. Life is a presentation. This is how bad I was at marketing myself at Lehman—in 2007, I made $8 million day-trading S&P 500 futures over the course of a year—a herculean feat. Except I did it in my old index arb futures account, so the bosses just assumed I was still doing index arb. It never occurred to me to tell them that I was a fucking market wizard trading S&P 500 futures. So I never got paid on that.

I'm a slow learner. I rode the short bus to school. I didn't start figuring this out until my 40s, when it was too late to matter. One thing I have learned in my old age is that friends are really important. I don't go around making enemies with people like I used to in the past. Though I have to say that writing a tell-all book about Lehman Brothers hasn't gotten me invited to any Lehman Brothers reunions.

This may sound like a bunch of Machiavellian bullshit, but really all it comes down to is being a decent human being. You treat people with love and respect, and patience and tolerance, and it will boomerang back to you. The ETF trader two guys before me, Tom, was allegedly a sweetheart of a guy, a sunny optimist who was friends with everyone. That guy hadn't been in the building in ten years and people would still talk about him. He probably got paid more than me, too.

If you're interested in another interesting read on the topic, check out Neil Strauss. Yes, that Neil Strauss. I read *The Game* in the 2000s— his memoir about being part of a pick-up artist cult, and then I read *Rules of the Game* in the 2010s, a how-to manual on how to pick up girls. Wait—what does picking up girls have to do with office politics? It has to do with a lot of things. Even though I was happily married, *Rules of the Game* was one of the most influential books I have ever read. This is an oversimplification, but here goes: girls like rockstars. So be a rockstar! You can be whoever you want to be. This biggest takeaway I got from that book is that oftentimes, our outsides match our insides. If you're wearing dad jeans with a FUPA, a woven leather belt, and New Balance sneakers, you probably don't have a very high opinion of yourself—and it shows. That was about the time that I started paying more attention to my personal appearance. I started buying better clothes, I whitened my teeth, I went tanning, I went to the gym—I looked and felt great. I wasn't doing it for sex appeal; I was doing it for myself, and it was interesting to see people's reactions to the new me. Anyway, Neil Strauss almost died of too much sex and wrote his last memoir, *The Truth*, about how all his other memoirs were misguided and false. I still like *Rules of the Game*. Not for nothing, Strauss is an excellent writer, a compliment I don't give out lightly.

I'm going to say that social media is important. It is a contrarian thing to say, because most people say that social media is the devil. I have about 1,250 Facebook friends, and I am not one of these people who collects Facebook randos right and left. I know pretty much all of them fairly well. I think staying in contact with people is a good thing. I could do without all the memes and politics and crap, but I like seeing wedding photos and vacation photos, and I especially like celebrating other people's achievements. I have a Facebook friend who posts videos of himself playing the guitar. I never thought much of that until I started taking guitar lessons, and I realized how fucking hard it is, so now I like his guitar-playing videos. I am generous with the like button. Look—ideally, we would have more meaningful contact than pressing the stupid like button, but you can't realistically go deep with 1,250 people, so the like button it is. Trust me, people will remember (and like) that you pressed the like button. Don't be so fucking stingy with it.

As is usually the case with these essays, spread good in the world, don't be a hater, and great things will happen. You will get paid and promoted. Your boss isn't a menacing authority figure, he's just a guy trying to find his way in the world. You can be there.

I LOVE PAIN

I SPENT A GOOD part of this afternoon reading Phil Stutz's *The Tools*. I was turned onto Stutz two years ago, but I still haven't watched his Netflix series, though I will soon, right after football is over.

The first of the tools is called "Reversal of Desire," and it is basically for people who can't get out of their own way, which is practically everyone. It goes something like this: There is something you want. But you will have to go through a lot of pain to get it. Since most people avoid pain, you instead choose to spend time within your comfort zone, which sounds fine, except if you spend your entire life within your comfort zone, you won't have accomplished anything, and you will have crippling regret. Again, this is practically everyone.

Stutz says that the solution to this is to run headfirst into the pain. He actually suggests you say to yourself, "I love pain," and then go do the hard thing. I have written about doing hard things before. So you run headfirst into the pain, without a helmet, you do the hard thing, and a whole new world opens up to you.

It will not come as a surprise to you that I like Stutz and I like this idea of getting outside your comfort zone and I also like this idea of running headfirst into pain. Now, the most famous person who loves pain is retired Navy SEAL turned self-help memoirist David Goggins. It's not that David Goggins doesn't feel pain, it's that he actually likes it. He takes it to an extreme—he's borderline masochistic. But he is a model of the idea that you can do pretty much anything if you put your mind to it, which resonates with a lot of people. But since I don't see five million David Gogginses running around, I am guessing that most people decided it was too hard and went back to eating Harvest Cheddar SunChips.

So when you think about people who love pain, the first people who come to mind are naturally the elite athletes. The long-distance runners, the swimmers, the gymnasts, the weightlifters, the MMA fighters, etc. If you are stepping into the octagon, you have gone through a lot of pain to get where you are, and you are probably going to be in a lot of pain after that fight. You are doing something that not a lot of people are willing to do, and that's great! One thing I've found about athletes, though, is that they look down on non-athletes for being unwilling to go through that kind of pain. Correspondingly, non-athletes treat elite athletes with a reverence that is probably unwarranted, as physical pain is not the only kind of pain out there. There is also psychic pain, otherwise known as mental pain or emotional pain, and sometimes, both. But an athlete will look at a fat person and say, *that guy is a pussy*, without realizing that Mr. Fat Guy is one of the leading mathematicians in the world. Or is a legendary trader, or a world-famous musician, or has a phone number in his bank account. No, we place physical pain on a higher plane than psychic pain, because it is visible.

It's funny—I'm not in the best physical shape, and sometimes people make assumptions about me that I am weak or lazy. Being weak or lazy would imply that I have a desire to be in shape, but that I refuse to endure the pain. In that case, I would be weak or lazy. The reality is that at one point in my life, I actually was an elite athlete, and my attitude is *been there, done that*, and I'd prefer to spend that time doing something else, like writing books. An athlete could not do what I do (write books). The funny thing is that Goggins wrote a book and it was so goddamned poorly written that his editor just threw up his hands and published it as is, and the voice was so compelling that it became a bestseller. But, in general, most athletes aren't willing to go through the psychic pain it takes to write a book, and I'm not just talking about the writing part. I'm talking about querying 300 agents, spending eight months on a proposal, getting turned down by 25 different publishers, going through a brutal editing process, and then hustling up 100 different podcasts when it is released. No, that process is painful. I'm not saying it's superior to physical pain, but I'm certainly not saying that physical pain is superior to psychic pain. They are *pari passu*. Don't assume that someone else's life is easy because they can't do five sets of 47 push-ups.

For example, everyone thinks that actors have it good. Oh really? Have you ever been in an audition? Have you ever been in a situation where how you perform for 120 seconds is going to determine the trajectory of the rest of your life? And, by the way, you are in competition with 500 other people? You want to talk about pressure? You want to talk about pain? The last six months of rehearsing comes down to two minutes? I don't think so.

But really what we are talking about here is the athlete who won't put in the extra effort, the writer who doomscrolls instead of writing, and the actor who bails on auditions because of the pressure. The people who aren't getting what they want out of their lives because they are living in their comfort zone. And within the comfort zone are opiates—not actual opiates, mind you, but mind-numbing habits like weed, booze, social media, TV, and porn, all of which can be psychological crutches, excuses to not go through the pain we need to learn and grow. Even one minute spent on any of these things will move your further away from your goal. You're either moving towards your goal, or away from your goal. If I am being honest, I spend a little too much time on social media. I have to use Twitter a bit for my job, but I don't need to spend a half hour scrolling to the bottom of Facebook where all the underwear ads live. I spent about three hours writing my novel today. I also spent about an hour on social media. Shame on me. I will say that writing the novel is painful much in the way that lifting weights in painful. Not fun while you're doing it, but you feel great afterwards.

Aside from the opiates, a lot of the reason that people don't run headfirst into the pain is because it is scary. They have fear. Usually fear of rejection. I am one of the lucky microscopic few who never had to query an agent, but I know plenty of people who have. Eighty percent of the time, you never get a response. 0.99% of the time, you might get some helpful feedback. And .01% of the time, you sign a deal. Of course, we all go through this, right? The kids in college trying to land investment banking internships are doing the same thing, sending out 3,000 cold emails or LinkedIn messages. You have to have zero fear of rejection. Talk to anyone in sales—same thing. I will tell you a story. When I published *All the Evil of This World*, I had 100 galleys printed, and I started DMing people on Twitter to help me promote the book. Practically no one responded. One person actually made fun of my pitch in a tweet. Kept going. Got no help from anyone. The book ended up being a cult favorite, and is one of my proudest achievements. Also: You are not in charge of what other people think of you. People will have negative feelings about you, and that's okay. You can't control other people—you can only control you.

Maybe you decide to take my advice and run headfirst into the pain, yelling *I LOVE PAIN*, and you do the thing and it is a failure. Well, doing something doesn't guarantee success. I have failed at a whole bunch of things over the years, and I'm failing at stuff as I write. When you take on a challenge, there are only two outcomes: it succeeds, or you learn something. Both of those are excellent outcomes. After 20 years of failure, I am one smart motherfucker. And success is often a matter of perspective. I sold 2,250 copies of my short story collection, *Night Moves*. That book was my baby. Now, 2,250 copies doesn't sound like a lot, but it is when you consider that the average short story collection sells about 500. I am guessing that *The Best American Short Stories* series sells about 4,000-5,000. So I feel pretty good about it. And even if I only sold one copy to my mom, I would still be proud of it.

So. The short version of this:

- Get out of your comfort zone.
- Run headfirst into the pain.
- Win.

The one thing unsuccessful people have in common? They don't love pain.

Back to the novel tomorrow.

FEAR

Wouldn't it be nice to be fearless?

People like to engage in catastrophic thinking. What is catastrophic thinking? When you think that the worst possible outcome is going to happen to you—all the time. I used to do this in my Wall Street days. I'd push the wrong button, or put a trade in the wrong account, and I'd think to myself: *that's it, I'm going to jail*. Every one of my catastrophic thinking fantasies ended up with me in jail. For a period of about ten years, I thought I was going to jail all the time.

Now, clearly, I didn't end up in jail. Obviously, that was irrational. And if you told me at the time that it was irrational, I wouldn't have believed you. People did tell me at the time that it was irrational, and I didn't believe them. I really, truly believed that I was going to jail. I went to the worst possible outcome, and believed it as if it were really happening.

The thing about these irrational fears is that you can't simply explain to someone that they are irrational. Because to them, it feels real. And then, the bad thing ends up not happening, and they are onto the next fear, making up a story and believing it. And it cycles over and over again.

Wouldn't you like to stop? Wouldn't you like to be happy?

Some people are absolutely crippled with anxiety. It goes way beyond worrying, into sheer, unrelenting terror that lasts for years. Some people are on a dose of Klonopin that would kill a giraffe. But that is not the answer.

Around 2013, I decided I wanted to stop. And the episodes of catastrophic thinking became less and less frequent. In my piece, "The Cure for Anxiety," I talked about the mechanical, procedural steps I took to reduce my anxiety. Small habits that I made and practiced on a daily basis to squash the catastrophic thinking. And it was a process.

But that is not the whole story.

You can do the mechanical, procedural things that I described in that essay, but more than that is involved. The solution is ultimately spiritual. You have to go from believing that the world is a dangerous place to believing that the world is a safe, forgiving place. You have to believe that even if these awful, terrible things you dreamed up happened to you, *you would still be okay*. People have anxiety about losing things— loss of money, loss of property, loss of reputation, loss of relationships. I guess when you've been through it all, like I have, and come out the other side, you don't fear these things anymore.

It is about faith, but it is more than just about faith. Lots of people believe in a higher power. That's level one of the videogame. Level 72 of the videogame is trusting the higher power, and knowing that God isn't going to give you anything you can't handle, and also, that the tough stuff that we go through isn't without purpose. It's all for a reason. I believe that God has a purpose for me now, but I couldn't see it in the 2000s. The suicide attempts, the psych wards; at the time, I believed it was unnecessary suffering. There is literally no such thing as unnecessary suffering. I went through all that, at the time I went through it, at the place I went through it, so that I could get the help that I so desperately needed so that it would unlock my potential and I could go on to live a life that most people only dream of. At the time, all I wanted was to not kill myself. Nineteen years later, I'm doing all kinds of amazing stuff and living in a huge house that is pretty close to being paid for. In 2006, my biggest ambition was to not kill myself. If you had told me in 2006 that this is where I would be in 18 years, I would have… cried? I wouldn't have dreamed it was possible.

We don't know what the future holds, but no matter what you are going through, no matter how awful it is, I can tell you one thing for sure: *this, too, shall pass*. It will get better. A lot of people were trying to help me back then, and people said a lot of dumb shit to me, but the truest thing that anyone ever said, while I was crying on the sidewalk at 87th and Lex, when I thought I had lost everything, was this: *it gets better*. Boy, did it fucking get better. And boy, do I have a lot of gratitude.

So it gets better—if you want it to. There are two parts to this: a decision, and action. First, you make a *decision* that you want to get better. This is harder than it sounds, because sick people want to stay sick. I wrote about this earlier, too. Being miserable is easy. Getting better is hard. So first, you must make a decision that you want to get better. And then you have to take action. Don't worry, you won't have to change much—just absolutely everything in your life. People don't change—but when they do, it is glorious. Becoming mentally healthy is one of the hardest things you will ever do. And it is a multi-decade process. The first place people usually go is the medication, but the medication is often a short-term fix, a band-aid. In the beginning, the medication will allow you to function. But you can't realistically be taking Xanax or Valium for 20 years. Once on the medication, the goal should be to get off the medication. I absolutely believe in modern medicine—the last thing I am going to tell people is that they should forget the meds and go find God. But it can be a psychological crutch over time, and it doesn't allow you to reach your full potential.

There is a saying: *Fear knocked. Faith answered. No one was there.* Took me about 20 years to understand that. I've been through some rough stuff, but I know people who have been through a lot rougher stuff than me, and they made it through with their faith intact. In fact, their faith carried them through. Combat. Dead spouses. Dead children. Bankruptcies. Divorces. Arrests. Jail time. If I find myself losing conviction that everything is going to be okay, I can borrow some of their conviction. Everything is going to be okay. And even if it's not okay, it's still okay.

There was a dumb movie that came out in 1998 called *Sphere*, with Dustin Hoffman, Sharon Stone, and Samuel L. Jackson. It's like an underwater alien movie or something; I forget the details. Like I said, it's dumb. But the movie is all about fear. And there is a scene towards the end where the three of them are in a mini-sub, and they have to undock so they can escape the base which is being overrun with aliens or something, but they're paralyzed with fear. Shit is blowing up all over the place, and they're just sitting in the mini-sub with their fear. I've probably done a poor job of explaining this, but if you've seen the movie, you know what I'm talking about. That's what fear is. Fear prevents you from living and enjoying life. Fear prevents you from doing the things you want to do. Fear prevents you from realizing your full potential. And the amazing thing is—it's all self-inflicted. We do it to ourselves; we are trapped within our own minds. God strike me down for bringing up Elon Musk again, but the guy literally has no fear. And look what he does! He literally told the SEC to go fuck themselves. And got away with it! Who does that? That is what a life lived without fear looks like. I'm not saying that we should all emulate his ketamine consumption, or suggest that is what is responsible for his fearlessness, and clearly, he has some other character defects, but the man has no fucking fear. That is what is possible when you don't have fear and anxiety—you can literally do anything.

So why not try?

I write all kinds of stuff, some funny stuff, some sad stuff, some uplifting stuff, but I swear to God, this will be the most important piece I ever write. Text someone and they don't text back? *He hates me.* Get an email from compliance? *I'm getting fired.* Child gets sick? *He's going to die.* Stop fucking doing this stuff—it's all in your head. And it's destroying your dreams one day at a time. Make a decision. Take action. Use the tools. Talk to people. Have faith. It really will be okay.

RESENTMENT

Let's say somebody pisses you off. Let's say somebody backstabs you at work. What are you going to do about it?

You go home, you lay in bed at night, and you engage in all these revenge fantasies. *I'm gonna fuck that guy over,* you think. You are caught in a maze of resentment, thinking of all the ways you're going to get even. Consequently, you can't sleep. You toss and turn until two in the morning, trying to send hate through the universe tubes, and you finally drift off to sleep, and then your alarm goes off at 5:30, and you're still thinking about this guy. You're thinking about him as you take a shower. You're thinking about him as you get dressed. You're thinking about him in the car on the way to work.

Guess what? He isn't thinking about you!

You are spending all this mental energy thinking about Mr. Public Enemy #1, and he isn't thinking about you. He's spending his time thinking about more productive things, like his family, or his pets, or how to make more money.

That's the way resentment goes—it's usually one-way.

But resentment is no joke. There are basically only two types of spiritual disturbances—fear and resentment. I addressed fear earlier. In

RESENTMENT

many ways, resentment is worse. Resentment will consume your soul and make you do things you'd never imagine you'd do, and I'm not just talking about getting revenge. I'm talking about hurting yourself. You'll engage in self-destructive behavior, like excessive drinking, overeating, acting out sexually, or anything else. You'll torpedo your own career. You'll torpedo your marriage. No exaggeration—resentment can ruin your life.

Now, sometimes we have what is known as *justified anger* at another person. Anytime you have a conflict with another person, you always have to ask yourself what your part in it was. And if you are really introspective about it, you might come to the conclusion that you had no part in it at all. You just got steamrolled by some random jerk, which happens sometimes. So if you are totally blameless, how can you not be angry at the other person? My friends, not even I am qualified to handle justified anger. As I have written before, I try not to ever get angry, because getting angry disturbs my peace and serenity. You might read from some other self-help dickhead that anger is a good thing and can actually be used to your advantage. I basically spent all of my 20s in a state of anger more or less all the time. It was exhausting. It would be really dumb to acquire wisdom from *Star Wars*, but *don't give in to the dark side, Luke*. Hate has never, ever accomplished anything. Sometimes people don't follow the script that I have written for them. They will, or they won't. And this gets to the core of why resentment is the worst of all spiritual disturbances—*you can't control other people*—and if you try, you will drive yourself nuts. Let them be dickheads. They're on their path, and you're on your path.

I want to take a brief detour here and talk about how unproductive it is to try to control the entire universe with our minds. We worry about bad things happening, thinking that if we worry hard enough, that if we pray for a bad outcome, then it won't happen. We resent other people, thinking that if we resent them hard enough, they'll change and we will get what we want. Virtually all forms of non-heritable mental illness come from a desire to control other people and our surroundings. Virtually all forms of non-heritable mental illness come from an inability to accept other people and the world as they are. You can't control your kid dropping out of college. You can't control your husband letting out a loud fart when he gets out of bed in the morning. You can't control the county when they hand you a property tax increase. You can't control the airport that just rerouted flight patterns over your house. You can't control who becomes president. The number of things you actually can control is shockingly small. You take the action, and you leave the results up to somebody else. That's how this game works. Read this paragraph a few times. If you understand it and internalize it, you will never need a therapist again.

So back to resentment. You can't control other people with your mind. It probably seems silly to read that—you're probably thinking, *I never do that*. Well, yes, you do. If someone's behavior disturbs you, you basically have two options. Option one is you talk to them about it, honestly and respectfully, and tell them how their behavior makes you feel. Option two is to decide it's not that important, and forget about it. There are no other options. But most people go to option three—they don't talk about it, they don't forget about it, and instead, engage in trench warfare in their minds—which does nothing! Except—it makes you feel bad. You have probably heard the quote that resentment is like drinking poison and waiting for the other person to die. People die because of resentment. People end up sitting in jail because of resentment. Again: you have option one or option two. There is no third option. One caveat here—if you try option two, and it doesn't work, and you can't forget about it, then go back to option one.

Or! There is another solution. This is not easy. So let's say that Mr. Dickhead has pissed you off, and you're hating his guts, and it's consuming all your thoughts, and you can't get any peace. Here is what you do: *You pray for them to have all the things in life you would want for yourself.*

If you want more money, you pray for them to have more money. If you want more fame, pray for them to have more fame. If you want better health, you pray for them to have better health. If you want a bigger house, you pray for them to live in a fucking mansion.

You send love to them. Find a quiet spot in your house, your bedroom, your library, a special place, and send love to them. Do this once a day for two weeks, and let me know how it turns out.

I can tell you how it will turn out—your resentment will be gone.

But I'm right! you say. Who gives a fuck if you are right? Do you want to be right, or do you want to feel better? Do you want to be right, or do you want to be happy? We have a need to be right all the time so that we can protect our egos. Financial Twitter is full of people who want to be right so they can protect their egos—and people see right through it. Acceptance is the answer. I mean, look. None of this means that you have to have a relationship with the person who wronged you. You could be past the point of no return with this person. You don't need to have a relationship with them—but you do need to be free of the resentment. You need to be free of the resentment so you can thrive. I don't think there's a therapist alive who will tell you that you need to go back into a toxic relationship. You don't to be friends with them—but if they're taking up space rent-free in your head, then you need to do something about it.

When you free yourself of fear, when you free yourself of resentment, you have so much space in your heart to be of service to other people. When you are consumed by fear or resentment, you don't have room for things like empathy and generosity. You are too jammed up in your own bullshit. Let's say you get divorced. Are you going to spend the next 20 years hating your ex-wife? That sounds like a good plan. Keep it up. You will be the guy in the office who has no friends.

Some people (like myself) had difficult childhoods. Are you going to be 40, resenting your parents, and the things they did to you? This is what therapists mean when they talk about moving on. They talk about the power of forgiveness, which, by the way, is a central tenet of Christianity. You don't forgive other people for their sakes, you forgive them for yours. A lot of people look at forgiveness as a sign of weakness, that it's win/lose, and you're losing. Again, how insane does it sound to wish for good things to happen to the person that you hate? I don't wish for bad things to happen to anyone—even the people who I dislike, even the people who have wronged me. I truly hope they go on to live happy, productive lives filled with joy. It's not a matter of whether they deserve it or not. Somewhere out there, someone has a resentment against me, and is wishing for shit to rain down on me, and it's not working.

Why should you listen to me? I don't have a PhD in psychology. I'm not an LCSW. I'm not a therapist. Let's just say that 20 years ago, I was the most psychologically unhealthy person in the world, and I've spent every day of the last 20 years thinking about how to get better. I'm a pretty happy guy, and I wish the same for you.

SIGNS

MY WIFE IS a big M. Night Shyamalan fan. She loves all his movies, even the terrible ones, and there have been some terrible ones. My personal favorite is *Signs*, from 2002, about an Episcopal priest (Mel Gibson) who loses his faith after his wife dies in an accident, and regains it after an alien invasion. The movie is also a nifty IQ test—dumb people will watch it and say, "The aliens looked stupid!" And smart people will watch it and just be in awe of the writing and the plot. I cry every time.

The plot is a bit too complicated to go into here, but basically (spoiler alert), the family is saved from the aliens by three coincidences— Mel Gibson's daughter's habit of leaving half-empty glasses of water around the house, his son's asthma, which prevents from inhaling the alien's poison, and Mel Gibson's wife's dying words, telling his brother Merrill, a former minor league baseball player, to "swing away." Mel Gibson can't comprehend the heaps and heaps of coincidences that led to his family being saved, and in the final scene, you see him putting his clerical collar back on. It's a move about faith, obviously, and the fact that there are no coincidences.

Carl Jung first explored the concept of coincidences and something he called "synchronicity." From *Perplexity*:

Carl Jung introduced the concept of synchronicity to describe meaningful coincidences that appear to have no causal connection. He defined synchronicity as "meaningful coincidences that cannot be explained by cause and effect." Jung believed these events were not random occurrences but manifestations of a deeper order in the universe.

Jung's most well-known example of synchronicity involved a patient describing a dream about a golden scarab beetle. At that precise moment, a real scarab beetle (similar to a golden scarab) flew into Jung's office window. Jung caught the beetle and presented it to the patient, stating, "Here is your scarab." This event had a transformative impact on the patient, breaking through her defensive rationalism. Jung believed that synchronicity could serve as a tool for personal growth and self-understanding. He suggested that most people experience synchronicities at moments when they most need them, and rather than over-intellectualizing these occurrences, one should remain open to their potential significance. In essence, Jung's concept of synchronicity invites us to consider a broader perspective on reality, one that acknowledges the potential for meaningful connections beyond simple cause and effect relationships.

I have experienced several such moments in my life, some of which I can't even talk about because they are so personal, but the one I like to talk about all the time is when I was touring the P. Coast Options Exchange in 1999, and someone went to throw a water bottle in the trash which almost hit me in the head, which led to a job offer—and that's how my Wall Street career began. Back then, I was a very rational person, and I didn't see the synchronicity. Looking back, I can see how there is a greater order in the universe, that it was meant to happen, that God or someone else had a plan for me, which I was not aware of at the time. But like I said, I've had several of these, including a few where I was "saved" during times of distress. You can be religious and say that

God did it, or you can be secular and say that there is a greater order in the universe, but the older I get, the more I believe that nothing happens by accident in God's world.

Last week I listened to the "This is Water" commencement speech by David Foster Wallace. First of all, let me say that David Foster Wallace had an absolutely superhuman intelligence. *Infinite Jest* is 577,608 words, using 20,584 unique words—absolutely unheard of. *Infinite Jest* is sitting on my shelf, waiting for me to dig into it, but I read a bunch of his essays in my MFA program. Anyway, Wallace tells the following story in his commencement speech (paraphrasing):

> There are two men deep in the wilderness of Alaska. There is a bar in town, and they go to the bar to drink and argue about the existence of God. One of them is a believer, and the other is an atheist. They're about six beers deep and arguing about the existence of God in the way that people on the way to getting drunk often do.
>
> "Look," says the atheist, "I've tried the whole God thing, I really have. Just last week, I was lost in the wilderness, and it was 50 below, and it was dark, and I was lost, and I really thought I was going to die, so I was in the snow and I raised up my arms and said, 'God, I believe in you, just save me now!'"
>
> And the believer says to him, "Well, you must believe, then, right? Because you're here!"
>
> And the atheist says, "No, man, two Eskimos just happened to be walking by, found me, and took me back to camp."

As I like to say, "Life is full of miracles, if your eyes are open."

I think about this a lot. Maybe some things aren't meant to happen? I'm going to say something a bit egotistical—I've had many people tell me that I'm the best "undiscovered" writer they've ever seen. They can't believe that a book like *Night Moves* only sold 2,250 copies when absolute dreck goes on to be a bestseller. Yeah, I agree. But what if it isn't meant to happen? What if God doesn't want me to become a bestselling author? What if I'm meant to be doing something else? What if I'm supposed to be a legendary trader? What if I'm supposed to be a radio show host? What if I'm supposed to be none of these things, and my purpose is to serve my fellow man? What if my purpose is to rescue cats? The point is that I am constantly looking for signs, those moments of synchronicity to give me guidance.

That moment in March of 2006—when I was sitting at my desk having a meltdown—and I picked a psychiatrist "randomly" off the internet and went to her office, and landed on her couch, sobbing, and she checked me into New York Presbyterian, where I would be given the best possible medical care, and given the lifesaving medication that would sustain me to this day—did I really choose that psychiatrist randomly? Why would I pick a psychiatrist with an unpronounceable 12-letter Russian name when there were other alternatives? The answer: it's not random. I've done pieces about luck, and I will tell anyone who will listen how lucky I am, except the thing is—it's not luck. It's meant to happen, or it's not meant to happen. We don't get to choose. We do the work and leave the results up to someone else. So maybe I will never get that bestseller, even though I want it with every cell in my body. You know why I am not getting it, probably? Because my ego wants it. Because I want to go on a 96-city book tour with TV appearances and red carpets. If it is meant to happen, it will happen. Barry Hannah sold no more than 7,000 copies of any of his books while he was alive. In his death, he was considered one of the greatest writers in history. Maybe that is my path. Or maybe not!

David Foster Wallace died on September 12th, 2008 (ironically, three days before the Lehman bankruptcy) by suicide. He hanged himself off his back porch in Claremont, California. He had struggled with depression for 20 years. He left a two-page suicide note and arranged the manuscript of his unfinished novel, *The Pale King*. He had been on and off his medication and even underwent ECT. So—was this "supposed to happen" in God's world, where a bright, shining light like David Foster Wallace was taken from us prematurely, without explanation? What about other tragedies? What about 9/11? Was that supposed to happen? What about mass shootings? If you believe in good synchronicity, do you believe in bad synchronicity? If your child dies from an overdose, and someone tells you that it was "God's will," you pretty much want to land an uppercut to their chin.

Going further, do you believe that the bullet in Butler, Pennsylvania, missed Trump's head by a whisker—by accident? Too good to be true, right?

The rationalists will tell you that this is all human beings being irrational trying to make sense of randomness. If you read enough Taleb, you will believe this to be true. As someone who trades, I deal with a lot of randomness. But one of the weird things about technical analysis is that when it works, which it often does, you start believing in deterministic markets—stuff is meant to happen. And so there is a lot of faith in my financial writing—when there is absolutely no reason for a stock, a currency, a bond, or a commodity to go down, when the fundamental bull case is as bullish as ever—it does. You had no reason to believe that it would. Shorting it was an article of faith—but it worked.

Go ahead and try raising money for a faith-based hedge fund, and see how well you do. There is no place for faith in finance, right? Is there a faith section in the CFA? It's not crazy talk. There is faith in every trade. Anytime you buy something, it is an act of faith, because we can't possibly know the future. Even when you have an ironclad investment case, markets are unpredictable. The people who fail are the ones who doubt.

I am writing this at the car dealership, waiting for my car to get serviced. They told me I needed new tires, brakes, and spark plugs. It will take three hours. Instead of resisting, and saying, *I'll do it later*, I said to myself, *well, I don't really have anything going on today, and I can sit in the waiting room and write something.* It was meant to be. All the pain in my life comes from when I am resisting. And so it was meant to be that you are getting this essay.

Life is full of miracles, if your eyes are open.

HAPPINESS IS A CHOICE

First, we will talk about therapy.

People go to therapists when they are spiritually disturbed. They hope that the therapist will quiet the disturbance. I am not against talk therapy, but the reality is that the vast majority of therapists are patently unqualified to be in charge of another person's spiritual well-being. They're people with intractable problems just like you or me. The good thing about therapy is that it helps to simply talk about your problems, to articulate them and get them out in the open; the bad thing about therapy is that most therapists are mirrors and will simply reflect their patient's narcissism and self-absorption back at them. People have ended perfectly good marriages and jobs because of therapists, resulting in huge amounts of chaos. But a good one can be immeasurably helpful for spiritual growth, or to end compulsive behaviors.

Anyway, the point here is that people go to therapists to get happy, but how many of them get happy? How many people have told you that they owe their life and their happiness to their therapist? A few, I suppose. But happiness is an inside job. As discussed before, it comes from work and achievements, relationships with others, and your relationship with a higher power. Everything else is ego.

I'm sure you've had this experience with a friend who is always lurching from one crisis to another. Somebody's sick, the job is going down the tubes, the marriage is on the rocks, everything's hard. Interesting. I've been sick, my job has gone down the tubes, and my marriage has been on the rocks at various times in my life. I'm not really sure what to say, other than that we get to choose our response to every situation. Life is difficult. Ninety-nine percent of spiritual disturbances occur when we think that life should not be difficult, and then it turns out to be difficult. I will make an observation: poor people are generally happier than rich people, because when your basic material needs are not met, you don't have the time or mental energy to worry about your financial advisor not returning your emails. If you told poor people your problems, they would laugh at your problems. People lack perspective, which is putting it lightly. The good news: you have food and a house and a TV and a washing machine and a dishwasher and the internet. Everything else is ego. Now, that's not to say that money doesn't have the ability to make people happy, because it absolutely does—I write a lot about how more material things make us happy. But nothing can compete with the spiritual disturbance that arises from an old friend not returning your calls.

And that's not to say that an old friend not returning your calls isn't a big deal, because it is. And that's not to say that having our basic needs met should make us content, because as you know, we have a hierarchy of needs, and spiritual needs are at the top. I'm just saying that most of the stuff that people get spiritually disturbed about... is not really a big deal. Unhappy people stay unhappy. Happy people stay happy. That is my experience. If you give an unhappy person everything they want, they will still find ways to be unhappy. I know, because I used to be an unhappy person. And then I chose happiness.

So wait—I'm telling you that the secret of happiness is just to choose to be happy? In a way, yes. How does it work? Most unhappiness centers around fear or resentment. You are afraid of something. You ask your higher power for the willingness to be released from the fear. Why? So you can be more useful to others. You have a resentment. You ask your higher power for the willingness to be released from the resentment. Why? So you can be more useful to others. This is a fact: I spend 99% of the time thinking about myself. If I instead spend 98% of my time thinking about myself, thereby doubling the amount of time I think about other people, I will be twice as happy. What is this higher power nonsense? You don't have to be religious to believe in a higher power. You don't have to go to church. You simply have to believe in a *power greater than yourself*. You can call it God, or you can call it Clyde for all I care. The key point is that it has to be a power greater than yourself. In other words, *you are not God*. And I can tell you that all spiritual disturbances come from when we think we are God. Also, if you are going to choose something as a higher power, don't choose a person, like your therapist or your spouse. People will always find a way to fail you. A higher power will not.

So wait—you're saying that the answer to the happiness problem is religion? I am not saying that at all. I have not set foot in a church since 2010. But I think I have had deeper and more meaningful spiritual experiences than most people who go to church. Remember, in the beginning of this essay, I talked about the phenomenon of the spiritual disturbance. The antidote to a spiritual disturbance is a spiritual experience. It doesn't have to be a "white light" moment. It could be something as simple as praying for the willingness to accept the outcome of something stressful—like taking the CFA exam—with grace and dignity. And regardless of whether you pass or fail the CFA exam, you will handle it with grace and dignity. Prayers answered. Note that you should not pray that you will pass the CFA exam—that's not how prayers work. We are not in the results business. Imagine failing the CFA exam—*and you are happy*. That's how happiness works. Maybe you weren't meant to pass that God-forsaken exam. Maybe you will do something else with your life that will be even better. Maybe you will get a life-changing opportunity that you could not have predicted. You don't pray for the outcome—you pray to be happy with the outcome.

How many therapists will tell you this? Probably not many.

Happiness is internal, not external. Here's the internal monologue: *I won't be happy unless I get that million-dollar bonus.* And then they get an $800,000 bonus, and they're miserable. Do we all realize how insane this is? How about, *I will be happy no matter what bonus I get.* That's not to say that you shouldn't aspire to be financially successful; money is important, but not enough to ruin your life for an entire year until the next bonus comes around, which will ruin your life for another year. How about: *I won't be happy unless my kid gets into Harvard.* Rejected. My friend, high school dropouts start billion-dollar companies. It really is going to be okay. I am successful in a lot of ways, including financially, but I have taken a rather unorthodox path, starting out with the military. There are a million ways to be successful in this country. These days, getting rejected by Harvard is a badge of honor.

I recently built a very large house. It is 10,000 square feet. Yes, I am happier in the house, but not in the way that you might think. The house makes me a better man. Better at my job, better at my marriage, better with my friends. It's as if I want to live up to the house. So yes, it is a huge fucking house, and there are creature comforts that go along with living in a huge fucking house, but it really makes me want to be a better person, which is something that I did not expect. And so I tell people that building the house was the smartest thing I have ever done. I owe some money on it, and there is some stress about the debt, but it's just a mortgage, and I can afford it, so there is nothing to worry about.

I didn't always have this perspective. I used to be one of those guys who was pissed at his bonus. I used to be consumed with fear and resentment. Whether I get $100 million is not up to me. Whether I have a book that sells a million copies is not up to me. I would like both of those things, but it is not up to me. I really want a book that sells a million copies. I thought *No Worries* would be the one. It was not. Maybe the next one will be. Maybe it will never happen. I can tell you something: I will be happy no matter what. Maybe a million-copy-selling book would turn me into a black-belt asshole. Maybe it isn't meant to happen. I will keep trying, and I will pray for dignity and grace no matter what the outcome. That's all I can do.

Write it down 100 times: *Happiness is a choice.* Took me 50 years to figure that out. Most people never do.

ACKNOWLEDGMENTS

FIRST, I WANT to thank my cats Stripe, Tars, Vesper, Wendy, Xenia, Yellow, and Zeus. The little fuzzballs keep me going.

Then, I want to thank my wife, Carolyn, for reading all of these essays and damning them with faint praise. In all seriousness, she read most of these before I published them and occasionally encouraged me to take out the riskier bits. People pay good money for sensitivity readers these days.

I want to thank my book designer and editor, Christopher Parker—I honestly don't know what I'd do if we hadn't met while working on *No Worries*.

I want to thank my higher power who I call God, who for some reason has saved me a bunch of times and who ultimately made this book possible.

And you, the reader, for believing my BS.

ABOUT THE AUTHOR

Author photograph by Emily Munn.

JARED DILLIAN IS the author of six books. He is the founder and principal of Armington Capital, LLC, a registered commodity trading advisor, editor of *The Daily Dirtnap*, an investment newsletter published since 2008, and a founding partner of Jared Dillian Money. He has degrees in mathematics, finance, and writing, and had a Wall Street career that spanned nine years. He is also an adjunct professor of finance, and was an op-ed columnist at *Reason* and *Bloomberg Opinion*. He lives in Pawleys Island, South Carolina with his wife and seven cats, where he practices the principles of *Rule 62* in all his affairs.

Printed in Dunstable, United Kingdom

64144604R10208